Teacher as Activator of Learning

I dedicate this book to children everywhere and especially those most dear to me, Megan and Jessica, that they will always find the joy of learning and reach their potential to meet the challenges of this ever-changing world. And to teachers present and future, that they always consider their vocation as a mission of passion and determination to be and do their best.

Teacher as Activator of Learning

Gayle H. Gregory

CORWIN
A SAGE Publishing Company

FOR INFORMATION:

Corwin
A SAGE Company
2455 Teller Road
Thousand Oaks, California 91320
(800) 233-9936
www.corwin.com

SAGE Publications Ltd.
1 Oliver's Yard
55 City Road
London EC1Y 1SP
United Kingdom

SAGE Publications India Pvt. Ltd.
B 1/I 1 Mohan Cooperative Industrial Area
Mathura Road, New Delhi 110 044
India

SAGE Publications Asia-Pacific Pte. Ltd.
3 Church Street
#10-04 Samsung Hub
Singapore 049483

Senior Acquisitions Editor: Jessica Allan
Senior Associate Editor: Kimberly Greenberg
Editorial Assistant: Katie Crilley
Production Editor: Melanie Birdsall
Copy Editor: Lynn Weber
Typesetter: C&M Digitals (P) Ltd.
Proofreader: Alison Syring
Indexer: Maria Sosnowski
Cover Designer: Michael Dubowe
Marketing Manager: Jill S. Margulies

Printed in the United States of America

Library of Congress Cataloging-in-Publication Data

Names: Gregory, Gayle, author.

Title: Teacher as activator of learning / Gayle H. Gregory.

Description: Thousand Oaks, California : Corwin, a SAGE Company, [2016] | Includes bibliographical references and index.

Identifiers: LCCN 2015034876 | ISBN 9781483381855 (pbk. : acid-free paper)

Subjects: LCSH: Teaching. | Classroom environment.

Classification: LCC LB1025.3.G738 2016 | DDC 371.102—dc23 LC record available at http://lccn.loc.gov/2015034876

This book is printed on acid-free paper.

16 17 18 19 20 10 9 8 7 6 5 4 3 2 1

Contents

Acknowledgments   ix

About the Author   xi

Introduction: Activating Student Thinking   1

Chapter 1. Activating Classroom Climate   17
  Brain Research and the Classroom   17
  The Problem of Stress   18
    How Stress Shuts Down Learning   18
    The Goal: Appropriate Stress Levels   19
    The Strategy: Managing Stress in the Classroom   20
  The Problem of Social Isolation   26
    How Social Isolation Shuts Down Learning   26
    The Goal: Identifying Social Isolation and
      Balancing Social and Learning Needs   28
    The Strategy: Managing Social Isolation in the Classroom   28
  Assessing Your Own Classroom Climate   39
  Summary   40
  Discussion Points   40

Chapter 2. Activating Teachers   43
  Personal Attitude   43
    Attitude 1: Enthusiasm   44
    Attitude 2: Credibility   46
    Attitude 3: Caring   50
  The Growth Mindset   55
    Mindset 1: Belief in Students' Potential   55
    Mindset 2: Practice and Effort   56
    Mindset 3: Errors and Obstacles   56
    Mindset 4: Growth-Friendly Techniques   57

Fostering Happiness 59
Instructional Techniques 60
   Instructional Technique 1: Clarity 60
   Instructional Technique 2: Multimodal
     Presentation 62
   Instructional Technique 3: Direct Instruction 65
Summary 70
Discussion Points 70

Chapter 3. Activating the Power of Peers **72**
The Importance of Peer Relationships in the Classroom 72
   Friendship 72
   General Social Interaction 73
Activating Learning Through Peer Relationships 75
   Monologue Versus Dialogue 75
   Evaluating Versus Extending 78
   Bloom's Revised Thinking Taxonomy 80
   Cubing 81
   Partners 81
   Orchestrating an Appointment Card 86
   Turn and Talk 88
   Tips to Better Ensure Productive Dialogue 90
Activating Learning Through Peer Tutoring 91
   Benefits for Students 92
Activating Learning Through Reciprocal Teaching 93
   Strategy 1: Questioning 94
   Strategy 2: Clarifying 94
   Strategy 3: Summarizing 95
   Strategy 4: Predicting 95
   Instructional Format for Reciprocal Teaching 95
Summary 97
Discussion Points 97

Chapter 4. Activating Cooperative Learning **99**
Why Teachers Can Be Skeptical of CGL 100
Why the Brain Loves CGL 100
Start Small 103
Designing Small Groups 104
Elements of Successful Group Work 107
   Element 1: Positive Interdependence 107
   Element 2: Individual Accountability 108
   Element 3: Social Skills 109
   Element 4: Group Processing 111
   Element 5: Face-to-Face Interaction 112

Implementing CGL: Jigsaw, Academic Controversy,
   and Group Investigation 112
   Jigsaw 112
   Academic Controversy 115
   Group Investigation 118
Summary 121
Discussion Points 121

Chapter 5. Activating the Power of Goals and Standards ... **122**
The Power of Goals: Tapping the Unconscious Mind ... 123
   Setting Broad Goals With Learning Progressions ... 126
Setting Daily Learning Goals 132
   Clarity 132
   Specificity 133
   Rubrics 135
   Flexibility 135
   Personalization 137
The Goal of Goals: Flow 138
   The Zone of Proximal Development 140
   Piaget's Stages 141
   Support 142
   Conceptual Understanding 143
Summary 146
Discussion Points 146

Chapter 6. Activating Assessment **147**
Assessment Basics 148
   Encouragement 148
   Learner Participation 148
   Formative Assessment 149
How to Incorporate Assessment in the Classroom ... 151
   Prior Knowledge Assessment (Pre-Assessment) ... 152
   Current Progress Assessment (Formative Assessment) ... 158
Summary 168
Discussion Points 168

Chapter 7. Activating Feedback **169**
Ineffective Feedback: What to Avoid 170
   Overly General Feedback 170
   Written Feedback 170
   Summative Feedback 171
   Praise 171
Instructional Feedback: Feedback Done Right 171
   Promoting a Growth Mindset 174
   The Power of the Particular 176

Positive Language   178
What Students Think About Feedback   178
Peer Feedback   179
Student Feedback: Giving Students a Voice   180
Surveys   182
Focus Groups   183
Video Diaries   183
Exit Cards   183
Metacognition: The Key to Self-Feedback   184
Metacognitive Thinking Prompts   186
Think-Alouds   188
The Recovery Strategy   188
Right Angles   189
Mindfulness   190
Summary   191
Discussion Points   191

Chapter 8. Final Thoughts   **193**
Student Centered   193
What Students Want From Teachers   194
Parents and the Growth Mindset   195
Collaboration   196
Microteaching   198
Hope and Self-Perception   198

References   **199**

Index   **219**

Acknowledgments

I wish to thank, first of all, Jessica Allan, senior acquisitions editor at Corwin. Her advice, encouragement, and enthusiasm for the project helped see me through to completion. Melanie Birdsall, senior project editor, and Lynn Weber and Katie Crilley were diligent in their monitoring and shepherding of the editing process. Jill Margulies and David Galinato are to be commended for their attention to the details of cover design and marketing materials.

Thanks too to Kristin Anderson and Ainsley Rose for their knowledge and expertise in Visible Learning Plus. Without these talented dedicated professionals this book couldn't have come to fruition. Also to Michael Fullan and John Hattie for their brilliance in writing and championing change for the better for children everywhere.

PUBLISHER'S ACKNOWLEDGMENTS

Corwin would like to thank the following individuals for their editorial insight and guidance:

Ellen E. Coulson, Teacher
Sig Rogich Middle School
Las Vegas, NV

Tara Howell, Instructional Leader
University City High School
San Diego, CA

Stacy Lemongelli, Teacher
Perth Amboy High School
Perth Amboy, NJ

Debbie Smith, Math Coach
Beaufort Elementary School
Beaufort, SC

Robert Wallon, Doctoral Student
University of Illinois at
    Urbana-Champaign
Champaign, IL

Colleen Winkler, Principal
Chateau Estates School
Kenner, LA

About the Author

Gayle H. Gregory is first and foremost a teacher, having experienced teaching and learning in elementary, middle, and secondary schools; community colleges; and universities.

She has had extensive district-wide experience as a curriculum consultant and staff development coordinator. Gayle was principal/course director at York University for the Faculty of Education, teaching in the teacher education program.

Her areas of expertise include brain-compatible learning, differentiated instructional and assessment strategies, block scheduling, emotional intelligence, student motivation, RTI Tier One, collaborative learning, common core, renewal of secondary schools, enhancing teacher quality, coaching and mentoring, managing change, and building professional learning communities. She also a trainer for Visible Learning Plus with Corwin.

She is an author of numerous books related to educational neuroscience and differentiated instruction, assessment, and curriculum, including the following titles:

- *Data Driven Differentiation in the Standards-Based Classroom, Second Edition* (2014, with Lin Kuzmich)
- *Differentiated Instructional Strategies: One Size Doesn't Fit All, Third Edition* (2013, with Carolyn Chapman)
- *Differentiated Instructional Strategies Professional Learning Guide: One Size Doesn't Fit All,* Third Edition (2013)
- *Differentiated Literacy Strategies for English Language Learners, Grades K–6* and *Differentiated Literacy Strategies for English Language Learners, Grades 7–12* (2011, with Amy Burkman)
- *Differentiated Instructional Strategies for the Block Schedule* (2010, with Lynne E. Herndon)

- *Student Teams That Get Results: Teaching Tools for the Differentiated Classroom* (2009, with Lin Kuzmich)
- *Teacher Teams That Get Results: 61 Strategies for Sustaining and Renewing Professional Learning Communities* (2009, with Lin Kuzmich)
- *Differentiated Instructional Strategies for Science, Grades K–8* (2009, with Elizabeth Hammerman)
- *Differentiating Instruction With Style: Aligning Teacher and Learner Intelligences for Maximum Achievement* (2005)

She is affiliated with organizations such as ASCD and Learning Forward. Her ASCD publication is *The Motivated Brain: Improving Student Attention, Engagement, and Perseverance* (2015).

Gayle consults internationally with teachers, administrators, and staff developers.

She and her family of two daughters and two granddaughters all reside in Burlington, Ontario.

Gayle is committed to lifelong learning and professional growth for herself and others. She may be contacted at gregorygayle@netscape.net, www.gaylehgregory.com, and @gaylegregory6.

Introduction

Activating Student Thinking

As I entered the classroom I immediately noticed the bustle of high energy and positive chatter. I couldn't find the teacher in the midst of the focused activity that was evident. Students were not in rows but in clusters of two or three, discussing and working together. I found the teacher engaged with a small group, questioning, suggesting, and giving specific feedback so students could proceed. I eavesdropped on several groups and asked questions myself; the students were very clear about what they were trying to accomplish, some of the roadblocks they had overcome, and what they would do next. As I scanned the room, the students were generally self-directed and productive, using technology seamlessly as needed . . . tablets, computers, cell phones.

Of course all this didn't just happen. The teacher had orchestrated it with careful planning and excellent classroom management. Materials were organized, charts showed expectations related to standards, and students had rubrics with success criteria to guide their success. These students were not recipients of knowledge; they were constructing it, monitoring their progress, and taking responsibility for their learning. This teacher had successfully activated the *thinking* in this classroom. How did she do it? What were the strategies used to turn these students into active, thoughtful learners?

THE TEACHER AS ACTIVATOR

This book is about all the ways that teachers can activate student learning. But when we use the phrase "activate student learning," what do we really mean? There is no single switch for learning but skillful teachers have discovered over time what will activate their students' learning. To activate is to cause to act, not to sit passively listening and writing down notes.

The reticular activating system (RAS) in the brain is vital to the ability to attend to and ultimately filter new information and experiences. The RAS helps us engage our curiosity and interest in meaningful opportunities. Some things will inhibit the engagement and activation. One is the learning environment. Some things are already innate in the learner to help with the activation issue, primarily, the SEEKING system.

THE SEEKING SYSTEM

According to Jaak Panksepp (1998), humans have a natural SEEKING system (always printed in uppercase by Panksepp). By studying the emotions of other mammals, Panksepp determined there are seven basic, primitive emotional processing systems found in the oldest area of human brains. These are primal levels and help us understand what we currently define as motivation. Panksepp calls the most powerful of the seven systems the SEEKING / EXPECTANCY system, which includes *curiosity, interest, foraging, anticipation*, and *craving*.

This is a primal survival system in all of us. The other systems are FEAR, RAGE, LUST, CARE, GRIEF, and PLAY. Panksepp emphasizes that the SEEKING system is the granddaddy of the emotional systems and will naturally engage and activate exploration, experimentation, and thinking from the learners' innate need to know and understand (Gregory & Kaufeldt, 2015). This critical primary emotion is innate and important for humans to connect, cooperate, and collaborate. It keeps people motivated and interested in examining the world for survival and learning. It is vital for survival and is there for all teachers use as a motivational tool. Educators can activate their students' SEEKING system and allow it to flourish by providing them with opportunities to explore, examine, and play, and also by offering them strategies they enjoy plus metacognition related to learning and success. Thus it helps generate enthusiasm and release dopamine in the brain as we SEEK. The dopamine is not so much a reward as a motivator, providing a sense of eagerness to continue. The dopamine release and resulting euphoria occur during the foraging process, not at the end result. This keeps us intensely involved in the process. It is the expectancy of completion and a sense of "wanting" that creates conditions for continued attention to the task. When the exploring is complete there is a brief squirt from the opioid system (liking) that is actually less significant than the ongoing dopamine release as we SEEK. There are three basic processing levels in the SEEKING system as seen in Figure I.1.

The primary SEEKING process is "appetitive" and related to expectancy. This is the initial phase of SEEKING; as we forage and explore we

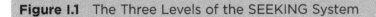

Figure I.1 The Three Levels of the SEEKING System

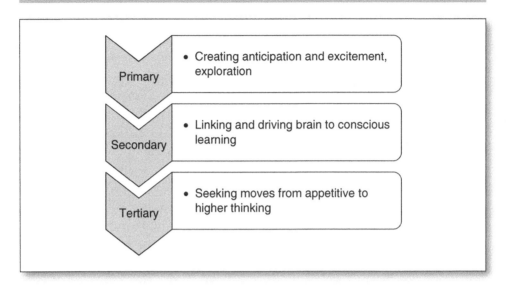

Primary
- Creating anticipation and excitement, exploration

Secondary
- Linking and driving brain to conscious learning

Tertiary
- Seeking moves from appetitive to higher thinking

create curiosity, anticipation, and enthusiasm and constant dopamine release that keeps us motivated. This is unconscious and emotion-driven and is referred to as *anoetic consciousness* (or without conscious knowledge of what is occurring). There is no higher-order thinking or reflection. In young children this is spontaneous play.

When the secondary processing system kicks in, there is conscious thought process or *noetic consciousness* including awareness and knowing. It is at this point that we are aware and real learning begins. We make connections from prior knowledge or to our own reality and anticipate next steps related to the exploration phase. If we have had previous pleasure or success we are "wanting" to seek that again. This stage includes active processing or practice to become proficient and grow dendritic connections between neurons through repetition. Thus memories are made. We can foster this phase by providing an enriched environment of resources, multisensory, and interesting activities. Hebb (1949) suggests that neurons that fire together will wire together and thus form memories. Brain growth is dependent on the interaction among genes, the environment and quality experiences.

The third level of processing develops with maturity. This level of processing is evident when the learner can think beyond the present and is able to create, imagine, and synthesize information and use it in a productive way to solve problems and make plans (Panksepp & Biven, 2012). This more complex thinking is referred to as executive function, which includes ability to consciously control thinking and to self-regulate. Multiple opportunities are needed to continue to develop executive function through asking learners to apply knowledge and higher-order thinking through the use of projects and problems (Gregory & Kaufeldt, 2015).

For the last number of years educators have talked about teachers moving from the "sage on the stage" to the "guide on the side," from lecturer to facilitator. Professor John Hattie (2009) now suggests that facilitation is not enough. He recommends that we distinguish between the roles of *facilitator* and *activator*. Facilitation is only the guide on the side, but activation means being integrally involved with students as a partner in learning. This also implies a new learning relationship between and among teachers and students. Not an I/You but a We.

How does facilitation contrast with activation in practice in the day-to-day classroom? Hattie gives some examples. In classrooms where the teacher acts as a facilitator, you might find gaming and simulations, inquiry-based activities, smaller class sizes, problem-based learning, individualized instruction, and web-based and inductive teaching. In classrooms where the teacher acts as an activator, you might find reciprocal teaching, teacher-student self-verbalization, metacognitive strategies, appropriate level of challenging tasks, and checks for understanding, feedback, and effectiveness. Figure I.2 shows these strategies in greater detail. The impact of teacher as activator has an effect size of 0.60 and that of teacher as a facilitator is only 0.17.

This book gives teachers a chance to learn about the high-impact strategies that are most effective according to Hattie and others, and it also offers practical ways to put these strategies into our daily work in classrooms and schools. Although research is helpful and promising, we need to operationalize the research so that teachers can use it in the classroom. Educational neuroscience has and will continue to inform our practice and cause us to question past methods and engage in new

Figure I.2 Teacher Facilitator and Activator Strategies

Facilitator	Activator
• Providing games and simulations • Problems and projects • Attention to gender issues • Online learning • Whole language programs • Inductive and inquiry methods	• Peer interaction and teaching • Quality feedback • Fostering self-reflection and metacognition • Using direct instruction • Attention to mastery • Appropriate level of challenge • Thoughtful assessment and evaluation methods

Source: Hattie (2009).

ones to better serve our diverse students. Brains have some similarities but also some unique characteristics. All this should take place, of course, in a climate of safety and invitation where errors are accepted as a part of the learning process. The environment should also be welcoming and nurturing.

Making a shift from facilitation to activation doesn't require hefty funding or output, the way new textbooks or computers would. It just requires a mind shift about what we believe schools should be like—changing our vision from a factory model to a thinking model. Here are some of the factors in education that need to be changed for students to be activated and reach their potential.

CHANGING SCHOOLS

Many schools have not changed much in the last century. In a lot of classrooms the teaching mode is still "sit and get." It becomes even more that way as we move up the grades with the guise of getting the student ready to handle college or university (even though many may have no intention of attending university and enduring long lectures). Teachers continue to rely on "talk and chalk" (or perhaps "talk and overhead" or PowerPoint) methods, and we expect students to endure it. Some teachers even suggest that if it was good enough for them when they were in school, it's good enough for their current students.

Teachers always find that there is a group of compliant learners in a class who learn in spite of us. They will do whatever it takes to graduate at a high level. They are somewhat self-sufficient, self-starters who follow routines and expectations and succeed whether learning is engaging or interesting.

But times are changing, and we now want more than a measly quarter of students—those on the high end of the bell curve who are highly internally motivated—to be successful. From No Child Left Behind to Race to the Top, expectations are that *all* students can and should do well. We should no longer blame failure on the students' lack of commitment and perseverance. If students are not committed, it's often because they are confronted with a boring and unchallenging curriculum filled with "drill and kill" assignments and preparations for test taking. Surveys of thousands of teachers from all grade levels as to the level of enthusiasm in their students garnered interesting information. About 95% reported teacher satisfaction with their students' enthusiasm at the kindergarten level, but that satisfaction plummets to 37% by ninth grade. Research sponsored by the MetLife Foundation (2012) showed a downward trend in teacher satisfaction as well, from 54% to 40% or even less. So we are losing hearts and minds of both our students and our teachers.

How can we turn this around? Cognitive scientist Daniel Willingham in the book *Why Don't Students Like School?* (2009) proposes that students don't like school because teachers don't understand the brain and therefore don't teach as well as they could. We have had over 30 years of neuroscience discoveries that we should be paying attention to, because after all it is the brains of these learners that are our main area of concern. Marian Diamond years ago suggested that all educators needed to know and should want to know how brains work. Lesley Hart (1983) stated that a teacher who doesn't know how the brain works is like a mechanic who doesn't know how engines work. Willingham likewise suggests that students could love school if we would use what we know about brains to plan learning. Currently, he suggests, school is more like prison. The only difference is the school is age mandatory and to get into school prison you don't have to commit a crime.

In the early years in elementary schools we are much more brain friendly, consciously or unconsciously. But as children move up the grades there is less and less movement, spontaneous application, novelty, fun, exploration, and autonomy. Students become less and less engaged and actively involved and often only endure passively in classrooms. The fact that many children don't like school is not because it really is a prison; it's because the "wardens" may not keep the students' minds activated. And it really isn't that hard to do.

It all comes down to student engagement, activating thinking, and challenging students just beyond their zone of proximal development.

CHANGING INSTRUCTIONAL STRATEGIES

Outside of the traditional classroom the world is rapidly changing. This millennium generation is living and learning in the information age, and students need to know how to access information and be practical, analytical, and creative with it (Sternberg, 1996). Students' brains are not the same either. The technology-rich, fast-paced real world is far more engaging than many classrooms. Schools are competing for attention and engagement with the digital world. Students will appreciate classrooms where there is more interaction, discussion, and *doing* with problem/project-based, hands-on application, creativity, and deep learning. There is a large evidence base of proven instructional strategies that not only activate and engage students but also increase student achievement. Teachers who use these strategies will be more engaged as well.

Not all teachers are effective, not all teachers are experts, and not all teachers have powerful effects on students. (Hattie, 2009, p. 34)

In order to make the shift to activated learning, teachers also need different types of support. Current teacher evaluation is usually based on their students' test scores, and that is not the message we want to send when we are endeavoring to encourage educators to take some risks to change practice and collaborate to unearth better approaches for all learners.

Educational change depends on what teachers do and think—it's as simple and complex as that. (Sarason, 1971, p. 193)

Therefore it is imperative that we help activate teachers and students *together* to become passionate learners. Teacher skills need to move beyond current evidence-based instructional strategies and learn to be "instructionally intelligent" (Bennett & Rolheiser, 2001). They need to know how to match strategies to content, skills, and student preferences; to know when learning has been achieved; to experiment and adjust strategies as needed; and to seek and give feedback in professional learning communities.

CHANGING CURRICULA

Madeline Hunter (1967) suggested years ago that if we are just going to "cover the curriculum" we might a well just dig a hole and bury it. Unfortunately there is a lot of "covering" going on in classrooms because of the demands of standardized testing. If we were to spend only 30 minutes on each K–12 standard we would need nine more years of school simply to review each standard (Marzano, Pickering, & Pollock, 2001). Marzano's suggestion is to concentrate on *power standards*—those enduring subject areas whose relevance has stood the test of time (McTighe & Wiggins, 2013; Ainsworth, 2003a)—and to go deeper to develop major concepts so that real long-term deep understanding takes place. When deep learning takes place, a lot of the other standards will be subsumed and understood simultaneously. Meaningfulness and relevancy are important to the brain and learning something "because it is on the test" does not engage the brain the way connecting learning to their lives would.

In day-to-day dealings with students, teachers might be overwhelmed and frustrated with the different levels of readiness, preferences, and interests that students have (Gregory & Chapman, 2013). When faced with the momentous task of differentiating instruction for students with various skill levels, some teachers may project the problem onto the students and may even unconsciously believe that some students just can't achieve. But students aren't the problem. Every student can learn and flourish if the curriculum activates their engagement. Here is what we know:

- Social class/prior achievement is surmountable. It has little impact on student success.
- All students can be challenged. Differentiation meets students where they are.
- Strategies, not styles, make the difference. Mixed modality strategies benefit all learners.
- Students flourish under high expectations.
- Coaching is important. Success follows when we monitor student progress and encourage students to seek help when needed.
- Students can learn to self-assess. They need to know where they are in relationship to the target so they can plan what to do next.
- Peer interactions and social support works.
- Feedback is the breakfast of champions. Critique and feedback are powerful.
- Self-regulation and seeing students as teachers is key. Students need to know, "If it is to be, it's up to me."

CHANGING LEARNING VISIBILITY

John Hattie in his work with visible learning suggests that teachers need to *see* learning through the eyes of the learner and students need to *see* themselves as teachers. In other words students take an active role in the learning process, identifying and setting goals, and planning and assessing their progress toward their goals.

Over the course of his 15 years of research Hattie synthesized over 1,200 meta-analyses (and counting) and described what most influences K–12 student achievement. This research included over a quarter of a billion students and is the largest collection of evidence-based findings of what is promising to improve learning. In his books he shares what one needs to pay attention to in order to achieve success for teachers and students. Three things stand out: clear and challenging learning expectations, making success overt and visible, and using learning strategies that develop conceptual comprehension for teachers and students.

Hattie uses a baseline of 0.40 standard deviation growth in a school year—this is the "typical effect" hinge point recommended (Hattie, 2009).

With no instruction at all (just life experience) the average student's academic achievement will increase yearly by 0.10. He also found that if a teacher possesses an average level of competence, then an average student's academic achievement would increase by 0.30. With these two factors combined, the average student will improve by 0.40 a year simply by living and experiencing average schooling. In other words, with little intervention and random placement, 0.40 is what we can expect. However, to improve beyond that we need to seek out practices that have a higher than 0.40 impact. Figure I.3 illustrates the possibilities.

> What is most important is that teaching is visible to the student, and that the learning is visible to the teacher. The more the student becomes the teacher and the more the teacher becomes the learner, then the more successful are the outcomes. (Hattie, 2009, p. 25)

We know that we want to get above the 0.40 hinge point. But what strategies will get us there? Hattie analyzed and ranked 150, and counting,

Figure I.3 Above and Below the Hinge

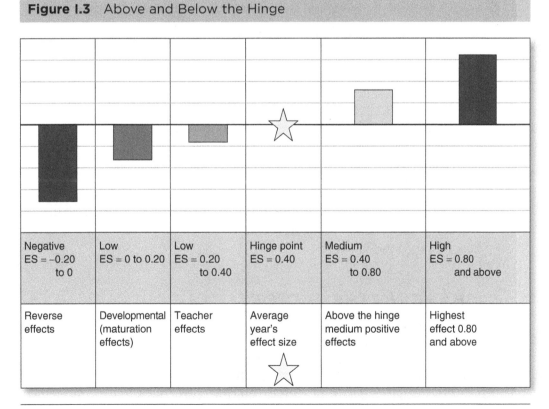

Negative ES = –0.20 to 0	Low ES = 0 to 0.20	Low ES = 0.20 to 0.40	Hinge point ES = 0.40	Medium ES = 0.40 to 0.80	High ES = 0.80 and above
Reverse effects	Developmental (maturation effects)	Teacher effects	Average year's effect size ☆	Above the hinge medium positive effects	Highest effect 0.80 and above

Source: Based on Hattie (2009).

influences on student growth, and he assigned each influence to one of six potential factors: the child, the home, the school, the teacher, the curriculum, and the approaches to teaching.

1. Hattie reminds us that **children** bring to school factors that influence achievement from nature (genetics) to nurture and personal dispositions that influence their school success.

2. Students are either supported by a positive **home** or hindered by a destructive one. Positive expectations of parents are critical to student success. They need to be involved and supportive and help develop the child's love of learning. It takes a village to raise a child.

3. The **school** effects include the climate of the classroom and peer influences that are embedded in the culture.

4. **Teachers** are a critical factor in terms of their expectations, quality of teaching, openness, classroom climate, clarity, encouragement, and engagement of students.

5. The **curricula** should offer a balance of surface and deep learning and should allow students to construct meaning with multiple opportunities for practice.

6. **Approaches to teaching** includes setting goals, identifying criteria for success, fostering student involvement, direct instruction, group work, technology, and out-of-school learning.

Hattie's research suggests that school has the most powerful effects by creating the most nurturing climate in the classroom, fostering peer influences, and minimizing the instances of students' disruptive behavior. Teachers also set the stage with their own expectations, their teaching and openness to students. Most critical, though, is the quality of the teaching through the students' eyes.

CHANGING THE FACTORS THAT MATTER MOST

In this book I've tried to start small and think big and will examine the most promising domains those that have moderate to high impact with effect sizes greater than the hinge point of 0.40. The complete rank order and extensive list of these effect sizes may seem daunting to a classroom teacher. But many of these can be clustered and linked together and are mutually supportive, as you will see throughout the book.

Group 1: Classroom Climate

This first grouping is crucial in developing a brain-friendly learning environment where students can feel secure, are supported, and thrive. All domains are beyond the hinge point with moderate to high impact.

- Self-efficacy related to learning: 0.80
- Developing teacher–student relationships: 0.72
- Classroom and student behavior: 0.68
- Eliminating labeling students: 0.61
- Classroom management—routines and expectations: 0.52
- Teacher expectations for students' success: 0.43

Group 2: Collaboration and Peer Support

It makes sense to focus on several domains together to develop peer interaction and facilitate dialogue in the classroom to activate a collaborative community.

- Class discussion rather than teacher monologue: 0.82
- Reciprocal teaching between and among students: 0.82
- Cooperative learning vs. individualistic learning: 0.59
- Peer tutoring: 0.56
- Collaboration vs. competitive learning: 0.54
- Peer influences toward positive climate: 0.53
- Cooperative group learning: 0.42

Group 3: Teacher Qualities

The qualities and expertise of teachers have a great impact on student success. The teacher does indeed make a huge difference by attending to a variety of high impact strategies and continuing to develop the knowledge, skills, and dispositions that make a difference in student learning and achievement.

- Teacher credibility: whether or not the teacher comes across knowledgeable, capable, and respectful: 0.90
- Teacher clarity in providing information, expectations, and worked examples in student language: 0.65
- Teaching strategies (instructional repertoire that varies instruction): 0.62

Group 4: Assessment and Feedback

Being clear about the learning intentions, offering quality feedback, and fostering metacognition are key to developing assessment-capable learners, all of which teachers can foster and nurture in their classrooms.

- Student self-report grades related to clear goals and students are assessment capable learners using assessment to progress: 1.44
- Providing formative evaluation: 0.90
- Feedback provided from multiple sources, teachers, peers, and self: 0.75
- Metacognition and self assessment considering their work and progress and redirecting as a result of reflection: 0.69

CHANGING OUR DEMEANOR: THE IMPORTANCE OF PASSION

It is not a crime to be joyful and emotional about learning. Yet by doing so teachers may be regarded as trivial and lacking cognitive focus and seriousness about learning (Neumann, 2006). Passion includes the sheer thrill of learning, a deep commitment to the process and the sensations and willingness involved in their experience. Passion is infectious and transferable and can be modeled and taught. Young children seem able to express passion and the thrill of learning. They exude joy when involved in the challenge of developing new skills and knowledge (Willis, 2007). It is amazing to see the passion and joy that is obvious at 7 or 9 years of age, whether it's discovering a new gymnastic routine, swimming dive, Tai Kwon Do technique, reading a challenging chapter in a book, or demonstrating a new skill in the kitchen. Life provides endless challenges for us to engage and persist in a new ability until we achieve mastery. Children are tenacious in their quest. It doesn't take much to activate their learning and SEEKING systems.

Doug Reeves (2002) suggests in these challenging economic times where resources for schools are scarce that passion is the commodity that is natural and renewable. Learning isn't always easy or pleasurable for that matter, but with deliberate practice and concentration one can meet challenges and achieve success.

CHANGING OUR MINDSET

Henry Ford famously said that whether you think you can or think you can't, you're right. And research since his time has only solidified the notion that expectation is everything. World-renowned Stanford University psychologist Carol Dweck (2006), after years of research, developed a perspective on expectations that backs this up. Everyone has beliefs about their potential and capabilities. People attribute their achievement or lack of achievement to mindsets or beliefs that they hold about themselves and their own personal qualities. Dweck identified the two basic mindsets that people have related to their abilities: a *fixed mindset* and a *growth mindset*.

Those who have a fixed mindset believe that they (and others) are born with certain capabilities—IQ, talent, resourcefulness, and so on—and that those don't change. Students who have a fixed mindset tend to avoid challenges for fear that they won't be able to surmount them. Teachers who have a fixed mindset tend to label students based on their assumptions about how smart they think they are; they expect and foster success for some students and hold lower expectations and offer lesser and mediocre tasks for others.

People who have a growth mindset believe that everyone has potential for developing traits and skills and effort can change one's abilities. Students with a growth mindset believe that effort and "grit" is the path to mastery. Teachers with a growth mindset invest time and effort in their students and give students opportunities to try, redo, and choose alternate approaches until they are successful.

These mindsets are not cut and dry, of course. Dweck offers that students tend to fall into three groupings: 43% have fixed mindsets, 43% have growth mindsets, and 15% are undecided. Students' mindsets can vary dependent on the situation. Some have fixed mindsets to some aspects of school work (e.g., "I can't do math") but growth mindsets related to others (e.g., extracurricular activities such as playing hockey or learning the guitar). (See Figure I.4.)

As educators we have a powerful influence in the classroom and can help students activate and attain their potential. If we don't have a growth mindset, we excuse our students' failures by saying that they just don't get it instead of looking at the misstep as a challenge and developing new approaches. Our challenge as educators is to change minds: our own and the students', especially about who we are and what we can accomplish.

Dweck suggests that children have developed a mindset by the time they enter school; however, mindset can be influenced and activated by skillful teachers. Experiences such as learning new skills actually change our brains: Dendrites—the tree-branch-like bunches of cell that connect neurons—are known to grow and strengthen with practice. The way our brains change through experience is called neuroplasticity. It is proof

Figure I.4 A Comparison of Growth and Fixed Mindsets

	Fixed Mindset: Intelligence Is Static *Desire to look smart, a tendency to . . .*	**Growth Mindset: Intelligence Can Be Developed** *Desire to learn and a tendency to . . .*
Challenges	Avoid	Enjoy challenges
Obstacles	Be defensive, give up	Persist despite setbacks
Effort	Not be impressed by effort	See effort as crucial
Criticism	Ignore feedback	Appreciate feedback
Success of Others	Be threatened by others	Learn from others
Students . . .	Don't reach potential	Exceed beyond expectations

positive of the growth mindset (Diamond, 1967). This growth of brain connections is prolific in an optimum environment rich with activity, resources, multisensory appeal, and interactions in collaboration with others, all of which is engaging and satisfying to the brain (Greenhough & Volkmar, 1973).

This book represents an attempt to respect the natural neuroplasticity of our brains—to bring together all of the things that can activate learning and allow students to achieve success, despite their own expectations and the expectations of others. Using Hattie's research base of meta-analyses and our knowledge of neuroscience, the book will investigate the factors that most impact learning, including brain-friendly strategies and the all-important step of putting students in charge of their learning.

HOW THIS BOOK IS ORGANIZED

Chapter 1. Activating Classroom Climate

Chapter 1 focuses on the relationship between the latest neuroscience information that supports the need for a brain-friendly classroom—what has become educational neuroscience. An environment that supports how the brain operates is not simply "nice to have"; it is essential for individuals to thrive and survive. The antiquated notion of control, pressure, punishment, and one size fits all have been disproven by recent advances in brain science. Practical strategies are provided to orchestrate a learning environment that supports trial and error, risk taking, and collaboration, one that avoids undue stress and allows students to activate thinking and continue toward self-regulation and success. Findings of classroom behavior with 0.68 effect size and classroom management at 0.52 as well as reducing anxiety 0.40 bear this out.

Chapter 2. Activating Teachers

It's about learning, not about teaching. But the teacher is key to activating and orchestrating quality experiences that enable learners to learn. Many attributes contribute to teachers being able to make the difference.

Chapter 3. Activating the Power of Peers

This chapter builds on the influence of peers in a supportive brain-friendly environment (ES of $d = 0.55$ from the meta-analysis). The neuroscience that supports this notion and how we as educators foster peer support and interactions in the classroom are included.

Chapter 4. Activating Cooperative Learning

One of the most highly researched instructional strategies, which unfortunately is not prevalent in all classrooms, is cooperative group learning. Students are often put in groups that fail to function well. As a result, there are classroom management issues and few academic and social gains, and teachers may eventually abandon the group format. These chapter reviews how to make cooperate learning really work.

Chapter 5. Activating the Power of Goals and Standards

Visible learning suggests that students should navigate their own learning experience using three key questions: Where am I going? How am I doing? Where to next? This chapter looks at the power of intentions and how we help students activate, monitor, and assess the process to success.

Chapter 6. Activating Assessment

Many classrooms and schools are data rich and information poor. Standardized testing provides lots of statistics, but they are not very helpful to teachers. This chapter reviews how to evaluate the whole student and how to give productive feedback (to both students and teachers) that will help them adjust the course and design the next steps. In this chapter the focus is "how are we doing" and "where to next" through collecting formative assessment including pre-assessment and ongoing checking for understanding.

Chapter 7. Activating Feedback

For students to continually monitor their progress and become more assessment capable learners, feedback is key—feedback from the teacher and peers as well as self-assessment and metacognition. Teachers need feedback too, and student voices are imperative for success.

Chapter 8. Final Thoughts

This final chapter pulls the pieces together and suggests how to use your professional learning communities to focus on student learning and developing assessment capable learners.

1 Activating Classroom Climate

Classroom climate (sometimes called the classroom culture) is made up of a constellation of factors that can sometimes go unnoticed. In laymen's terms, it's how the classroom *feels* or "how we do things around here." It includes everything from the paint on the wall, how many physical objects are in the room, and how the space is organized to the dominant emotions being expressed, the teaching strategies used, and how much students speak or are quiet (Ambrose et al., 2010).

Neuroscience has taught us a lot about how the brain works. And one thing has become clear: the setting in which learning takes place affects the brain. Children are not robots, whose parts function independently of the world around them. The elements of classroom climate will concretely affect children's brains and influence how well they learn.

In this chapter we'll look at the elements of classroom climate and the myriad ways they can affect the learning brain of students, particularly in regard to two common classroom problems: stress and social isolation.

BRAIN RESEARCH AND THE CLASSROOM

Brain research has huge implications for the classroom. Neuroscience can never tell us exactly what to do in the classroom, but its findings can help us determine best approaches to teaching. The term *neuroeducation* or *educational neuroscience* refers to how educators use the findings of neuroscience to shape their educational practices. Neuro-educators like John Geake, a professor and cofounder of the Oxford Cognitive Neuroscience Education Forum, have spoken about the importance of neuro-education as a field:

> Relevant and useful professional and classroom applications of educational neuroscience will increasingly become available as we gradually come to understand more about brain function through neuroscience research, which answers educational questions about learning, memory, motivation and so on. (Geake, 2009, p.10)

In the sections that follow, we'll examine two of the biggest impediments to student learning—stress and social isolation—and explore how classroom climate inhibit or ameliorate these two problems. Each problem has its particular challenges, but the base principle is the same: Learning requires a safe, supportive, nurturing climate in the classroom so that students are able to activate their prefrontal lobes and focus on learning, not just survival.

THE PROBLEM OF STRESS

How Stress Shuts Down Learning

The brain was put in the head for survival, not to go to school. And one of the primary ways it guards survival is by scanning the environment for threats. When a threat appears—whether it's a saber-tooth tiger crouching in the grass, the shake of the ground before an earthquake, or the approach of a threatening-looking person with a weapon—the brain reacts by releasing stress hormones like cortisol and adrenalin. This flood of stress hormones gear up the body to take action.

The amygdala is often called the emotional sentinel of the brain. It is part of the brain's limbic system and it helps deal with incoming data about a person's environment. Under normal conditions the amygdala directs incoming data to the prefrontal cortex (PFC), which is the seat of executive function and long-term memory. The PFC uses the data to formulate a logical response to outward events. In a normal setting a person can monitor their own responses and make a decision to engage or ignore the stimuli.

However, in situations of high stress, where there is a sense of threat or fear, the PFC shuts down and the limbic system takes over. There is no time to carefully consider all the data and options and work out a solution. The brain tells the person to act now, and there are two options for action: fight or flight (Gregory & Parry, 2006; Zull, 2002; Posner & Rothbart, 2007). Stress hormones are released, thought processing and language virtually stop, and the entire brain is geared toward monitoring and dealing with the perceived threat.

So how does stress affect learning in a contemporary classroom? Most classrooms are free of saber-tooth tigers, but not all threats are physical or life-threatening. For children in school, the fear may be of humiliation, ridicule, bullying, embarrassment, failure, or confusion. The stimuli may be a mean classmate, an insensitive teacher, a task that is too hard for the student at his or her current abilities or readiness, or even a stressful home environment. These things put a child in a state of constant alert, ever scanning the environment for danger, and ever reacting with anger, fear, or sadness. These emotions emanate from the primitive brain, and we know that when the primitive limbic brain is in control, the PFC with its higher functioning shuts down (Raz & Buhle, 2006). The person cannot focus on learning because the limbic system is too busy. In this case, it's not that the students aren't paying attention. They just aren't paying attention to learning because they are on high alert in their limbic system. They're in survival mode.

Hattie's meta-analysis research on anxiety shows an impact with effect size of $d = 0.40$ (although most of the research used focused on test anxiety and mathematics). Given the impact of undue stress on the ability of the brain to process new information creating appropriate challenges and offering emotional support to students may be one of the most important strategies for any teacher. Jensen (1998) theorizes that excess stress and threat could be the single highest contributor to inhibiting academic success in schools. So it is crucial that this be recognized and monitored by all teachers so that learning can be activated.

The Goal: Appropriate Stress Levels

Some level of stress is desirable. Stress can help people thrive and survive by contributing a high motivation and engagement with the task at hand; in reasonable amounts and for short time periods, those stress hormones help get the job done. Without any pressure there is little motivation. Neuroscientist Antonio Damasio (2003) defines appropriate stress as that which occurs when a challenge is just beyond the person's current skill level. He calls this *maximal cognitive efficiency*. Likewise, Kirby et al. (2013) found that the onset of stress entices the brain into growing new cells responsible for improved memory.

However, when stress levels become too high or last too long, they become harmful (Goleman, 2006b). Kirby's research found the benefits of stress only accrued when stress was intermittent. As soon as the stress continued into a prolonged state, it began to *suppress* the brain's ability to develop new cells. And for some children, the level of stress that they are under—the amount of cortisol and adrenalin churning through their bodies on a daily basis—is similar to that of a combat soldier. They simply cannot engage their PFC and learn under a condition of constant stress.

The Strategy: Managing Stress in the Classroom

Teachers cannot eliminate all the stress from children's lives. But they can reduce the stress that children are subject to within the classroom. It's a constant balancing act to create just the right amount of low-level, intermittent stress—the good kind of stress that Kirby and Goleman say aids in achievement—but not so much that it shuts down the PFC.

So how can teachers achieve this optimal balance? Here are just some of the things that teachers can monitor and adjust:

- **The physical climate:** Some students have a hard time staying seated for long periods of time. If a student appears to need more opportunities to move and speak, find ways to make that happen. If a child is constantly told to sit down and be quiet, the continual negative feedback can put his brain in a state of stress. Another aspect of the physical climate can be classroom layout; some children may feel isolated and need to interact with classmates more.

- **The intellectual climate:** Students experience stress when the tasks before them are too far out of their current range of capabilities or when instructions are unclear. They experience boredom when the tasks are too far below their capabilities or the work feels purposeless. Boredom or frustration will inhibit the information flow. In these situations students will either "zone out" or "act out." Their reduced academic success affects their self-confidence and reinforces a fixed mindset of failure and often learned helplessness.

- **The emotional climate:** Students find it stressful when they are isolated from their peers or have no emotional or cognitive support systems and structures. Understanding how to establish and maintain a positive classroom climate is crucial to the quality of learning and time on task. Even basic courtesy and kindness are important. As Hirschy and Braxton (2004) indicate, "Incivilities that are not addressed properly not only negatively impact learning within the course in which it is experienced, but may also negatively influence a student's success at an institution."

Teachers can create a positive classroom environment by keeping the door to the PFC open. They can provide stimulation—without undue stress—by introducing novelty and interesting ideas and items that create curiosity. Exploring novel experiences activates the SEEKING system for mammals that is important for survival, and engaging it releases dopamine, a great motivator. This sense of engagement and reward helps to "Velcro" information or concepts to the mind and transfer learning to long-term memory. All the attention-getting devices at our disposal, from music, color, stimulating curiosity, discrepant events, anomalies, and questions, not only activate the brain but also allow the brain to pay attention, take in information, and process it if there is an absence of threat (Wang et al., 2005).

Students are intrigued when there are opportunities to explore and connect with new materials and concepts. For example, a teacher may provide students with a variety of tools and utensils borrowed from a pioneer museum. The students can examine them and speculate on how they had been used by pioneers and then brainstorm which tools we use today to do the same functions. The collaboration and speculation in this activity can create high interest and further investigation at the secondary processing conscious level of the SEEKING system.

A classroom that balances appropriate challenge and creates an environment and climate that are supportive and safe allow students to take risks and be themselves. It allows for that state that Damasio calls maximal cognitive efficiency and Caine and Caine (1994, 1997) call *relaxed alertness,* where students are attending to tasks without undue pressure and with full support of peers and teachers, satisfying the brain's innate need to know.

Strategy 1: Routine and the Importance of Clear Expectations

Many students take the unexpected twists and turns of life in stride. But others feel great stress when they experience uncertainty—a reaction to a mostly imagined threat often referred to as "anticipatory anxiety." These students become anxious if they are unsure about what is going to happen, conditions are unclear and expectations of their performance ambiguous.

Students do better in classrooms where they know what to expect. There are consistent, clear, and predictable processes for "how we do things around here." Not to say that surprises and deviations don't or won't happen, and often add novelty that the brain loves and pays attention to, but when they do we can ease students through the unknown with clarity and scaffolding supports. If we provide this environment we will lower stress and reduce distractions and anxiety and produce a more brain-friendly place to learn with more focused attention to learning.

Many of my students would come into class asking, "What are we doing today?" I was glad for their enthusiasm and knew that they were seeking clarity of purpose and some knowledge of what we were going to be doing and learning and perhaps also to decide if this was going to be an interesting day. Knowing what to expect brings clarity to the day and helps students anticipate what they enjoy as well as prepare them for the challenges they may have.

Providing agendas for the class and/or unit of study will foreshadow what the content, tasks, or activities that students will be exposed to in the classroom (see Figure 1.1). Brains like to know where they are going and it creates curiosity, opens mental files to prior knowledge, and helps with transitions. Posting the materials, books, and resources that students will need to get ready for the learning is helpful too. This can be done by taking a photo of the materials and posting them on a white board so students see what materials they will need for the class without a lot of teacher aural direction and students tuning out. Visuals have much greater clarity and consistency than the teacher repeating and repeating "Take out your . . . " We know the brain pays attention to visuals more of the time than auditory stimulus (Sousa, 2006). Figure 1.1 shows some examples of agendas.

Strategy 2: Standards and Expectations

Along with the agenda students also need to know and be clear about the standards and objectives as well as the tasks and criteria for success. These need to be clear and also presented in student verbiage with perhaps rubrics that help them focus on criteria so that they can monitor their progress (more in Chapter 5). This will also help reduce anticipatory anxiety and lower stress. Having a choice of assessment methods also gives student a sense of control and lowers anxiety. Control over process and progress will give students the autonomy they need to develop as life long and assessment capable learners. Choice is a great activator and motivator.

The use of rubrics and scoring scales help students focus and monitor their own progress toward goals and personal success.

Strategy 3: Routines and Procedures

Setting up routines and establishing procedures will also dissipate "anticipatory anxiety" and help keep the prefrontal lobe rather than the ancient brain centers engaged. This will alleviate stress and unnecessary distraction. Procedures and routines also set up patterns for the brain and facilitate smooth transitions and management of materials, resources, and student interactions that are positive and as a result increase on task behavior.

Figure 1.1 Agenda Samples

Agenda: January 15, 2015

1. Learning intentions for cells
2. Cell Game: Review terminology and structures
3. Write cell analogies to explain cell part functions

Agenda: Thursday, January 15, 2015

NO notebooks needed today

1. POP quiz
2. Review with I have . . . Who has?
3. Jeopardy game on Illinois history

Agenda for Today

Meet with 9:00 partner and review your homework.
Meet in project groups and create a timeline for your project.
Generate a "to-do" list with group member commitment.

Review Columbus's journey with your partner.
Pairs squared: Complete the jigsaw reading and timeline graphic.
Create a group mind map of his accomplishments.

Sign up for the center where you want to start.
Review the directions for the center with the group there.
Work in the center for 20 minutes.
Be ready to report on your work.

Source: Images courtesy of jannoon028/Shutterstock.com.

Establish procedures and behaviors (with student input if possible) for

- Class entry and exit
- Accessing resources and materials
- Options when work is finished
- What to do when you don't know what to do
- Accessing help and support
- Forming groups
- Respectful behavior

Having students discuss these procedures and routines and offer suggestions and ideas is a great way to include them in their reality. It fosters a sense of community as they contribute suggestions. They often have great ideas and are more willing to support them if they have had input and own the decisions. This buys in to their need for a sense of control and autonomy.

These procedures can be posted in the classroom so that students have a reference point and can access them when needed. This saves a lot of time and off task behavior when the teacher doesn't have to keep reiterating them (often falling on the ears of tuned out students). The brain pays attention to what it needs at the moment. Relevancy is a reality. A comfort level and sense of support can help students feel emotionally and psychologically safe and cognitively enabled. These routines and procedures also create a sense of self-efficacy and autonomy that is motivating and self-satisfying to students.

Initially these procedures should be reviewed, perhaps demonstrated and practiced so that they are clear to the students; also this will give students an opportunity to revise them if things aren't working for them or the class. Repetition reinforces the probability that knowledge and skills will become automatic over time, as the neural connections in the cerebellum are strengthened and myelinated (dendrites grow thicker with a fatty coating of myelin that protects and insulates the dendrites and increases their connection speed).

Some routines can be shared visually. The ASCD has examples of visuals for procedures at their website (ASCD, n.d.).

An example of establishing a procedure might be: "What to do when you're stuck." In a whole-class discussion students can offer suggestions for getting help or resources when they are stuck. These can be brainstormed in the whole group or students can work in small groups to generate options. This is also an example of student input and voice that builds trust and consensus.

Sample items might be those shown in Figure 1.2.

Behavior guidelines for how to work alone, in a group, or as a class will greater ensure a stable environment and contribute to organization

Figure 1.2 Student Signboards

What to Do When You're Stuck
- Check for a chart with directions.
- Ask someone in your group quietly.
- Think about what would help and where it might be.
- Conduct an Internet search.
- Check your text.
- Check your notes.

When You Come Into Class
- Enter quietly.
- Pick up the Do Now assignment and any supplies you need.
- Sharpen your pencil if needed.
- Be seated.
- Read the day's learning objective.
- Read the agenda.
- Begin your Do Now.

Leaving the Class
- Turn in all assignments.
- Return any supplies, books, or pencils.
- Put your notebook on the shelf.
- Have your things ready to go.
- Make sure your desk and floor around your desk is clean.
- Remain quiet and stay seated until dismissed.

and orderliness. These guidelines free the self-preservation mode and allow students to engage fully in pursuit of learning. "How we work together" in this classroom is important as it reduces potential conflict that may arise in collaborative work situations and creates an orderly atmosphere of predictability and safety. Establishing classroom norms or behaviors is crucial to positive social interaction. Norms are a good way to go rather than rules. Rules sound more punitive and rigid whereas norms indicate what is normal behavior that we all expect. Students can also create their own norms. *Tribes* and Gibbs provide a program of building classroom community that has a set of fixed norms.

Strategy 4: Movement

Movement is valuable in the classroom and contributes to the overall climate as it creates both a sense of freedom and self control—and it ultimately lowers stress. As we sit it becomes more of a stress on the body to pump oxygenated blood to the brain. The brain needs 20% of the body's glucose and oxygen. It is a small organ comparatively but needs nourishing to keep it working optimally. Moving helps pump the blood to the brain. This creates a wake-up surge. When we move we reduce stress and release endorphins and dopamine, as well as lower the levels of cortisol and adrenaline (the stress hormones). A renewed sense of well-being and comfort is achieved (Ratey, 2008).

In Finland children have 15 minutes of exercise for every hour of instruction. Nations that are eliminating physical education and recess for more seat time are missing the boat. It is counterintuitive to eliminate movement when we know how important it is for the brain and learning. Students moving to form a group or moving tables and chairs to work together is a natural movement. A standing partner dialogue will work as well. A movement song such as "Head, Shoulders, Knees and Toes" or a game of Simon Says would be a stress reliever and energy booster. Brain Gym (Dennison & Dennison, 1986) offers plenty of movements that re-oxygenate the brain and energize the learners.

Physically and psychologically movement helps create a climate that is less stressful and more brain-friendly.

THE PROBLEM OF SOCIAL ISOLATION

How Social Isolation Shuts Down Learning

School is not a comfortable place for all students. They may feel unsafe emotionally, physically, and mentally. Isolation can grow out of socioeconomic differences, racial issues, bullying, or a student's lack of social skills. Social isolation affects learning in much the same way that stress does: by engaging the brain in activities other than learning. Students may be more concerned with saving face or self-protection than academic quests.

Two cognitive psychologists contributed to our understanding of how people prioritize their attention. The first, Abraham Maslow, in 1968 suggested a hierarchy of human needs. Maslow believed that basic needs must be met before other needs can be addressed, in this order:

- Physiological needs: water, food, air, shelter
- Safety needs: order, security, freedom from fear
- Belongingness and love: family, spouse, children, friends
- Self-esteem: self-respect, reputation, achievement
- Self-actualization: achieving one's potential

The second theorist, William Glasser (1990, 1999), developed his own array of five needs, which are similar to Maslow's in many ways but not hierarchically arranged. The five need categories are as follows:

	The need to survive and procreate: health, relaxation, sex
	The need to belong and love: respect, friendship
	The need to have some power: recognition, success
	The need for freedom: choice, independence
	The need to have fun: enjoyment, laughter

Source: Survival, belonging, freedom, and fun images courtesy of Dynamic Graphics/Liquid Library/ThinkStock; power image courtesy of Medioimages/Photodisc/ThinkStock.

Glasser's choice theory of motivation emphasizes people's abilities to choose which needs they address. For Glasser, the need to belong is the most important; it parallels Maslow's categories of belonging and love.

The Goal: Identifying Social Isolation and Balancing Social and Learning Needs

Although the theories of Maslow and Glasser are slightly different, both theorists demonstrate that needs occur in a context and are often competing with other needs that are just as pressing—or even more pressing. This explains why a problem like social isolation can impede the learning process. For most children, the need to belong will far outweigh the need to learn multiplication tables or the process of creating a PowerPoint presentation. If concern about meeting the need to belong is preoccupying a young mind, learning will take a back seat.

Social isolation can stem from many causes. For example, if a student's primary language is not English, he or she may be shy about engaging in social interactions or may have trouble understanding concepts, leading to frustration and embarrassment. Some students may be migrants or in the country illegally and, if transient, feel like it's not worth connecting with classmates. Sexual orientation may create isolation if students feel they must hide their orientation. Some students of different cultural backgrounds find it challenging to connect with academic material that is outside their prior knowledge or experience. Bullying and racism are other isolating factors that cause students to be traumatized daily.

When students' social needs are not being met, they are too focused on self-preservation (emotional, psychological, and physical) to care about learning.

These situations prevent students from focusing on learning for very real reasons (National Research Council, 2003). Teachers need to manage the classroom and make sure that socializing doesn't take precedence over learning. But they also need to ensure that students have their social needs met so that fears about social isolation don't hobble their ability to concentrate and learn. This balancing act is the goal.

The Strategy: Managing Social Isolation in the Classroom

It's crucial that teachers create a positive, warm climate in the classroom by developing a community of supportive learners and peer-positive relationships (Charney, 2002; Donohue, Perry, & Weinstein, 2003). This will increase the comfort level of students so that they can then activate the PFC and focus on learning rather than personal or emotional safety. It also promotes learning by avoiding the negative behaviors that can result from social isolation. If a person doesn't feel included, he or she will create his own inclusion by grabbing influence-attracting attention, creating a controversy, demanding power, or withdrawing into passive belligerence (Gibbs, 2006a).

The following sections offer activities that may help build classroom inclusion and a supportive, positive climate for thinking.

Strategy 1: Creating Classroom Norms

Working together on a shared goal is one way to mitigate social isolation. One project students can work on together is developing classroom norms. To do this, the teacher can have students work in groups of three or four. A large piece of newspaper divided into sections (Figures 1.3 and 1.4 on the next page) allows each student to write down what is important to them when they are working in the classroom. After each student writes down his or her ideas, the small group can share and discuss their needs and then come to consensus about one or two statements that they think are most important. These are written in the center box and presented to the class. The statements are refined and/or combined to come up with five or six norms that the whole class agrees to. Everyone has a voice and input into the master list, and often this satisfies the individual that they have been heard and respected. People are much more likely to support norms if they are part of the creation.

Strategy 2: Tribes

Jeanne Gibbs was an educator in Santa Rosa in the 1980s who was attempting to implement cooperative group learning in her classroom. Her classroom was made up of African American, Caucasian, and Hispanic children, and Gibbs found that they were not working well together. She developed the program called *Tribes* (2006) in order to build classroom community and collaboration. Students were placed in culturally and ability heterogeneous groups as base groups. She began using team-building activities to forge relationships and find commonalities among students. The more students interacted with everyone in the class as well as their base groups, the more they developed an understanding and tolerance not seen before. They realized they were more similar than different and began

Figure 1.3 Placemat for a Group of Four

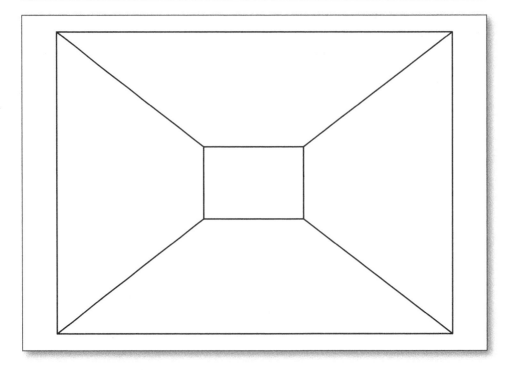

Figure 1.4 Placemat for a Group of Three

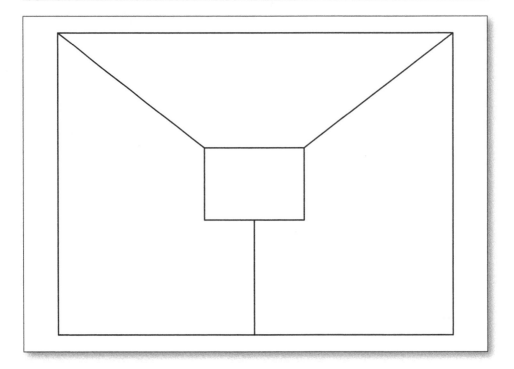

to appreciate each other's traits and skills and work better together in a respectful, supportive, complementary way. This made a huge difference for the climate of the classroom and the productivity that ensued without resentment and conflict. They became a WE community. The program has become so popular that Gibbs recently published a 30-year anniversary edition of *Tribes*.

Tribes describes four classroom norms that help build inclusion and safety. They are as follows:

1. Attentive listening: giving full attention

2. Showing appreciation/no put-downs

3. Right to pass—right to participate

4. Mutual respect: personal regard

These norms need to be understood and agreed on by all members and monitored by the teacher and each member of the group so that they enhance the learning climate with the sensitivity and respect needed to give the brain opportunity to fully activate and learning to take place. Let's take a look at these four norms and how they can be encouraged in the classroom.

1. Attentive Listening

Attentive listening is an important skill that is becoming harder and harder for children to master as their lives are bombarded with media and technology that moves at a rapid pace, and as people are constantly flipping from screen to screen and not giving full attention to anything. These digital natives have brains that are used to "switching screens" and may not give full attention to anything.

Although one might expect to be more efficient by multitasking, one study (Rubinstein, Evans, & Meyer, 2001) showed that people lost large amounts of time as they jumped from task to task. And even more time was lost when the tasks were challenging. Meyer says that productivity may be reduced nearly 40% when people switch tasks.

Contrary to popular thought, the brain is not good at multitasking. Research at Stanford University (Ophir, Nass, & Wagner, 2009) showed that it is better to do one thing at a time and focus without trying to divide your attention. People who are receiving several streams of electronic information cannot recall, pay full attention, or transition from one task to the next as well as those who focus on one task at a time. Multitasking actually reduces your efficiency and performance. Your brain lacks the capacity to simultaneously perform two tasks well.

Not only does multitasking slow you down, it lowers your IQ. Adults who multitasked during cognitive thinking showed IQ score declines close to those of someone who had stayed up all night or smoked marijuana, sometimes to the average range of an eight year old. Cognitive impairment from multitasking was thought to be temporary, but researchers at the University of Sussex in the UK (Loh & Kanai, 2014) compared the amount of time people spend on multiple devices (such as watching TV and using a tablet) to MRI scans of their brains which showed that high media multitasking is associated with smaller gray-matter density in the anterior cingulate cortex. Surprisingly high multitaskers had less brain density in the anterior cingulate cortex. This area is responsible for cognitive and emotional control and empathy.

Teaching students to listen attentively may take some time but is a critical skill in the classroom whether in large groups, small cooperative groups, or partners. Each person is encouraged to pay close attention to one another's ideas, opinions, and expressions; to let others know they are heard and to check for clarification instead of formulating a rebuttal, or multitasking. This shows a supportive climate for learning. If we began this effort in early elementary we would probably have a lot greater on task behavior from students when working in groups throughout the subsequent years of school. And it's not just important for school; it's a critical life skill as well.

To encourage attentive listening, teachers can use an activity similar to that described in "Creating Classroom Norms." They can also use a T chart, which takes a subject like attentive listening and asks students what the activity "Looks Like" and what it "Sounds Like" (see Figure 1.5).

Figure 1.5 Looks Like/Sounds Like T Chart

Skill: Attentive Listening	
What It Looks Like:	**What It Sounds Like:**

It's important to have students contribute ideas in their own words so that they can "own and adhere" to the behaviors they deem important.

2. Showing Appreciation/No Put-Downs

Expressing appreciation of others in concrete terms; using kind words; and avoiding negative remarks, hurtful name-calling, and rude gestures are other ways to promote a climate of safety and inclusion. This may seem like common sense, but these simple rules for positive communication may be foreign to some students, having engaged with the media and TV situation comedies that ridicule and use sarcasm and put-downs as the norm. Some students don't know how to give and receive a compliment.

Using a T chart for put-downs and "put-ups" is a good technique for making students more aware of their communication choices (see Figure 1.6). Students are generally much better at coming up with put-downs and may really have to think about what an alternative put-up might be. Teachers can record student suggestions as they are voiced; it's key to use the students' own language because the language that a first grader may use will be different than what an eighth grader may use. For every put-down, the students should be asked to think of an alternate put-up that is more respectful.

After completing the T chart, students need to develop a system for monitoring the use of put-downs and put-ups. One teacher asked students to create a signal or gesture to use when they heard a put down. The students chose a thumbs-down signal. Then, whenever they heard a put-down, the students gave a thumbs-down signal, and the one who used the put-down had to come up with a put-up instead. This transferred the

Figure 1.6 Turning Put-Downs Into Put-Ups!

Put-Downs	Put-Ups
That's stupid.	I don't agree.
Dumb answer.	I'm not sure that's correct.
DUH!	Oh, are you sure?
Who are you?	Why do you think so?
That's crazy!	That's different.
Never heard of such a thing.	That's new to me.

responsibility of monitoring to the students, and they were better at changing behavior than the teacher could ever be. In a couple of months the put-downs were eradicated from the classroom.

3. Right to Pass—Right to Participate

We all want our students to participate in the classroom. But the truth is that sometimes students are caught off-guard by a question; their mind goes blank, and under pressure they can't think of anything to say. This can be an embarrassing incident for a sensitive student and can increase their sense of social isolation.

In this situation, the teacher should respect the students' "right to pass." This allows the students a break to compose themselves. This is not a "free pass" that excuses them from the requirement of class participation; the teacher or group should return to them later. It's just a recognition that sometimes students need "wait time" (Rowe, 1986) to access the information. Our brain needs at least 5–7 seconds to access information stored in long-term memory, and in a fast-paced classroom there is sometimes split seconds given to respond. Often too, a student may be in a pensive stance and need time to process new ideas or concepts. A pass gives them time to do that and lowers the stress and anxiety that may occur in the learner. Time allows students to activate the long-term memory files and feel more confident in their ability to answer.

4. Mutual Respect

The *Tribes* program emphasizes affirmation and valuing the uniqueness of each individual. This may mean appreciating cultural differences or offering encouraging feedback for growth. This builds caring and support for all learners and allows them to activate the PFC and higher-order thinking.

Affirming mutual respect can come from activities we've already discussed, like put-ups and attentive listening. It can also come through group processing at the end of an activity when the group is talking about how they did that day working together. They can practice the social skills of "disagreeing with ideas, not people" and "disagreeing agreeably," both of which are valuable skills for students to foster mutual respect.

Tribes also describes team-building activities that help students know each other better. These are short exercises that can help students get to know one another and find commonalities and differences that will also facilitate inclusion and mutual respect. They can be tied to subject content for extra effectiveness. Here are some examples of these team-building activities:

- **Shoes:** One of the most moving and useful of these activities that I used was "My Favorite Shoe," and interestingly it was in an eighth grade classroom. Students were asked to bring a shoe that was important to them and be ready to share why this was so. A couple of students brought ballet or tap shoes. One brought a pair of football cleats, another flippers (although not really a shoe, scuba diving was his passion). One young girl brought a tiny pair of well-worn moccasins that she explained her grandfather made for her as a little girl. She said she would always keep them as he had passed recently and they made her feel close to him.

This powerful sharing did a lot to create social bonding for those students. Recognizing others interests and special moments went beyond regular classroom discussions. We all need to know one another at a personal level, sometimes "heart before mind." Some may think this is fluff and a waste of good instructional time; but you actually gain time in the long run as students are more comfortable working with others and fewer conflicts erupt as students have developed respect and tolerance for one another in a brain-safe climate.

- **P.I.T.:** Often when students would get with a new partner, teachers can encourage P.I.T.: Personal, Interpersonal, and Task. Students would have 90 seconds to share something personal and make an interpersonal connection. The brain needs to feel safe and comfortable and these types of exercises forge connections and help prevent isolation.

- **Names:** Another such strategy is "How I got my Name." Here a student would ask their parents or guardian what decisions were made when naming them. Origin? Named after? Why a particular spelling? I modeled this for the students. I was named Gayle because my mother liked the actress Gale Storm, and Gale was not very common. I think she used Gayle with a "y" perhaps to be different (I've had to spell it all my life for clarity on documents) or perhaps the "y" was added for balance with the "tail" letters in Gregory. Gregory would appear to be Anglo-Saxon in origin, but it's actually not. My dad was Ukrainian and the original family name was Gregorky. Removing the "k" made it less foreign. My middle name is Helen after my maternal grandmother. Her maiden name was Duncan (which my cousin got as a middle name). I was glad to be born first and get Helen.

All of these activities allow students to share personal information with class members—and they have students talking at home and learning to value their heritage. This activity serves to expand students' knowledge of cultures and traditions of their classmates and hopefully continues to help them develop mutual respect.

The *Tribes* program is a wonderful aid in reducing social isolation in classrooms. There are editions of *Tribes* for elementary, middle, and high schools and a Spanish edition as well. I also highly recommend Gibbs' companion volume, *Reaching All by Creating Tribes Learning Communities*, which is a wonderful resource for team-building activities.

Strategy 3: Personal Interest in Students

Each student in our classrooms is a whole human being. Each has a life beyond the classroom, and knowing something about that helps us know him/her better as a learner as well. It helps to know their likes and dislikes, extracurricular activities, talents, and interests. The more we know about the student the more we can relate to them, and relate the classroom experience to their real world. The more we know about them the better we can tap into their areas of interest. We are able to forge connections and create bonds by commenting on things in their real world that interest them (McCombs & Whisler, 1997; Combs, 1982). Invisible students who don't feel noticed or welcomed may act out to receive the recognition they desire in a negative way (Sheets & Gay 1996) or withdraw further as they don't see themselves as part of the classroom community. Exhibiting consideration, patience, and interest in our students make teachers seem more likeable and approachable (Barr, 1958; Good & Brophy, 1995)

Teachers sometimes use interest surveys to get to know students quickly. Figures 1.7 and 1.8 are two samples of ones you might use or adjust.

Showing a personal interest in students is very cost effective and meets with big payoffs in winning them over. Making an effort through some of the following:

- Welcome students as they come into your classroom.
- Use high-fives or elbow or fist bumps to make a connection.
- Engage in conversation before, during, and after class.
- Comment on the extracurricular activities they are involved with.
- Drop by the cafeteria and speak to them informally.
- Ask about the events in their lives such as drama, sports, and music.
- Mention their out-of-school successes such as sports or other achievements.

Figure 1.7 Student Interest Survey

Name: _____ Date: _____

Please answer each question so I can get to know you better.

What is your favorite sport to watch or play?	What is the most interesting place you've been?
What is your favorite movie and why?	What is your favorite thing to do?
What clubs or groups do you attend?	What is your favorite meal or snack?
Who would you like to meet in person and why?	What would you say is best about school?
What do you do for fun with your friends?	How much time each day do you spend watching a "screen" of any kind?
What kind of stores do you like to visit?	What is your favorite kind of music?
What is something you are interested in globally?	In the future what would be your choice of career or area of interest where you would like to work?

Figure 1.8 A Few of My Favorite Things . . .

Name: _____ Date: _____

1. My favorite show on TV is _____ .
2. My favorite food is _____ .
3. My favorite sport is _____ .
4. My favorite snack is _____ .
5. My favorite movie is _____ .
6. My favorite book is _____ .
7. My favorite place to go is _____ .
8. My favorite game to play is _____ .
9. My favorite pet is/would be _____ .
10. My BFFs are _____ and _____ .

- Call them by their name and acknowledge them in the hall or schoolyard.
- Call or text if they are absent. When they return to school tell them that they were missed.

Share your attention with everyone and be as equitable as you can with your contacts by considering the following:

- Provide "wait time" for students when questioning.
- The "power zone" (proximity to students) is important to help learners feel connected, so remove physical barriers; move about the room during the class to be close at some time to all students.
- Show appreciation and acknowledge their ideas.
- Make eye contact; look at them when they speak and truly listen to them.
- Respect their opinions and encourage involvement.

Strategy 4: Catching Them Being Good

Students are used to hearing corrections, rules, and criticism in the guise of constructive criticism. However negativity is rarely encouraging. Try finding something that they did each day that might be positive. It is especially important for those students who receive a lot of criticism or are estranged from their peers. It's the premise of "finding their stars before their scars." Even small things can forge a bond.

An easy way to "find their stars" and catch them being good is to display student work on the walls of the classroom. The bulletin boards should be teeming with art and writing samples—and not just with the best samples (or you may end up with the same students' work being displayed all the time). There should be a space for work by students who have shown great improvement and effort as well. Some teachers divide up the bulletin board space in a self-contained classroom or on the class website so that there is a space for everyone.

In a middle or high school classrooms teachers can dedicate a bulletin board for each class they teach. High school teachers often think this is an elementary thing and not appropriate for high school. However it really helps students feel that the classroom is home, that they belong here, this is what they are learning, and this is what they have achieved. Orderliness in helpful in the classroom as well so that students feel comfortable and can access resources easily. I taught elementary school before I was in a high school. In elementary classrooms everyone displayed their students' work. When I went to the high school I naturally used the bulletin boards for charts, student work, interesting articles, and lots of other things unlike most other classrooms.

ASSESSING YOUR OWN CLASSROOM CLIMATE

Marzano (2003) found that the achievement effects of a well-managed classroom was $d = 0.52$ and in terms of engagement $d = 0.62$. Teachers who had the correct mental set and a great influence on the management of the classroom and reducing disruption had an effect of $d = 1.29$. Teachers who could assess and quickly react to prevent behavior problems without emotional investment had an effect size of $d = 1.42$. This trait is also referred to as situational awareness or mindfulness by Langer (1989). Hattie's meta-analysis rated ES 0.68 for classroom behavior and 0.52 for classroom management.

The statistics reaffirm how important classroom climate is. Teachers who know how to create a positive climate make a huge difference in student learning, not because they are acting as an information source but because their classroom climate helps activate students by creating a safe, warm, nurturing environment where brains can flourish.

The checklist in Figure 1.9 can help teachers evaluate their own classroom culture and target areas for improvement for a brain-friendly environment.

SUMMARY

Brains can't learn in hostile environments. It's like setting the stage in the theater: everything must be just right with resources, props, and scenery that will enhance the experience along with appropriate stage directions. When we know that undue stress is detrimental to the learning process, we as educators should do everything we can to provide an appropriate positive climate that will allow students to feel comfortable, meet challenges, and learn in a risk-free, safe environment.

DISCUSSION POINTS

- Discuss how educational neuroscience has or could influence your decisions about classroom tasks and management techniques. What research in this chapter has intrigued you, and what might you do as a result?

- Discuss the notion of classroom climate and its implications for student learning.

- Examine ways to reduce anxiety and create a climate that supports brain safety, including attention to routines and norms.

- Consider the social isolation of students in the classroom that often leads to bullying. How can teachers minimize social isolation and foster student relationships? What do Maslow and Glass consider to be people's basic needs, and how can teachers help meet those needs?

- Do some further investigation of *Tribes*, especially strategies for team-building and the development of social skills.

- How does movement increase the sense of well-being in a classroom? Discuss some strategies to include movement as part of stress-free classroom.

Figure 1.9 Classroom Climate Self-Assessment

Read the statements below. Mark the response that most closely describes the extent that you consider this in your classroom on a regular basis

1 = never   2 = seldom   3 = occasionally   4 = regularly

	Statement	Self-Assessment Response (1–4)
1.	I believe all students can learn.	
2.	I create norms with my students to identify acceptable behaviors.	
3.	I share expectations for procedures and processes.	
4.	I try to understand my students' personal lives if possible.	
5.	I have the students submit an interest survey or self-assessment.	
6.	Students give their input about how the class satisfies their needs.	
7.	I try to treat students fairly and equitably.	
8.	I believe in the potential for success for my students.	
9.	My students know I like them.	
10.	I respect the multiculturalism of my students.	
11.	My students feel safe in my classroom.	
12.	My students feel confident in taking risks and making errors.	
13.	I recognize the uniqueness of each of my students.	
14.	I try to organize the classroom so students can get the resources they need.	
15.	The class decor reflects the students' work and efforts.	
16.	The environment is orderly and comfortable.	
17.	I try to keep the students engaged in interesting and challenging activities.	
18.	I try to be a learner alongside my students.	
19.	I listen to my students, empathize, and respond.	
20.	I do not ridicule or humiliate my students.	
21.	I use a variety of multimodal instructional strategies in my teaching.	
22.	I provide choices in topics, processes, or products to increase motivation.	
23.	I adjust the curriculum topics to fit my students' interests and readiness.	
24.	I am sensitive to my students' physical, emotional, and social needs.	
25.	I remember how it feels to be a student.	

- Discuss the section on student interests. How do you find out what students do beyond school, and how might you tap into their interests to increase their comfort and connectedness?

- Use the Classroom Climate Teacher Self-Assessment, and identify one or two things you want to improve or focus on.

2 Activating Teachers

The act of teaching requires deliberate interventions to ensure that there is cognitive change in the student . . . aware of the learning intentions, knowing when a student is successful . . . , having understanding of student's prior understanding as he or she comes to the task, and knowing enough about the content to provide meaningful and challenging experiences.

—Hattie (2012, p. 19)

Teaching is no small feat. It requires that the teacher have a full repertoire of proven instructional strategies, be able to provide helpful feedback, and create a safe, caring, nurturing environment, rich in ideas and resources where one is permitted to be vulnerable and risk errors in the quest of learning.

Teachers are the principal resource for student learning. And teachers have a hand in all of the aspects of activated learning that this book discusses—from classroom climate to developing peer relationships. But this chapter focuses specifically on the ways that teachers can activate learning in the classroom—in particular, personal attitude, growth mindset, and instructional techniques.

PERSONAL ATTITUDE

Students come to school each day and are flooded with messages from everyone around them. Neuroscience tells us that the brain works at a conscious and unconscious level; sensory information is processed continually with or without awareness (Ornstein & Thompson, 1984). In the classroom, students process not only what is heard (what the teacher and others say out loud) but also multiple messages that come through a teacher's tone, gestures, body language, and facial clues (O'Keefe & Nadel, 1978). They notice smiles and expressions as well as eye rolling, exasperated looks, and sarcasm (Pianta & Hamre, 2001; Rimm-Kaufman et al., 2002). Students, based on how they are treated or spoken to, make assumptions about what the teacher thinks or feels about them. These assumptions prevail and influence the student's self concept and feelings of welcome and acceptance. The messages students receive can determine whether they persevere or give up, take risks or avoid risks, allow themselves to be vulnerable by speaking up in class or hide in the corner hoping never to be called on. Teachers have a lot of power over young impressionable psyches.

The following sections discuss some of the messages that we as educators need to send to students about how we value them academically and personally.

Attitude 1: Enthusiasm

A teacher's enthusiasm is one of the most valuable messages she can deliver to students. Students are watching your expressions. Enthusiasm lets students know that the teacher believes good and exciting things are about to happen. Students need both routine and novelty: routine to help them feel safe and in control, and novelty to stimulate them. Enthusiasm conveys both safety and a sense of fun and adventure.

There are several things teachers can do to enhance the expression of their enthusiasm. One is almost ridiculously easy: smile. Smiling seems to be the most recognizable social cue even at a distance. The old cliché "Don't smile before Christmas" is a fallacy. Smiling has many benefits in interpersonal relationships because the smiler is presumed to be more likeable, friendly, approachable, and socially competent. The impact is also notable; exposure to a smile may alter another's mind to being more positive and favorable. A genuine smile from the teacher is a powerful tool. It shows welcome, respect, appreciation, and that you are glad to be there and glad that they are too (LaFrance, 2011).

Smiling is rarely displayed when isolated. It is a social interaction that has split-second recognition and elicits an instant response from most people. It is contagious. I have often smiled at a child who seems unhappy. Looking at their sad face, I add "NO smiling" and they immediately break into a smile or a giggle. (Interestingly, frowns do not appear to be contagious.) Smiles also convey understanding. A gentle low-level smile with only a slight movement around the mouth is a cue that the brain understands whatever it is engaged in.

Cultures may vary as to whom they smile at or the appropriateness of a smile. For example, the extended length of a smile for Russians may be taken as insincerity, and many Koreans think that a man who smiles a lot is not a real man. Cultural and facial expressions do vary. But smiles are important and needed. They send a powerful nonverbal message and help prep students' brain to welcome the learning that will follow.

Another important messenger is gestures. It is amazing what impact gestures have on student thinking. Studies by Dr. Goldin-Meadow et al. (2005, 2009) show that teachers who use gestures find students more actively use the information presented. Hand gestures as a teaching strategy increases learning during a lesson, and young children think the teacher is more knowledgeable if she uses her arms to punctuate key points. One teacher raised her arm and index finger whenever there was an important thing to pay attention to, essentially using her whole body as a teaching tool.

Gestures also convey commitment, emphasis, and enthusiasm. Facial expressions and intonational pitch also helps punctuate learning. Speaking softly will often cause students to pay closer attention. Moving about the room and using arms in expressive ways punctuates key ideas. A more animated teacher conveys enthusiasm and intensity related to the subject material.

A third tool is humor. Laugh a little. Learning is serious business, but, as G. K. Chesterfield wrote, "angels can fly because they take themselves lightly." Emphasizing humor and laughter may seem like a generic feel-good recommendation. But there's science behind it: Laughter raises endorphins, which release pleasurable feelings and help associate learning with enjoyment. It helps the memory processing system because it is a form of novelty, which increases attention, and it activates the hippocampus, which aids in putting information into long-term memory.

Humor also helps unify the group that laughs together. Teachers can tell humorous stories related to the topic or event, and this also increases memory as the brain loves stories and also remembers the anomalies, inconsistencies, and juxtaposition that humor presents. I remember little of my ancient history class but do remember the day the teacher talked about the first marathon runner in ancient Greece, a man named Phidippides. The teacher said we could remember his name by imagining him looking at his dirty socks at the end of a long day of running in sandals. He told us that at the end of the day Phidippides said "Phi dippi des socks in Tide, they will be clean for the morning." I remembered this in Greece when the tour guide asked us about the first runner even though it was 30 years later. Humor sticks.

Laughter can also help as a tension breaker when there appears to be a power struggle between teacher and student. A colleague was very skillful with taking the sail out of students' wind. One day a student, frustrated at the time, commented out loud that "math sucks"; the teacher quickly responded, "So does a vacuum cleaner and we need them both." Laughter ensued and then dissipated, and everyone resumed working as the teacher went on to help the student with some worked examples. This kind of humor worked because the comment wasn't personal. Everyone saved face and a tense moment was lightened. It also reinforced for the student that the teacher had his best interests at heart, and after that episode the student was never disrespectful in class again.

It is critical to remember that some types of humor are inappropriate in the classroom. Humor at a student's expense is never a good or positive step. Sarcasm is never acceptable. Sarcasm comes from the Greek *sarkazein*, which translated means "to tear or strip the flesh off." A math teacher trying to be humorous and perhaps trying to lighten the moment once told my daughter that she had a vegetable brain when she couldn't grasp a problem; he said he thought it perhaps was spinach. Everyone laughed except her. We needed a math tutor for her after that incident, as she was so traumatized in front of her peers that she had trouble concentrating on math for the rest of that semester in that class for fear that she would again be humiliated by her teacher. It's possible that another student may not have reacted as she did, but that just emphasizes that as teachers, we really have to know the learner before we risk humor that may affect the relationship. Sarcasm or negative humor can send students into flight-or-fight mode, which deactivates the prefrontal cortex, the primary site of learning, judgment, and memory making.

Attitude 2: Credibility

A second key attitude for teachers is credibility. Credibility encompasses many traits, including not just subject matter expertise but personal attributes like trust and fairness that lend authority to the teacher's position as an educator. Professor Hattie's latest research, published in his book *Visible Learning for Teachers* (2012), suggests that teacher credibility is one of the most important factors in all of learning. Hattie cautions us that students will turn off if a teacher is perceived as not being credible. Students are behind for most of their school lives if they haven't developed the value of education by about age eight. Having one ineffective teacher increases the probability of a student dropping out before graduating. Having two or more increases the probability even more.

According to Hattie, teacher credibility is vital to learning, and students are very perceptive about knowing which teachers can make a difference. The impact of teacher credibility is an effect size of $d = 0.90$, which is quite an impact based on perception. We know that the brain is working as a parallel processor taking in all data and can be intuitive at the subconscious level. Teachers can sometimes either have a "halo" effect or a "jerk" effect.

Subject matter expertise is necessary, of course, but that in and of itself has no positive effect on student achievement. In fact according to Hattie's research, teachers' subject matter knowledge may actually have a negative effect of $d = 0.09$, if the teachers' expertise makes them distant, unable to gauge how much the students know, or unable to convey knowledge that is so second nature to them and concepts and skills that have been so deeply internalized that they don't understand how someone could not "get it." It's not what they know but what they do with what they know that makes the difference. It's the quality of the instruction interactions and how students learn from the expert that increases student achievement. The effect size of teaching strategies is 0.62.

The second component of credibility, in addition to subject matter expertise, is those personal attributes that justify the teacher's authority. Dr. James McCroskey, who researched credibility in communication in the early 1980s, identified four key factors of credibility: trust, competence, dynamism, and immediacy (Haskins, 2000). Haskins used the term *ethos* to refer to these attributes collectively and noted that "Erosion of a teacher's ethos can quickly spell disaster. . . . Whether at the conscious or unconscious level, a student's perception of the teacher's ethos, or speaker's character, has an important impact on how he or she will react to the teacher and how effective the teacher will be in the classroom."

McCroskey's four key factors of credibility function in the classroom in specific ways:

1. **Trust:** Trust refers to the students' bedrock belief that the teacher can be relied upon to act in certain ways: to act in the students' best interests (wanting them to learn, not embarrassing them), to avoid favoritism, to display consistency and fairness (with classroom discipline, rules, and other activities), and so on. Teachers need to be counted on to say what they mean and mean what they say. That being said, students need to understand that "fair isn't always equal" and "equal isn't always fair."

Note that the trust level in the school community matters as well. Bryk and Schneider (2002) found in a seven-year study of 400 elementary schools that the higher the trust level among parents, teachers, students, and the administration, the better the students performed on standardized tests. Bryk and Schneider called this "relational trust," referring the interpersonal interactions that occur in the school and classroom.

2. **Competence:** A teacher must know their subject and be able to deliver it in a meaningful way. Competence includes good classroom management skills (ES $d = 0.52$), the ability to answer questions, and the capacity to explain complex material in multiple ways. Expertise is tricky: You have to know your stuff but also know how to help others learn it. Sometimes an expert who has perfected his skills and knowledge over time may have forgotten how exactly he learned the information or skills. Empathy and understanding are key traits to help others grow.

3. **Dynamism:** Teachers who just go through the motions robotically with a laminated plan book, used year after year, lose credibility quickly as they do not engage learners with the enthusiasm and excitement that they should bring to the subject material. After all, if we as educators aren't excited, why should they be? Part of that excitement is novelty, variety, and creativity in the teaching/learning process. The brain loves it and responds with better attention and more active engagement. It energizes the learner and keeps them on their toes. "I wonder [can't wait to see] what we'll be doing today" is a great way for students to approach a class.

4. **Immediacy:** Immediacy refers to a feeling of closeness to students, everything from verbal traits (e.g., using collective pronouns such as "we" or "us") or nonverbal (e.g., making eye contact, rearranging the class into a community circle, utilizing the "power zone" of physical proximity to students). All of these things convey that the teacher is invested in the students. Moving about the room, commenting on their work, prompting, questioning, providing feedback, and showing genuine concern is so important and should be part of the guided practice that occurs as students are working independently or with partners and in small groups. If you can't find the teacher when you walk into the classroom, it's a good thing if she is among the students coaching and learning together.

It can be difficult for teachers to gauge their own credibility. The self-assessment in Figure 2.1 can help teachers think about credibility issues more objectively. Read the statement and decide whether you think you are at a 1, 2, 3, 4.

Figure 2.1 Teacher Self-Assessment

4 = always	3 = usually	2 = sometimes	1 = not often enough

Competency: Trust	4	3	2	1
I try to be sincere and honest in the presentation of information and adapt information for listeners.				
I try to identify strengths and weaknesses in information—and identify sources to demonstrate honesty.				
I introduce resources that can trusted by students to use in class.				
I explain complex materials with evidence and analogies.				
I show trust toward pupils and they generally reciprocate.				
I try to be myself. It's easier to maintain that over time.				
I am consistent, fair, and equitable.				

Competency: Competence, Organization	4	3	2	1
I try to be sincere and honest in the presentation of information and adapt information for listeners.				
I exhibit organization in the presentation of subject matter.				
I model quality messages that are as free from errors as possible, including grammar, pronunciation, and enunciation.				
I use organized and detailed lesson plans.				
I create an orderly environment that students can count on. A place for everything and everything in its place.				
I share relevant personal experiences to provide concrete examples for students.				

Competency: Dynamism	4	3	2	1
I use a confident style of speaking that is free of hesitancy and ahs, ums, and "you knows."				
I vary physical movements such as gestures, facial expressions, and eye contact.				
I vary vocal characteristics, such as rate, pitch, inflection, and tone.				

(Continued)

Figure 2.1 (Continued)

Competency: Dynamism (continued)	4	3	2	1
I use a variety of evidence, stories, visual aids, and computer programs.				
I display "relaxed alertness" and show that I am comfortable but attentive in my classroom with students.				

Competency: Immediacy	4	3	2	1
I move about the room and establish my presence and interactions with all students, so those in all areas of the room have a connection with me.				
I look at the students, scanning the class and looking into the students' faces. Eye contact may not be appropriate for some cultures but looking at the student and attentively listening is important.				
I get down to their level when helping them individually, face to face. The proximity increases the sense of concern and is a personal interaction that shows concern.				
I smile and laugh with my students and use humor to relieve tension and as an aid to memory making; I try to never ridicule or diminish them.				

Source: Adapted from Haskins (2000).

Attitude 3: Caring

In addition to attitudes of enthusiasm (which is directed to the class as a whole) and credibility (which projects a general sense of competency), a third supremely important attitude is how teachers interact with students on a one-on-one basis. An attitude of caring about the students as people, personally, is one of the most important attributes of a teacher who can activate learning.

Hamre and Pianta (2001) report that poor relationships between students and teachers were correlated with poor academic success and increased behavior problems, especially for boys. Middle school students actually had better social skills as a result of closer connections and fewer conflicts with their teachers from kindergarten to when they enter middle school (Berry & O'Connor, 2009). Hattie, in the Visible Learning research, suggests that teacher/student relationships have impact on student learning (effect size of $d = 0.72$).

Gopnik, Melzoff, and Kuhl (1999) remind us of the innate need we have to connect and interact with others. We are drawn to positive relationships. Positive relationships influence students to come to school, do better academically, and sustain perseverance (Battistich, Schaps, & Wilson, 2004; Birch & Ladd, 1997; Hamre & Pianta, 2001). Teachers who have positive relationships with students report that attendance is better, and pupils are more self-directed, motivated, and cooperative (Birch & Ladd, 1997; Klem & Connell, 2004). This helps deal with student isolation and their academic achievement improved as well. Student-directed learning helps create positive relationships and greater engagement (Daniels & Perry, 2003; Perry & Weinstein, 1998).

Positive teacher-student relationships are evident in observable ways through the following:

- Teachers genuinely find teaching enjoyable and students recognize this.
- Teachers are responsive, attentive, and respectful.
- Teachers are eager to be helpful and assist students.
- Teachers are patient and are not angry with students.
- Teachers take a personal interest in student and their lives beyond the classroom.
- Teachers foster reflection and metacognition in their students.

There are practical ways to connect with students as people, beyond their academic personas (Croninger & Lee, 2001). Some of these ways include using names, avoiding hiding, mentoring students, being cultural responsive, and eliminating labels.

Using Names

One of the simplest strategies is also one of the most powerful. Learn students' names and use them often. Names are very personal and help form a connection and bond. One teacher (who herself had felt invisible as a student in high school) made the effort to learn and use the names of all students in her class on the first day in school. It gives the students a powerful message: You belong here and I know who you are.

Avoiding Hiding

Classroom teachers are always cognizant of time and how precious it is. Yet taking some of that time to connect with students pays dividends with more on task time, better attendance, and student success. Some students are especially shy or challenging and sometimes want to be lost in the crowd and it is especially important for teachers to seek them out and have one-on-one time with those you have identified. Although they may be reluctant at first, students will ultimately appreciate it (Pianta, 1999; Rudasill, Rimm-Kaufman, Justice, & Pence, 2006).

In one school, teachers were asked to identify students who were often truant, tardy, and somewhat unresponsive learners. The entire school staff—custodians, cafeteria workers, teachers, office personnel, coaches, and administrators—were given a list of several students and for a month looked for them every school day. They said hello, asked how things were going, and engaged in a short conversation. After those 20 encounters they saw an improvement in attendance, less tardiness, and more positive attitude. If school is not welcoming and students have no advocate, they won't want to come.

Mentoring

Find time outside of class, such as lunchtime, when you can seek out a troubled or defiant student. Spend time getting to know them, talking about their extra curricular activities, hopes, and dreams, and family or friends. This sends a powerful message that they matter. It may take repeated encounters to break through some students' shells but it's worth it; it may change their outlook and their life. If students feel that someone actually cares about them, they will feel more included and more willing to make an effort (Nolen-Hoeksema & Hilt, 2012).

Ray Wlodkowski developed a mentoring system that he calls the Two by Ten strategy (Smith & Lambert, 2008). Every day for two minutes for 10 consecutive school days (two weeks), the teacher has a personal conversation with a challenging or unresponsive student about an interest the student has. Smith and Lambert (2008) found that this simple strategy resulted in a noticeable improvement in the student's behavior and attitude in class. The student may even become an ally of the teacher and a positive influence on others.

Being attuned to mentoring can lead to all sorts of positive outcomes. One high school teacher had a first-period life skills class called Bachelor Survival. The class was composed of quite an eclectic group. One young man was always there bright and early, sometimes waiting for the teacher to unlock the classroom door. He was rather bedraggled, needed a good scrub, and often looked very tired. He'd come in and sit down and put his head on the table and kind of snooze until the rest of the students arrived. Busily getting things ready for the day, the teacher would chat away to him (partly to keep him awake!). Asking questions, she realized that he came straight to class from his overnight job at an automotive center in town. His single mother was on disability pension and he helped out. The teacher arranged for him to use the gym locker room to shower and freshen up in the morning and brought breakfast items for him as the cafeteria wasn't open yet. They quietly developed a relationship unbeknownst to the other class members. When he graduated he brought that teacher a gift and a thank you note for seeing him through, as he put it. It was a simple cake plate with lilacs on it that she still has in her china cabinet today. It reminds us what a difference listening, empathizing, and providing in a small way something that can matter to students to "see them through."

Fostering Relationships Through Cultural Responsiveness

Sometimes an attitude of caring is conveyed by taking the time to learn about a student's unique background or culture. For all students, knowing about their lives and showing a genuine interest is important. It's even more so for English language learners, immigrants, and minorities. The ability to relate respectfully to people from all cultures and also from them is referred to as *cultural responsivity*. *Cultural responsivity* has a huge impact on a young person coming to school where they don't always feel they fit in.

It is important to offer and establish a welcoming climate where they can activate their learning through their own culture and the worldview they have created. It has been noted that many teachers hold a negative perspective regarding minority groups (Gay, 2002). Teachers often have a mindset that these learners may not be as capable and may not succeed. They may use basic and low impact strategies for these learners, such as speaking louder and slower. Often these students are asked fewer and lower-level questions and aren't given enough wait time for them to construct an answer. Wait time needs to be greater for English language learners. Both teacher and students need to exhibit a growth mindset with higher expectations for these students (Dweck, 2006).

Awareness of the culture and ethnicity of our students is a first step to becoming culturally responsive. Invest time getting to know the cultures of students by having conversations, reading about their cultures, and consciously building their culture into the curriculum (Brown, 2003). Consider building in materials related to the cultures and ethnicity in the classroom (Montgomery, 2000). Become involved with community cultural celebrations, festivals, and organizations. Try their foods and learn some common phrases in their language.

The benefits of cultural responsivity by teachers are many. Students will exhibit growth in the these areas:

- Comfort level
- Knowledge and skill
- Ability to take risks and explore
- Teachers' ability to reach diverse learners, discover their interests and talents, and provide greater variety in instruction, resources, assessments, and active learning

Eliminating Labels

We in education have so many labels for programs and students. These labels can be quite adhesive, and once a label is used for a child it seems to stick forever. No matter how things may change or the student may evolve and grow, the label sticks.

Unfortunately the label was often developed to get funding or resources for the child instead of it being the place to start to teach that child. Often it's a barrier instead of a vehicle. It may limit them as it reinforces a fixed mindset. The research doesn't support the idea of various disorders or learning styles. Hattie calls it pop psychology. Even though students may have a predisposition or preference, they need to explore other ways of learning and thinking to increase their problem solving and creativity tool kit and developing multiple ways to learn that they haven't yet experienced. Let students know that there are many ways to be smart (Gardner, 2004) and that their talents may emerge at different times in their lives.

Observing the types of things that students enjoy participating in is a place to start to hook their engagement. But assessing their preferences and catering to them holds no promise in terms of effect size. It's better to design multisensory, pluralistic instructional approaches and offer choices. This will avoid labels and engage more learners. It also provides variety in the learning process, as students require multiple rehearsals and practices related to content and skills. In reflection after the learning process, give students a voice and foster metacognition by asking them to reflect on what they enjoyed, were good at, and would like to try again sometime or perhaps need to practice. Hattie suggests that as we identify strengths and needs in our learners, we see them as starting points and challenges that we rise to so that all may make progress. James Nottingham (2012) reminds us that "labels limit learning."

THE GROWTH MINDSET

If the first step in becoming a learning activator is developing and expressing personal attitudes like caring and credibility, the second is an intellectual attitude: the growth mindset. Conveying to students a growth mindset may be as important as any single piece of information you will pass along as a teacher.

Carol Dweck developed the idea of growth mindset versus fixed mindset in her book *Mindset: The New Psychology of Success* (2006). The growth mindset is one that recognizes that intelligence and talent are not set in stone. A person with a growth mindset is not easily discouraged by obstacles or failures because he recognizes that these are normal parts of life and learning. The fixed mindset believes that everyone has a set, limited amount of intelligence and talent and that failures are indicators of a person's limits.

The growth mindset is not just a feel-good concept. It is backed by neuroscience. We now know that brains change through our experiences, a phenomenon called *neuroplasticity*. In terms of education and learning, as we practice things, the neuron connections (dendrites) in our brain grow stronger and we find tasks easier.

Think about it: This means everyone's brain can grow and everyone can become competent in even difficult tasks. There is no stopping you if you work and make an effort and practice. Kids understand this when it comes to playing sports or videogames. But somehow when it comes to math or reading, it's hard for them to see. Your job as an activator of learning is to convey to your students a growth mindset that opens their mind to their own potential.

So how do you help convey the growth mindset in the classroom?

Mindset 1: Belief in Students' Potential

First, use encouraging phrases that convey, over and over again, your confidence in your students' potential. Reiterate and reinforce growth mindset thinking with statements such as "Everyone can become more intelligent"; "You learn with effort"; "Effort helps grow brain connections": "Your brain is like a muscle—it needs exercise and we all need to work out to get smarter." These phrases are suggested on the MindsetWorks website (mindsetworks.com/free-resources):

- You've made good progress; keep working.
- You're coming along. Speed isn't what matters. Remember the tortoise and the hare.
- I know you gave this a lot of time. It was so worth it.

Mindset 2: Practice and Effort

Second, emphasize that mastery requires practice and effort. Having to work at a skill or problem and having to practice that skill over and over is not an indication of failure or lack of talent. It's a normal part of learning. You get stuck; you practice, and figure out how to get past it. Liken learning to practicing a basketball, soccer, or hockey shot. Many practice sessions with a good coach can make you a star. Talk about, read, or view stories of people who became great through practice. One example is Michael Jordan, who once shared that he missed hundreds of baskets; but if he hadn't kept working, even missing, he never would have scored all the points he did (see Figure 2.2). Even Einstein was sent home from school because he appeared subnormal, and one of Einstein's college professors infamously remarked that he wouldn't amount to much. You can use phrases like this to help convey that everyone needs to practice and put forth effort:

- Even geniuses have to work hard. It's not easy.
- I'm happy that you're so dedicated. Good learners do that.
- You seem to be working really hard to figure that out. Nice job.

Figure 2.2 Fostering a Growth Mindset: Michael Jordan

I've missed 9,000 shots in my career.

I've lost almost 300 games.

Twenty-six times, I've been trusted to take the winning shot, and I missed.

I've failed over, and over, and over again in my life.

And that is why I succeed!

Mindset 3: Errors and Obstacles

Third, convey to students the role of obstacles. Obstacles, difficulties, and even failures are not dead ends. They are a normal step in solving any problem and should be embraced; they're an opportunity to use your brain, have fun, and be creative.

In addition, talk about the positive impact that mistakes or failures can offer. A great book called *The World's Greatest Mistakes* by Nigel Blundell (1980) chronicles the mistakes of remarkable people who are famous because of their mistakes and the amazing results. Another publication,

Mistakes That Worked by Charlotte Jones (1994), tells the story of many things we value in our society that came from an error or mistake, including potato chips, Velcro, and self-sticky notes. This helps students of all ages understand that it doesn't matter if you try and fail because who knows what you might find, discover, or invent as a result of an error. Life has mishaps and we can learn from them. As one first grader told me, "If you mess up, you fix it." Phrases like these can help convey that a moment of being stuck is not a permanent obstacle, that the student can puzzle it out:

- Any idea what you might try next?
- Wow, you chose some good ideas that will probably help you solve that. Try some of them.
- Is there anything I can do to help? You've really been trying hard.

Mindset 4: Growth-Friendly Techniques

Finally, use instructional techniques to help students see the way around a problem:

- Scaffold steps with prompts, supports, and resources to help learners attain appropriate challenges. Then be available as the guide and coach to provide resources and encouragement.
- Match up a student who appears to have a fixed mindset and a student with more of a growth mindset. The growth mindset student will influence and model their thinking and tenacity.
- Provide students with self-assessment strategies such as rubrics where students can see criteria and plot where they are and what to do next. This provides clear incremental goals and shows growth proving to them that they can get better. Even better, have students develop the criteria for success and then meet it.
- Teach students the process of goal setting where they would set an attainable goal and develop criteria for success, create a plan, and go for it. They should be able to make a list of things they need to be successful such as resources, technology, and people. Not only do they have a list of the steps they are going to take in their plan, they may also have a T chart and in the second column chronicle their path and in the third write down reflections or feelings as they worked through it (see Figure 2.3).
- Praise students who make an effort, not just those who succeed. It is imperative that students are comfortable making a mistake. They need to understand that it is through errors that we eliminate wrongs strategies and keep testing until we find a right one.

Figure 2.3 Goal-Setting T Chart

Steps in My Plan	How It Went	Thoughts, Feelings
1.	1.	1.
2.	2.	2.
3.	3.	3.
4.	4.	4.
5.	5.	5.
6.	6.	6.
7.	7.	7.
8.	8.	8.
9.	9.	9.
10.	10.	10.

These types of exercises provide students with processes to be a successful learner throughout life. Using these techniques to convey a growth mindset is one of the best things you can do to be a teacher activator. When students get praise for effort and persistence, they enjoy a dopamine rush and actually tackle more challenging tasks the next time. These students develop a growth mindset and learn to persevere in spite of obstacles. They are resilient and "gritty" (Duckworth et al., 2007).

Dweck (2015) cautions teachers that praising effort should not simply replicate the 1990s self-esteem concept in which parents and teachers made students feel good about just any effort they exerted, regardless of whether they learned or not as a result of the effort. The concept of effort should include their ability to try new techniques, approaches, and strategies as well as seek knowledgeable others to continue toward their learning goals. The growth mindset should help students close the learning gaps, not ignore them. It is being realistic about where you are, where you are going, and what to do next. It includes strategizing to succeed.

A fixed mindset (teacher's or student's) should not be an excuse to allow a student to underachieve. Dweck suggests in actuality we may be of "two minds"—fixed and growth—and that it's a journey to move more to the growth category. There are probably triggers that pull us back toward a more fixed mindset about ourselves, such as becoming defensive or angry when something doesn't go so well and creating excuses for our failure or inadequacies. Moving to a true growth mindset is a journey—not a decision but an awareness of the attributes of growth mindsets and monitoring where we are on the continuum.

As Caine and Caine (1997) wrote, "Teacher's beliefs about human potential and the children's ability to learn and achieve are critical. The teachers' mental models have a profound impact on the learning climate and learner states of mind that teachers create. Teachers need to understand students' feelings and attitudes, as they will profoundly influence student learning" (p. 124).

FOSTERING HAPPINESS

In *The Happiness Advantage* (2010) Shawn Achor, the Harvard researcher and bestselling author, suggests that a happy brain reaps a massive advantage in life. Happiness generates success, not the reverse. When we are positive, our brains respond with more engagement, creativity, motivation, energy, resiliency, and productivity.

Achor (2013) in his book *Before Happiness* further elaborates on factors for student success. We hopefully have discarded the notion that IQ is fixed yet there is still the lingering idea that IQ and expertise will account for success. In reality only 25% of success can be attributed to these factors, according to Achor. He suggests that 75% of success in life comes from three key factors: optimism level, social support and connections, and stress management.

- **Optimism level:** We generally put more effort and energy into our goals when we see the possibility of success. Our reality, in fact, is how we see the world, and we have the power to interpret it in negative or positive ways. "Positive geniuses," according to Achor, can look beyond the negative to see that there are still possibilities regardless of the challenge, if we are flexible and creative and allow ourselves to think outside the box. As teachers we can also transmit the positive vibes to students and help them be more optimistic about their success coupled with effort: effort in accessing other resources, trying alternate methods, and so on. It isn't about becoming a Pollyanna where we only see the good but consciously dealing with the negative and challenges in a problem solving way to achieve our goals.

- **Social support and connections:** Be ready to discuss with students the brain research related to social support and relationships and what an impact they can have on learning.

- **Stress management and seeing obstacles as a challenge:** Similar to Dweck's focus on effort in the growth mindset attributes, Achor offers that positive geniuses will persist to achieve goals by meeting challenges and problem solving, seeking resources, and persevering.

Achor says that being positive in the present gives us a "happiness advantage." Happiness provides:

- More resiliency
- More creative and productivity (31%)
- Lower stress
- Increased dopamine that turns on all learning centers

Because we are wirelessly connected to others through mirror neuron networks, positive teachers create positive students.

INSTRUCTIONAL TECHNIQUES

Thus far we've looked at two important ways a teacher can be an activator of learning: personal attitudes and the growth mindset. The third way is through instructional techniques that are designed to activate the students' own capability for learning. This section examines some of these concrete instructional techniques: clarity, multimodal presentation, and direct instruction.

Instructional Technique 1: Clarity

Fendick (1990) defines teacher clarity as organization, explanation, examples and guided practice, and assessment of student learning. It is the clarity of reciprocal communication between students and teacher. Of course part of teacher clarity is the ability to speak clearly without ambiguity, speak with appropriate volume, and use correct grammar in understandable English without vague terms and false starts or hesitations so students can focus on the content without distractions.

One of the most important aspects of teacher effectiveness includes clear learning intentions. Findings in the Hattie meta-analysis unearthed that teacher clarity had an impact with $d = 0.75$. Here are the key components of teacher clarity that Fendick explains.

Clarity of Organization

It is important that there is structure to the lesson. Beginning the lesson there needs to be clear intentions in student-friendly language with clear criteria for success. Teachers should connect the learning experiences to the outcomes intended, review what has been covered, and reflect on the progress. Tell them what they are going to learn, help them learn, and reflect on growth toward learning targets.

Clarity of Explanation

In order to explain a lesson clearly, teachers must do some of the following:

- Explain things simply and in a meaningful, interesting way.

- Repeat patiently as necessary, without exasperation, and stress directions and important or difficult points that are critical. It always amazes me when a teacher gets angry if someone asks a question for clarification or because they missed hearing something or didn't understand. First of all there are so many verbal directions that the brain can't hold them all in short-term memory. And sometimes the directions are not timely; in other words the student is not at that point yet so your instruction is not relevant or needed just now. That is why visual prompts that remain in view on charts, overhead, smart board, or tablets help learners to access directions or information when needed. This lowers the possibility of anxiety and prevents the teacher from rambling on repeatedly for every child that missed the information the first time. Often this is why students don't listen because the teacher's voice becomes *Wah, Wah, Wah* as in the Charlie Brown cartoons or they fall behind as they quit asking for clarity, as it seems to annoy the teacher.

- Chunk new content so students can manage it. The brain needs wholes to parts and parts to wholes. Give them the big picture and then break it down to manageable munchies. Make connections to prior learning, theories, or methods.

- Set your pace according to what students can manage. Adjust pace for more able learners and for those who need more processing time.

Clarity of Examples and Guided Practice

Encourage and answer questions as needed. Students don't necessarily ask questions because they didn't listen the first time but because it didn't click the first time or wasn't needed yet for them to continue. That is why flipping the classroom can be such an important strategy. Flipping the classroom means providing content outside of the class (through websites, homework, or videos) and using classroom time for activities and discussion around the concept. Flipping the classroom also can prime the pump by contributing background information that students may be lacking. Prior knowledge is essential for students to learn new material (Ausubel, 1968; Piaget, 1970). If there is no prior knowledge there are no neurons already connected on which to hook the new information.

Practice is also key for students to strengthen the brain's neuron connections (dendrites). Marzano, Pickering, and Pollock (2001) suggest that it may take 21 practice trials to get 80% mastery. If students don't get it, reteach to clarify before moving on. Otherwise we create cumulative ignorance, and students are not ready for the next learning. Give clear, precise, timely feedback on how well they are progressing. Revisit skills and concepts to strengthen their place in long-term memory.

Clarity of Assessment of Student Learning

Check for understanding of learning and about how you are doing as the teacher from feedback from students. Sometimes teachers check for understanding by having the students nod or shake their heads (or giving a thumbs up or down) in response to "Everyone understand?" Sometimes it's "Any questions?" and students shake their heads dutifully. But this isn't always an effective way to check for comprehension. It is more of a compliance move and also valuable for saving face. Why would I be vulnerable in front of my peers and admit I don't get it? Pat Wolfe, noted educator and author, suggests that the only thing we really know for sure with head nodding and shaking is that their neck muscles are working. Checking homework, asking students questions, and using quick formative assessment are generally more accurate (see Chapter 6 for more on assessment).

Instructional Technique 2: Multimodal Presentation

Teachers should be encouraged to become adaptive learning experts, who not only have a repertoire of proven effective strategies but also know when and where to use them flexibly to be innovative activators of learning (Bransford, Brown, & Cocking, 2000). They know when things are working for students and when to abandon what is not. According to Darling-Hammond (2006) adaptive experts are continually expanding and restructuring their knowledge and competencies. Expert teachers need to have a high level of empathy, see learning through the eyes of their learners, and show students that they can respond to their needs in the learning process. This requires keen skills of observation and listening to interpret student understanding and perspectives. This is adaptive expertise rather than routine expertise. It is the art of teaching based on the science of learning. Routine expertise will not serve all students, so teachers must be flexible and adjust tactics as necessary.

One important way of being adaptive is to use various types of presentation, known as *multimodal.* By appealing to multiple modes of learning and all our senses, we address students' learning preferences and greater ensure that students have the best chance at engaging with and retaining information. Graesset, Halpern, and Hakel (2008) summarized some of the major processes for learning into four major categories: multiple ways of knowing, multiple ways of interacting, multiple ways of practicing, and knowing that we are learning.

Multiple Ways of Knowing

There are multiple ways of presenting new information without taxing the cognitive load. *Cognitive load* is the amount of effort required of working memory to hold and manage information. When Sweller coined *cognitive load* in the late 1980s he suggested three types: intrinsic, extraneous, and germane. Intrinsic refers to the effort associated with the effort required. Extraneous refers to the way the information is presented. And germane cognitive load refers to the work or processing necessary to put the new learning into long-term memory (developing a schema). Miller (1956) suggested after extensive research that children of five years of age have two memory spaces, plus or minus two, and it increases one space every other year until fifteen years. People with a mental age of at least fifteen years have seven memory spaces, plus or minus two, at their disposal. More than seven pieces of information must be chunked in networks of association for the brain to be able to manage it. This should caution us as educators as to the amount of new information presented, how it is presented, and the schemas structured to support it.

Teachers should:

- Present information in patterns of association (chunks) so students can see connections.
- Provide rich sensory representations: visual, auditory, and multimedia forms to engage learners and activate thinking.
- Challenge with cognitive flexibility with different viewpoints that connect facts, skills, and processes.
- Make sure materials and multimedia are explicit and don't dazzle with distraction from the explicit learning.
- Not overload the working memory and cognitive load at any time.

Multiple Ways of Interacting

Processing new information to make sense of it is often best done through student interactions where students can begin to relate new learning by activating prior knowledge, questioning, and forging links. Students need explicit instruction in processes for interactions.

Teachers should:

- Have students outline, summarize, and discuss to help integrate new learning.
- Embed new information in stories and examples so it will "stick" in the memory.
- Create cognitive disequilibrium (challenges, problems, anomalies that create opportunities for deep reasoning and learning) and help students understand that this is typical of learning.
- Help students with self-regulation as needed.

Multiple Ways of Practicing

Everyone needs to practice a new skill and repeatedly interact with new ideas and concepts over time. This practice needs to occur recursively by looping back to new learning for review and reinforcement.

- Abstract concepts require multiple and varied examples.
- Spaced practice is better for long term retention.
- Students need to see purpose and value in learning to remain engaged.

Knowing That We Are Learning

Learning is not linear but often circuitous and messy. We make errors and get off track and face unforeseen challenges. Students need "just in time" and "just for me" feedback to keep moving toward success criteria. Here are some guidelines for providing this kind of helpful feedback:

- Feedback is most effective when it is tailored to the level of competency.
- Errors happen, and learners need a brain-safe environment to push beyond their comfort level to risk mistakes and continue trial and error.
- Feedback is necessary to keep students from learning incorrect information or developing skills poorly.
- Challenges are important to keep learners engaged. When learners produce results with effort, long-term retention is greater.

Bransford, Brown, and Cocking (2000) in their book *How People Learn* help teachers understand valuable information and issues about learning. They first recommend that teachers understand students' existing knowledge or skill level. This is necessary so there is a foundation or schemata on which to build. Accessing prior knowledge may be helpful in identifying misconceptions that need to be corrected to properly accommodate the new learning. Starting with students' existing knowledge does not begin just a linear process of adding more bricks of knowledge, but examining the relationship between what they know and what they are learning can produce new concepts and advance the schemas. Constant assessment to check for understanding is necessary to see if new information has been assimilated.

We also need to help students foster an awareness of their thinking: what they are doing, where they're going, how they're going, and what to do when they don't know. When we express that we want life-long learning for our students, it is the meta-cognitive and self-regulation skills we want them to develop, that help them to become their own teachers. These skills need to be embedded in the surface and deep learning we offer.

Instructional Technique 3: Direct Instruction

Direct instruction has gotten a bad rap recently. This is because direct instruction is sometimes interpreted as didactic teacher talk ("stand and deliver," "sit and get"). But direct instruction, done well, is one way to activate learning. Hattie's research assigns it a moderate effect size of 0.59.

In this section, we'll look at how to use effective direct instruction. Note that students are not passive receivers but fully engaged in the learning process and there is plenty of opportunity for multimodal, pluralized instruction.

Hunter's Seven

Adams and Engelmann (1996) and Hunter (1967, 2004) describe a type of direct instruction that is very brain friendly. It was often used ineffectively as a checklist for teacher evaluation instead of the powerful strategy it is. Hunter's method consists of seven steps:

1. **Anticipatory set:** A "hook" to engage the brain (sensory memory, novelty, attention getting) related to the topic and to reduce distractions

2. **Sharing the purpose:** Identifying and sharing the learning intentions and success criteria, relevance, and purpose

3. **Input and modeling:** Often from teacher, text, video, multimedia, etc.; modeling, demonstrating, discussing, showing successful examples (remember those mirror neurons)

4. **Checking for understanding (formative assessment):** Checking through questioning, observations, students reactions, and comfort levels

5. **Guided practice:** Students applying the new learning and the teacher monitoring with feedback and corrective suggestions or further examples as students develop new knowledge and skills

6. **Independent practice:** Moving from guided practice to attempting the new learning without support; moving from "we do" to "you do"

7. **Conclusion:** Using closure signals that indicate to the students that the lesson has come to an end and to revisit the learning objectives and purpose to help students see what progress they have made. This helps students create a coherent picture of the learning. Closure helps consolidate and affords an opportunity to clear up any misconceptions or gaps that signal next steps.

Extended practice occurs when students have a repeated look at the knowledge and/or skill over time to reinforce the dendritic connections made and rehearse new learning and then replace it into long-term memory

Often teachers think that direct instruction is only for the lower ability or youngest students, but not so. The effect size of direct instruction varied by learning group (0.99 for regular education students, 0.86 for special education students) and discipline (0.89 for reading, 0.50 for math) (Adams & Engelmann, 1996). But it made some difference for all students.

Marzano et al.'s Essential Nine

Marzano, Pickering, & Pollock (2001) shared meta-analysis of nine instructional strategies that have an impact on student achievement (see Figure 2.4). They were originally listed in a hierarchy delineated by their impact (effect size) from moderate to high effect size.

After the book and field book for *Classroom Instruction That Works* were published, additional research took place as teachers implemented the strategies. After ten years of experimentation the authors unearthed new information about the impact of the strategies as well as teacher practice when implementing them. The teachers found that when and where they used the strategies made a difference. Initially teachers would try to implement the strategy with the highest ES that shows most

Figure 2.4 Categories of Instructional Strategies That Affect Student Achievement

Category	Effect Size
Identifying similarities and differences	1.61
Summarizing and note taking	1.00
Reinforcing effort and providing recognition	0.80
Homework and practice	0.77
Nonlinguistic representations	0.75
Cooperative learning	0.73
Setting objectives and providing feedback	0.61
Generating and testing hypotheses	0.61
Questions, cues, and advance organizers	0.59

promise for student success such as similarities and differences. However this strategy is not a beginning surface level strategy as students need to have knowledge about two topics in order to be able to go deeper and make comparisons. They began to realize that where and when the strategies were used made some sense and garnered better student engagement and learning.

A framework emerged as it became evident that the "essential nine" have an impact on three areas in the learning process: (1) creating climate, (2) developing understanding, and (3) extending the learning. These categories (see Figure 2.5) were explored further in *Classroom Instruction That Works* (Dean et al., 2012).

Part I: Creating the Environment for Learning

The first category cluster is creating the environment for learning. This includes setting objectives and providing feedback; students should be aware of the common core standards that are targeted, and they should be easily adaptable to students' own objectives. The second strategy is reinforcing effort and providing recognition; this means clarifying the connection between effort and achievement and promoting a growth mindset. The third strategy is cooperative learning; research shows that organizing students into heterogeneous cooperative groups yields a positive effect on overall learning. Many of the strategies mentioned such as discussion and cooperative group learning will be attended to in Chapters 3 and 4.

Figure 2.5 Instructional Strategies Framework

Part I: Creating the Environment for Learning

1. Setting Objectives and Providing Feedback

2. Reinforcing Effort and Providing Recognition

3. Cooperative Learning

Part II: Helping Students Develop Understanding

4. Cues, Questions, and Advance Organizers

5. Nonlinguistic Representations

6. Summarizing and Note Taking

7. Assigning Homework and Providing Practice

Part III: Helping Students Extend and Apply Knowledge

8. Identifying Similarities and Differences

9. Generating and Testing Hypothesis

Part II: Helping Students Develop Understanding

The second category cluster is helping students develop understanding. These strategies activate student thinking to analyze and explore new information and skills. They facilitate the secondary level of processing of the SEEKING system. They facilitate the rehearsal processes needed to go deeper than surface coverage. The first item in this cluster is using cues, questions, and advance organizers to enhance learning; these are most effective when presented before a lesson so that they help prime the students' learning with prior exposure.

The second item is nonlinguistic representations. According to research, knowledge is stored in two forms: linguistic and visual. The more students use both forms in the classroom, the more opportunity students have to understand and comprehend. Recently, use of nonlinguistic representations has proven to not only stimulate but also increase brain activity. Physical engagement and role-play are also memorable and help long-term retention. The use of graphic organizers is important in this category as well.

The third item is summarizing and note taking. These skills promote greater comprehension by asking students to analyze a subject and then explain it in their own words. According to research, this requires substituting, deleting, and keeping some things and having an awareness of the basic structure of the information presented.

The fourth item is assigning homework and providing practice. Research shows that the amount of homework assigned should vary by grade level and that parent involvement should be minimal. Teachers should provide students with tips on homework like following a schedule and setting a time limit. Teachers should give feedback on all homework assigned, but grading homework is not recommended because the goal is safe practice. But students should be advised to practice until the skill is mastered. Homework can be detrimental if the practice is not "perfect practice." Having to unlearn a skill is sometimes more difficult than learning it in the first place. And if parents lack the skills that the students are learning, this puts a strain on the relationship. Hattie shows an effect size for homework of $d = 0.29$ but varies with the greatest impact being for secondary students, then middle school, and last elementary. Elementary students should spend time reading and practicing basic skills and playing rather than spending large amounts of time on homework. Amount of time and parental involvement also plays a part.

Part III: Helping Students Extend and Apply Knowledge

The third category cluster is helping students extend and apply knowledge. This moves information from surface learning to deeper understanding.

The first item in this cluster is identifying similarities and differences. The ability to break a concept into its similar and dissimilar characteristics allows students to understand (and often solve) complex problems by analyzing them in a more simple way. Teachers can either directly present similarities and differences, accompanied by deep discussion and inquiry, or simply ask students to identify similarities and differences on their own. While teacher-directed activities focus on identifying specific items, student-directed activities focus on identifying specific criteria. Student-directed activities encourage variation and broaden understanding as well. Graphic forms are a good way to represent similarities and differences. For example, you can use Venn diagrams to classify characters, genres, and situations in literature. You can ask students to create a chart of analogies and metaphors.

The second item in this cluster is generating and testing hypotheses. Research shows that a deductive approach (using a general rule to make a prediction) to this strategy works best. Whether hypotheses are induced or deduced, students should clearly explain their hypotheses and conclusions. This would include making predictions and using supportive evidence. This practice deepens surface knowledge. Dean et al. (2012) provides some examples: Ask students to predict what would happen if an aspect of a familiar system, such as the government or transportation, were changed. Or ask students to build something using limited resources. This task generates questions and hypotheses about what may or may not work.

Not only do these nine strategies have a moderate to high impact with effect sizes from $d = 0.59$ to 1.16, they can be integrated to increase their impact by responding to student preferences for learning through providing multimodal learning tasks.

Cooperative learning and advanced organizers paired with questions and cues (over 300 studies on various types of graphic organizers) have an effect size of 0.59 with an associated percentile gain on standardized assessments of 22. Students who use graphic organizers score better than 73% of peers who do not use organizers with questions and cues or organizers of any kind. Of course with cooperative learning there is also the addition of dialogue and creative and critical thinking. This multiplicity of strategies also naturally attends to and supports the diversity of preferences that students exhibit for their learning.

SUMMARY

While Chapter 1 examined how classroom climate can activate learning, this chapter turned to one of the most important elements of activated learning: the teacher. Through personal attitudes, a growth mindset, and brain-friendly instructional techniques like multimodal presentation, teachers can help their students feel safe so they can concentrate on learning, believe in their own potential, and engage with the curriculum in ways that have been proven to be effective. The challenge for teachers is to balance the surface learning (the facts) and deep learning (active processing and applying those facts). Processing new learning in multiple ways, over time, includes discussion with others so that long-term memory can be built and students are able to deepen their learning. If the experience is meaningful, relevant, and fun, the learner will actively seek it again and again.

DISCUSSION POINTS

- A quote from Hattie starts off this chapter. Discuss this quote in terms of the qualities of deliberate interventions.

- Discuss how students absorb messages from teachers about their abilities and self through both verbal and nonverbal means.

- Take the self-assessment on teacher credibility. Identify an area that you would like to focus on and set a goal of something you will consciously do over the next term.

- Discuss the benefits of a positive attitude toward students for you as the teacher and for students in your class.

- Think about how you would use and adapt some of the strategies for making connections with students, such as using names and avoiding labels. What are some ways you currently forge relationships in your classroom?

- How might you increase your cultural responsivity to students in the classroom? What are some activities you might do yourself to connect with a student's culture?

- In what ways do you currently strive for teacher clarity? Discuss clarity of organization, explanation, examples and guided practice, and assessment.

- View James Nottingham's lecture on Labels Limit Learning, and discuss.

- Discuss the following quote and whether or not you agree: "Teachers' beliefs in and about human potential and the children's ability to learn and achieve are critical. The teachers' mental models have a profound impact on the learning climate and learner states of mind that teachers create. Teachers need to understand students' feelings and attitudes, as they will profoundly influence student learning" (Caine & Caine, 1997, p. 124).

- Discuss the concept of a growth mindset. How can a teacher help students move from a fixed to a growth mindset?

- Teacher expertise generally has a positive impact on learning. But are there some ways in which teachers' expertise can be a hindrance?

- Discuss the role of direct instruction as a best practice.

- Develop some ideas for multimodal teaching for language, science, or any other class.

3 Activating the Power of Peers

Teachers are the teachers, and students are the learners: That's how many of us were trained to see our roles. But it turns out that peer relationships are some of the most important elements in learning. This chapter addresses the importance of peer relationships in the classroom, obstacles to peer relationships, and the many ways that teachers can use peer relationships to activate learning.

THE IMPORTANCE OF PEER RELATIONSHIPS IN THE CLASSROOM

Peers make a real difference for learning. Hattie (2009) identifies peer influence with an effect size of $d = 0.55$, citing the impact of helping, tutoring, offering friendship, and giving feedback.

Friendship

One of the simplest ways that peers make a difference is friendship. Positive peer relationships actually make students want to come to school (Wilkinson & Fung, 2002). Anderman and Anderman (1999) remind us that friendships play a large part in the classroom as they offer support, caring, and help; ease conflict resolution; and offer greater learning opportunities. My own children rarely missed school not always because of their passion of learning but because of the friendships they had and the interactions they might miss if they weren't there. If a friend was moving, it was the end of life as they knew it.

When children are transient and move from school to school, the greatest indicator of their success in assimilating and thriving will be if they make a friend in the first month (Galton et al., 2000; Pratt & George, 2005). Social relationships are especially important to young adolescents when coupling—the survival issue of procreating the species—kicks in as the hormones do (Levy-Tossman, Kaplan, & Assor, 2007). Sometimes this interferes with learning, as students fail to take risks to avoid losing face or appearing incompetent or too competent in front of others—especially the opposite sex, especially if they are teens or tweens.

Robert Sapolsky, in his book *Why Zebras Don't Get Ulcers* (1998), confirmed the role of friendship. Sapolsky describes watching primates and their interactions in a group. If they were exposed to undue stress and there were friends around, the stress wasn't as great. Contrarily, if the primate was in an unsupportive, unfamiliar group, the stress was much greater. The level of stress is more or less traumatic based on with whom we experience it.

Of course, there can be a dark side to our need for friendship. Buhs, Ladd, and Herald (2006) suggest that if students don't have peer acceptance there can be disengagement and it can affect achievement. These learners can become marginalized when partner work is expected. Many of these students lack social skills and are ostracized as a result. Also many students are not inclusive and lack empathy for others. A great little book called *You Can't Say You Can't Play*, written by Vivian Paley (1992), contains great suggestions to help students develop inclusion in classrooms and playgrounds. Although written by a kindergarten teacher, the principles are the same at any age. Social skills are necessary to be invited into a group, to include others, and to get along with other people.

General Social Interaction

It's important to note that our social needs as humans go beyond the need for individual friendship. Panksepp (1998) reminds us that humans need to connect, cooperate, and collaborate with others in a general way, not just in terms of the value of close friendships. We have an innate need to seek the contact of others (Gopnik, Meltzoff, & Kuhl, 1999); we need to both be alone sometimes and also have time to connect with others (Covey, 1989). Some students may enjoy social interaction but lack the skills to interact successfully with partners or small groups in a learning situation. Emotional intelligence is a key skill for success in life (Goleman, 2006b). Students need to develop emotional self-awareness and be able to self-manage as well as to self-motivate and regulate. Empathy and social skills are critical to get along in life in any setting with others.

The innate need to belong is an initiator for cooperation and interactive exploration. Baumeister and Leary's research (1995) shows that the need for belonging could drive our other needs such as power, achievement, intimacy, and approval. It is suggested that belonging is as compelling as the need for food and that human nature is conditioned to seek it. A group was needed for survival. It was a recursive loop, belongingness leads to cooperation and . . . cooperation fosters belongingness.

From a neuroscience point of view, our normal neurocognitive development *requires* social interaction time. We have an innate need to interact with others to satisfy our human biological needs (Hallowell, 2011). People deprived of this interaction will actually *lose* brain cells and not make vital connections. Our need for social interaction is built into humans' facility for what is known as *mirror neuroning*; neurologists discovered that our neurons have mirroring capabilities that are able to replicate the brain state of others. When you observe someone else, you are able to pattern yourself after him or her and what he or she does (Freedman, 2007).

Social interaction is also important to the brain because of stress. Chapter 1 discussed the extensive research on how undue stress reduces learning. With excessive stress, the learning brain suffers the flight-or-fight reaction and no real learning can take place. Adrenalin and cortisol are released and the individual is on high alert. When students experience stress, the concern with physical and emotional well-being consumes their attention, the prefrontal lobe of the brain is not engaged, and learning is blocked as the amygdala sends sensory input to the survival areas of the brain (Toga & Thompson, 2003). As a result the ability to access the memory bank is blocked by the overactive amygdala.

Social interaction prevents stress in several ways. At its best, positive interaction prevents the stress that results from being bullied or even *observing* someone else being bullied. Also, if social interaction takes the form of small-group or partner work, it prevents the stress that can come from students feeling put on the spot in a large classroom. There is much more "brain safety" for students if they're working with partners or in a small group because it feels less risky to offer ideas, ask questions, and make mistakes than to risk embarrassment in a large group setting (Gregory & Kaufeldt, 2012).

Positive social interactions also aid memory. Brain scans can actually show the information passage from intake areas to memory storage areas in the brain. Learning connected to positive emotions has a longer shelf life and is more memorable. Krashen (1982) suggests that when learners anticipate pleasurable states there is an increase in dopamine with the expectation of pleasure (Holroyd, Larsen, & Cohen, 2004). Teachers armed with this knowledge are able to consciously activate learning through peer interactions and cooperative tasks.

ACTIVATING LEARNING THROUGH PEER RELATIONSHIPS

Many researchers report the value of cooperative interactions in the classroom. Vygotsky (1978) proposed that we learn through interactions with knowledgeable and more capable teachers and peers. Collaboration offers students a chance to be appreciated and to feel important, influential, and powerful among peers.

Because cooperative learning motivates students' achievement, peer interaction, problem solving and decision making, research has found that cooperative structures enhance students' intrinsic motivation to learn, more so in a small group rather than in a large group (Shachar & Sharon, 1994). Slavin (1990) found, in reference to group work, that one behavioral indication of student motivational involvement is the proportion of their class time they spend on-task, or what Slavin called "engaged time." In terms of engagement, talking and doing trumps listening. Feeling safe and valued by peers will also intrinsically motivate students (Wasserman & Danforth, 1988).

Teachers are key to fostering community spirit by facilitating collaborative opportunities in partners and small groups. These couplings and small groups should, of course, be focused on rigorous, interesting, appropriately challenging academic tasks while simultaneously developing social skills. The following sections suggest some concrete ways to activate the power of peer relationships in the classroom.

Monologue Versus Dialogue

Teacher monologue is the age-old technique of "stand and deliver": The teacher delivers information to a listening classroom. Monologue has its place in pedagogy and can never be eliminated entirely. But it's a matter of balance. There is a huge push by eager parents to get their youngsters mobile and communicating; and then they send them to school where we expect them to sit still and be quiet unless spoken to. They say that teachers ask about 250 questions per day per week and students only ask 2 per class: clearly one sided and far from a dialogue. The Gates Foundation provided webcams in 3,000 classrooms in the United States for 3 months. Observing all those classrooms, the staff found that 65% of teachers recorded activated no discussion in their class for the three months observed.

Most teacher talk is in large-group configurations as part of the instructional process. It's a table tennis model: The teacher initiates a question, the student responds, the teacher evaluates (Meehan, 1979). Most of these questions are low-level factual and most talk is by the teacher (Alexander, 2008). Alexander found that less than 5% of class time in general is allowed for student discussion. The questions posed were usually a check that students were listening rather than open-ended questions to prompt real thinking. This practice allows students to hide or play the "odds game." It goes like this. The student thinks: "I hear the question and I'm not sure of the answer. There are six hands up so she has a choice. I already answered a question today, so if I look at my textbook or tie my sneaker, she won't ask me." Instead of really thinking about the answer they are checking to see the probability of being asked. Probability is a good math skill but not the best way for the brain to be engaged and information to be processed when a question is offered.

Extended periods of teacher monologue don't seem to be damaging to the more able learners, as they tend to be more able to self-talk regarding new learning. However, struggling learners do not have that capability. So teacher monologue is not satisfactory for struggling students who may be confused or disengaged. Of course, if monologue (usually 85% of the time) is simply replaced by low-level worksheets, complete meaningless simple tasks, or just random talk, it's not helpful for learning anymore than is constant sitting and listening. Students need real, engaging dialogue in order to learn. Visible learning research found that dialogue clearly increases student achievement (Hattie, 2009). Beyond the hinge point of $d = 0.40$, dialogue in classrooms as opposed to monologue has an impact of $d = 0.82$, increasing student achievement by almost two years.

How, then, can teachers replace monologue and low-level worksheets with productive, engaging tasks that include peer-oriented dialogue? Let's go back to the student playing the odds game above. Instead of allowing volunteers to raise their hands and all other students to hide, a better method is something that Lyman and McTighe (1988) call Think Pair Share. In Think Pair Share, the teacher presents the questions and specifies "no hands, please." Then she instructs students to think about the question for a minute and then turn to an elbow partner (someone close to them) and discuss the answer. Then after a quick discussion students can return their focus to the large-group discussion and be ready to contribute.

This simple strategy is extremely brain friendly and will increase engagement and thinking, especially because it has wait time built in (Rowe, 1986). Teachers generally wait tenths of seconds from the time the question is posed to selecting a student to answer. But it takes at least 5 to 7 seconds for the brain to access stored information from long-term memory, get it back to working memory, and then process it. Think Pair Share also lowers the stress the brain feels (time restraints and possible large group embarrassment if the student answers wrong) and opens up thinking instead of blocking the flow of information from the sensory system to the neocortex.

Wait time is extremely important in the classroom. If a question is simple and factual, it may be responded to quickly. However, higher-level answers require more time to formulate an answer because the students need to access stored information relevant to the level of thinking. For example, "Who were the characters in the story?" is much simpler than "In your opinion, which character had the most influence in how the plot twisted and give an example?" When we are striving to have students really think, we need to give them time.

Teachers are sometimes uncomfortable giving time to "dead air." It is uncomfortable to have that silent anticipation as we wait for an answer. But those moments of waiting are extremely important for students. It allows them to think and it also reminds them of some of the lessons of the growth mindset discussed in Chapter 2: that it's okay if you don't know the answer immediately and that learning takes time, effort, and *thinking*. Here are some ways teachers can avoid rushing to the answer stage by using these tactics:

- Be quiet. (Bite your tongue.)
- Stand still and look pensive.
- Remind students, "We all need time to think."
- Tell students, "No hands, please."
- Suggest everyone think of his or her best answer.
- Remind students of the question by restating it.
- Offer time to check their source.
- Don't add more pressure with prompts and leads.
- Ask students to take a moment to jot down an answer and come back to them.
- Allow them the "right to pass" and think about an answer. You can come back to them.

It is important for teachers to learn how to increase quality dialogue that deepens understanding and develops higher-order thinking. All students, including at-risk students, get the greatest benefits when students are offered instruction that is interesting, challenging, relevant, and demanding academically with higher engagement and less teacher monologue.

Dialogue is especially important for language learning, like developing understanding of vocabulary and being able to restate what they have learned; those who talk learn. And dialogue is especially important for foreign language acquisition. I don't speak French very well today even though I grew up in a bilingual country and took French for many years in school. But it was always . . . *ecoute, ecrivez,* rarely *parlez.* In order to develop language one must be immersed in it. We don't teach young children in any culture to speak; we speak to them and encourage them to respond.

My granddaughter Megan was very verbal at a young age of two years old, and a little boy about the same age was over swimming at our house. Keran didn't talk much. Megan never stopped. He was timid and sitting on the edge of the pool. She offered him a pool noodle to entice him into the water. He said *no no.* Megan turned to me and told me Keran didn't want a noodle. But his grandma said Keran calls the noodle a *no no.* Megan made her way over to Keran and offered him a green noodle, saying, "Here Keran, here is a noodle. Can you say *noodle* Keran, say *noodle?*" Megan is a child of two teachers and several grandparents who are also educators. She couldn't help herself. Although Keran knew what a noodle was, he needed prompting and opportunity to verbalize the word.

You have to speak to learn language. Especially English language learners should be talking more of the time in safe supportive pairs or small groups where they are included and feel comfortable to risk and practice their new language. Dialogue lets students develop vocabulary in context, deepen concepts, clarify misconceptions, and rehearse ideas. Plus, it is a great assessment tool for teachers as they eavesdrop when partners or small groups are discussing. We learn what students know, don't know, and any misconceptions that need clarifying or reteaching.

Evaluating Versus Extending

Evaluating student responses is a great way to shut down thinking and increase the tension and anxiety students feel. Back in "teacher school" some of us were told to praise answers: "well done," "great job." But those comments actually interfere with student thinking (Kohn, 1993). If a student has an idea that is different from the "great job" answer given by another student he or she will probably take down their eager arm. Praising answers stops others from thinking. It says the teacher was looking for [fill in the blank] and the students need to think about what the teacher wants—the right answer. This also comes from numerous recall questions. If there is only one right answer, the teacher tends to praise the student who found it. If there are many possibilities, the better responses to an answer might be:

- Thank you.
- That's one way to think about it.
- I never thought of that.
- Interesting.
- Possibly.
- Tell me more.
- Can you give me an example?
- Who else was thinking along those lines? What can you add?
- Who was thinking something else?
- Who can piggy back on that idea?
- What makes you think so?
- Have you evidence for that?
- What is another point of view?
- How are you deriving that?
- What do you think about what Sue has said?
- So you're saying . . . [paraphrase for clarity]
- What do you think Jay means by this?

Teachers need to listen (Parker, 2006). The old adage, we were given two ears and one mouth . . . use accordingly. Stephen Covey (1989) cautioned us to seek first to understand, then to be understood. By listening to student answers we are assessing and understanding their thinking, including prior knowledge as well as getting to know them better. We pick up anomalies and misconceptions that need to be redirected, preferences, and clarity of understanding. It also shows respect for student thinking and helps us respond with additional prompts for clarification and extension. It also helps us know the level of thinking students can handle and we can differentiate questions to the individual dependent on the level that will challenge them to keep them in the flow. This way you are not judging but creating a dialogue where each student can be engaged without fear of being wrong. Negativity in response to questions is the quickest way to shut down thinking.

They say 85% of the questions that teachers ask have only one right answer. So students are basically playing Trivial Pursuit trying to figure out what the teacher wants. Instead they should be thinking about the content at different levels and rationalizing their answers based on evidence. Black and Wiliam (1998b, 2004) conducted a study in UK secondary schools and found that students did better thinking and gave more complete, fuller, thorough answers when more wait time was given. As a result they had better conceptual knowledge that developed into long-term memory and did better on their tests. Black, Harrison, Lee, Marshall, and Wiliam (2004) found that there is greater retention and student achievement (up to 60%) with extended wait time. Often teachers feel an obligation to provide information as that is their job, but giving does not necessarily equate to receiving and storing. Doyle and Strauss (1976) suggest that "gum" is the content given to students and processing is "chewing the gum." Their suggestion is "less gum, more chewing." The more students talk, generate, and debate ideas, the more the ideas and concepts form and stick.

In the 21st century, skills like collaboration, communication, and critical and creative thinking are essential. Student dialogue fosters all of these. To be a critical thinker one needs to examine from a variety of angles. To move students to higher-order thinking our questions need to foster student thinking in these areas and also create potential tasks that include all levels of thinking. It also is important to ask open-ended questions for which there could be multiple answers to get students thinking.

Bloom's Revised Thinking Taxonomy

Bloom's taxonomy of thinking added a rich dimension for thinking in classrooms originally in 1956. It was revised in 2001 by Anderson and Krathwohl to include more elements of critical and creative thinking and includes the following processes:

1. **Remember:** Access long-term memory

2. **Understand:** Comprehend using words, symbols, and pictures

3. **Apply:** Ways to use

4. **Analyze:** Parts to whole, whole to part

5. **Evaluate:** Judge using criteria

6. **Create:** Go beyond, reconstruct, and innovate

Questions and activities can be generated at all levels in order to stretch student thinking. Using levels of thinking help students rehearse and interact with content to better internalize concepts. Figure 3.1 suggests prompts at all levels of the revised taxonomy.

Figure 3.2 on pages 82–83 charts off samples of the thinking levels with question prompts and potential activities that align with the various levels of thinking.

Figure 3.1 Bloom's Taxonomy Revised

Thinking Level	Process Verbs
Remember	Remember, define, list, tell, label, state
Understand	Discuss, describe, summarize, explain, calculate
Apply	Demonstrate, illustrate, dramatize, apply, solve, operate
Analyze	Analyze, compare, contrast, question, classify, experiment
Evaluate	Judge, select, evaluate, support, defend, advocate
Create	Create, invent, construct, develop, design, synthesize

Cubing

Cubing (Cowan & Cowan, 1980) is a way of having students examine a concept at each of the six levels of thinking. Teachers can create prompts for each of the six sides of the cube. Students can roll the cube and answer the prompt with their partner. Students may also create prompts for a cube and work with a partner to roll and respond to the prompts. It activates discussion with a partner or small group and gets students going deeper with concepts that they need to understand more than just a definition. See Figures 3.3 and 3.4 on pages 84–85.

Partners

Teachers sometimes get frustrated when allowing dialogue for a variety of reasons:

- Students get off task.
- Students waste time.
- Students get loud.
- It seems faster to simply tell students the answers, and the teacher can be sure of the accuracy of the information.
- It means that the teacher loses control.

It's hard to get left out of a pair. When students work with only one other person, face-to-face interaction is greater. There is more conversation between two. They get more airtime. It's safer than having many eyes on the student. There is greater reciprocity and the ability to build on one another's ideas and also question their thinking in a safe small space.

There are various ways to get a partner. We want students to work with many other students in the classroom to build community and practice social skills. We want random partners often, as we know that we

Figure 3.2 Question Starters and Classroom Activities Differentiated According to Bloom's Taxonomy

QUESTION STARTERS	POTENTIAL ACTIVITIES
Level I: REMEMBER (recall) 1. What is the definition for . . . ? 2. What happened after . . . ? 3. Recall the facts. 4. What were the characteristics of . . . ? 5. Which is true or false? 6. How many . . . ? 7. Who was the . . . ? 8. Tell in your own words.	1. Describe the . . . 2. Make a time line of events. 3. Make a facts chart. 4. Write a list of . . . steps in . . . facts about . . . 5. List all the people in the story. 6. Make a chart showing . . . 7. Make an acrostic. 8. Recite a poem.
Level II: UNDERSTAND 1. Why are these ideas similar? 2. In your own words retell the story of . . . 3. What do you think could happen? 4. How are these ideas different? 5. Explain what happened after. 6. What are some examples? 7. Can you provide a definition of . . . ? 8. Who was the key character?	1. Cut out or draw pictures to show an event. 2. Illustrate what you think the main idea was. 3. Make a cartoon strip showing the sequence of . . . 4. Write and perform a play based on the . . . 5. Compare this _____ with _____ 6. Construct a model of . . . 7. Write a news report. 8. Prepare a flow chart to show the sequence . . .
Level III: APPLICATION (applying without understanding is not effective) 1. What is another instance of . . . ? 2. Demonstrate the way to . . . 3. Which one is most like . . . ? 4. What questions would you ask? 5. Which factors would you change? 6. Could this have happened in . . . ? Why or why not? 7. How would you organize these ideas?	1. Construct a model to demonstrate using it. 2. Make a display to illustrate one event. 3. Make a collection about . . . 4. Design a relief map to include relevant information about an event. 5. Scan a collection of photographs to illustrate a particular aspect of the study. 6. Create a mural to depict . . .

QUESTION STARTERS

Level IV: ANALYSIS

1. What are the component parts of . . . ?
2. What steps are important in the process of . . . ?
3. If . . . then . . .
4. What other conclusions can you reach about . . . that have not been mentioned?
5. The difference between the fact and the hypothesis is . . .
6. The solution would be to . . .
7. What is the relationship between . . . and . . . ?

Level V: EVALUATE

1. In your opinion . . .
2. Appraise the chances for . . .
3. Grade or rank the . . .
4. What do you think should be the outcome?
5. What solution do you favor and why?
6. Which systems are best? Worst?
7. Rate the relative value of these ideas to . . .
8. Which is the better bargain?

Level VI: CREATE

1. Can you design a . . . ?
2. Why not compose a song about . . . ?
3. Why don't you devise your own way to . . . ?
4. Can you create new and unusual uses for . . . ?
5. Can you develop a proposal for . . . ?
6. How would you deal with . . . ?
7. Invent a scheme that would . . .

POTENTIAL ACTIVITIES

1. Design a questionnaire about . . .
2. Conduct an investigation to produce . . .
3. Make a flow chart to show . . .
4. Construct a graph to show . . .
5. Put on a play about . . .
6. Review . . . in terms of identified criteria.
7. Prepare a report about the area of study.

1. Prepare a list of criteria you would use to judge a . . . Indicate priority ratings you would give.
2. Conduct a debate about an issue.
3. Prepare an annotated bibliography . . .
4. Form a discussion panel on the topic of . . .
5. Prepare a case to present your opinions about . . .
6. List some common assumptions about . . . Rationalize your reactions.

1. Create a model that shows your new ideas.
2. Devise an original plan or experiment for . . .
3. Finish the incomplete . . .
4. Make a hypothesis about . . .
5. Change . . . so that it will . . .
6. Propose a method to . . .
7. Prescribe a way to . . .
8. Give the book a new title.

Source: Gregory and Chapman (2013).

Figure 3.3 Cubing Prompts

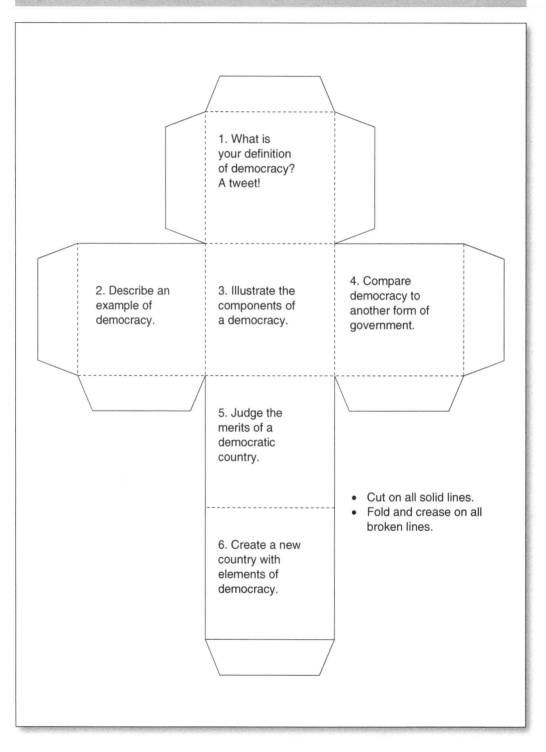

Figure 3.4 Cubing Template

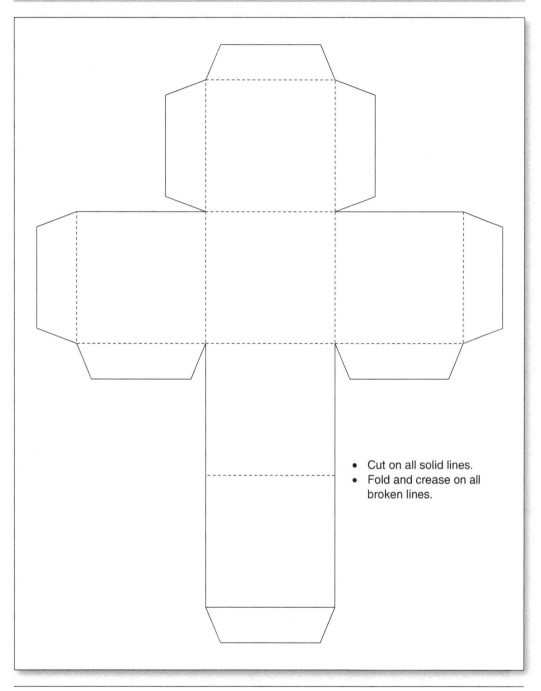

- Cut on all solid lines.
- Fold and crease on all broken lines.

learn from MKOs (more knowledgeable others) (Vygotsky, 1978) and also from those who are perhaps not as capable. So there are many ways to connect with a random partner. An easy way is to use the elbow or shoulder partner method, in which students turn to someone close by and start working together; they may be tasked with working on a problem or simply asked to say something about what the teacher just said. There's also point-and-go: Students look for someone close by that they haven't talked to today and point at each other. That's the signal that they are partners. They meet up and discuss whatever topic is proposed, question asked, or task given.

A more complex method is appointments. With the appointment method, students make appointments with three or four other students so that the teacher can ask students to meet with their partner for many different conversations as directed by the teacher. Here's how it works:

1. Prepare appointment cards such as small 4" × 4" cards with a symbol for each season such as a snowman, beach scene, blossoms, and autumn leaves (see Figure 3.5).

2. Student will put his or her name on their appointment card.

3. Then everyone will walk around and make appointments for each of the seasons.

4. As a student meets another student they will write their partner's name on the appointment card at the season when they plan to meet.

5. They will thank their partner and move on to make another appointment with someone else at a different season time.

6. When they have their four appointments (winter, spring, summer, and fall) they will go back to their table or desk.

7. The teacher can then use the appointment cards to get students together for a discussion or a task at anytime during the day, saying, for example, "Please meet up with your summer partner and complete the Venn diagram comparing the similarities and differences in the two theories."

Orchestrating an Appointment Card

Another way to have students fill in their appointment card is a more organized method that doesn't allow students to pick and choose or shun a partner. They line up in two lines facing another person. (See Figure 3.6.)

Figure 3.5 Appointment Cards

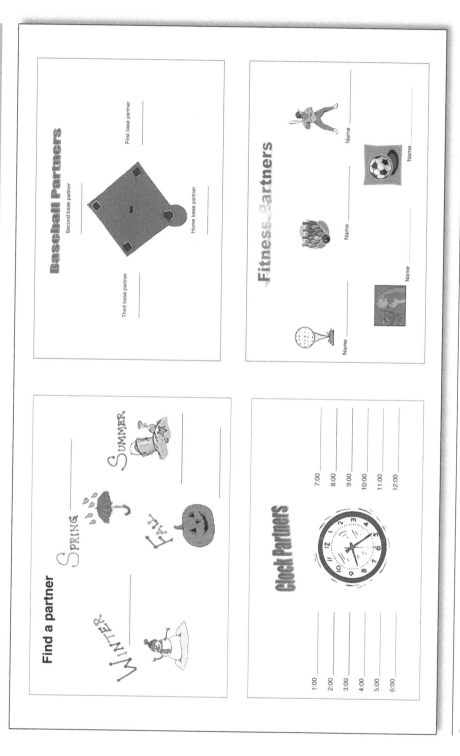

Source: Gregory and Kuzmich (2010).

Figure 3.6 Students in Two Lines Across From Each Other

Source: Gregory and Kuzmich (2010).

The first person across from them is their first partner and they will put their name on their card by the first appointment. Then the one line moves one place to the right. The person on the end will come down to the other end and then everyone will have a new partner. That will be their second appointment and so on.

Turn and Talk

"Turn and talk" is a cooperative structure that uses brief, focused conversations to allow students to check for understanding and practice new skills. The discussion eases students into cooperative relationships and helps them clarify their thinking before responding to the large group or to make connections from their perspective. The structure works well with any content or grade level and is particularly useful at intervals in a teacher-directed lesson.

1. Assign a problem, question, or task.

2. Ask students to turn to a partner nearby or to stand and make eye contact with another student and form a pair.

3. Students complete the task with the first partner and then move to find a second partner and continue the task.

4. Repeat as often as needed.

Once partners have been established, all sorts of partnering activities can take place. Here are just a few:

Talk a Mile a Minute

Students may get an elbow or eye contact partner. Then they proceed to take turns talking "a mile a minute" with hand gesture while their partner listens and encourages with nods and smiles. Partners reverse.

Say Something

This teacher could use this strategy so that students get to process what they have just heard or read. The teacher would ask them to think about the material and say something about the content to a partner. We get to hear what caught their interest as well as perhaps some misconceptions that were made as they listened. This also primes the pump and broadens students' perceptions for a large group discussion.

Say and Switch

This cooperative structure asks partners to respond to a prompt and then to switch the roles of speaker and listener at unexpected intervals. Say and switch (Kagan, 1992) is particularly useful for reviewing, rehearsing, or checking for understanding. The articulation helps the students to commit the ideas to long-term memory. Since each student must be ready to contribute they are both held accountable.

1. Form pairs.

2. Assign a discussion or review task.

3. Student A begins to respond while B listens carefully.

4. Call switch.

5. Student B must continue student A's train of thought before adding new information.

6. Repeat the switch as often as necessary.

Concentric Circles

This strategy ensures equal participation so all students are engaged simultaneously in a novel, active, social, kinesthetic way—all very brain friendly. They might be prompted with a question or asked to discuss information about a topic with a variety of peers in a structured way. Students create two concentric circles and stand facing one other person (Figure 3.7). They discuss the topic or question and at the signal from the teacher one of the circles moves so that everyone has a new partner.

1. **Split the Class:** One half of the students will form the inside circle and the other half will form the outside circle.

2. **Question:** Pose a question or statement. Give students time to think of an answer on their own.

3. **Share:** The students in the inside circle share their response with the student facing them in the outside circle. In response the student in the outside circle will share their response.

4. **Rotate:** Then have the outside circle move one person to the left or right and discuss the same question with their new partner. You could give a new question here.

This strategy is a good check for understanding any time a meaningful conversation is needed. It could be a good review strategy at the end of a lesson or a good recall discussion at the beginning or after a reading to discuss key ideas or questions (Kagan, 1994).

Figure 3.7 Concentric Circles

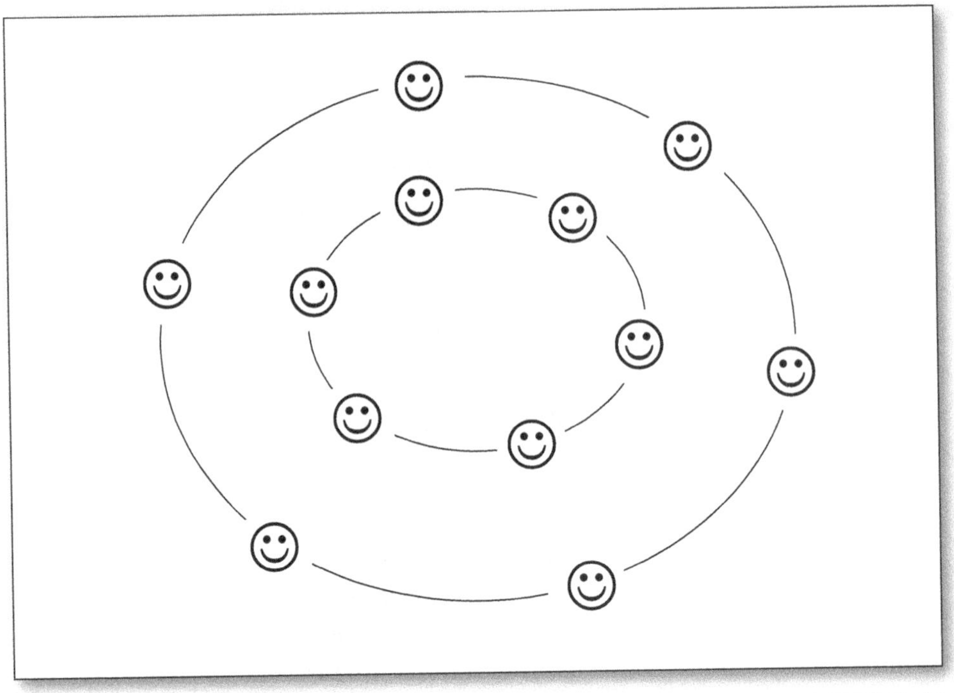

Source: Gregory and Kuzmich (2010).

Tips to Better Ensure Productive Dialogue

Some of the worries of teachers who are tenuous about allowing students to talk and perhaps waste time often prevent them from using powerful dialogue to deepen understanding. It is one thing to set up appointments and another to facilitate smooth transitions and activate thinking.

When you ask students to meet with their partners, give them five seconds to get there. Hold up your hand. Count down from 5, 4, 3, 2, 1 using finger prompts as well as aural. Students need to meet up with their partners, stand or find a place to sit, and be ready to listen to the instructions for whatever conversation or task that might be required. They will not be totally proficient at the transition the first time and it may take a few practice trials. We must persist longer than students resist so that this becomes a routine process and done effectively and with automaticity. Once the procedure is established, students get in and out of groups quickly and quietly so there is more time for dialogue. Don't give up as new ideas take time to implement and you may find creative ways to improve on the process.

Work the room. This is a time when teachers need to be in close proximity to the partners or groups, eavesdropping and with close presence helping students stay on topic. Eavesdropping is a great assessment tool as teachers pick up information on student understanding and misconceptions.

Working with many classmates over time builds the learning community and trust between and among all students. Working as a partner with everyone in the class, randomly at some time, creates a connection and familiarity that helps when students find themselves working in groups throughout the school year. Students will need a lot of time as partners to develop good listening skills, and when those have been established another member may be added to form trios for a cooperative task.

ACTIVATING LEARNING THROUGH PEER TUTORING

Peer tutoring offers unique benefits to both the tutors and the tutees. According to Hattie (2009), peer tutoring has a medium effect size of $d = 0.55$. Hattie stresses that visible learners need to see themselves as learners and teachers. The aim is to teach students self-regulation and control over their own learning as they must move from being only students to being teachers themselves.

Peer tutoring describes a variety of tutoring situations with students working in pairs to help one another learn new material or practice a skill or academic task. It works best with mixed-ability students in pairs (Kunsch, Jitendra, & Sood, 2007). Often student will switch roles halfway through so both have a chance to play the tutor and tutee roles.

Stephen Covey suggests, "To teach is to learn twice." Peer tutoring is beneficial for all students. While one student may excel in reading, another student may be excellent in math. These two students can work together to help each other understand difficult concepts in the subjects where they excel or struggle. Even if you are proficient, you deepen your own knowledge of the subject when you explain and revisit concepts.

In reviews of peer tutoring programs, it was found:

- Students who participated as a reading tutor saw improvements in reading achievement.
- Tutors who were explicitly trained in the tutoring process were far more effective and the students who were the tutees experienced significant advancement.
- Practically all students benefited from peer tutoring; same-age and cross-age tutors were equally effective (Burnish, Fuchs, & Fuchs, 2005; Topping, 2008).

Some benefits derived from peer tutoring include greater academic achievement, increased retention, improved interpersonal relationships, improved social and personal skills, increased motivation, and reduced failure and drop-out rates. The teacher also benefits from peer tutoring that fosters an opportunity to individualize and facilitates inclusion and chances of reducing inappropriate behaviors (Topping, 2008).

Students at all grade levels participating in tutorial programs improved their reading performance more than the expected gain for the typical student at that grade level (AmeriCorps, 2001). When students teach students, the result is marked improvement in their learning. In peer tutoring, students are "prosumers"—both producers and consumers of education. Peer tutoring is the most cost-effective way to improve both math and reading performance.

Peer tutoring also has benefits for the tutor. High school students raised their own reading scores by almost three years as a result of tutoring fourth graders in reading (Peer Research Laboratory, 2002).

Benefits for Students

Kalkowski (1995) reported the following additional benefits to students:

- Development of academic skills
- Development of social behaviors and overall discipline
- Improved peer relations
- Improved self-efficacy
- Development of skills transferable to employment or business
- Improved vocabulary skills and reading skills

Kalkowski (1995) also reported these benefits to the tutors:

- Strengthened understanding through frequent review of previously learned subject matter
- More higher-level thinking
- Confidence in one's ability to learn
- More motivation for studying
- Enhanced self-esteem and a sense of pride in service to others
- More communication skills and empathy
- Improved attitudes toward subject area
- Sense of responsibility

The Internet provides many ideas for peer tutoring; see, for example, http://www.wikihow.com/Be-a-Peer-Tutor and https://peers.aristotle circle.com/uploads/NTA_Peer_Tutoring_Factsheet_020107.pdf.

ACTIVATING LEARNING THROUGH RECIPROCAL TEACHING

Reciprocal teaching is an instructional activity that takes the form of a dialogue between teachers and students regarding segments of text for the purpose of constructing the meaning of text. Reciprocal teaching is a reading technique that is thought to promote the teaching process. Palincsar and Brown (1984) first developed reciprocal teaching. Its purpose was to help students move from decoding text to comprehension (Palincsar, Ransom, & Derber, 1989).

Palincsar suggests the purpose of reciprocal teaching is to facilitate a group effort between teacher and students or students to students with the goal to bring meaning to the text, as often students can sound out words but are unable to construct meaning.

Reciprocal teaching is best represented as a dialogue between teachers and students or students and students in which each take turns assuming the teacher's role in a collaborative group. Prediction is part of the process and students may predict before reading then read to verify accuracy or misconceptions or predict after reading as to what might come next (Stricklin, 2011).

A reciprocal approach offers students four specific reading strategies that are actively and consciously support comprehension:

1. **Generating Questions:** Teacher or students generate questions that they share and answer individually or collectively. Answers should use supportive evidence and rationale.

2. **Clarifying:** Restating or paraphrasing helps students deepen understanding because in doing so one must clearly comprehend the material. Language and terms need to be clarified as well.

3. **Summarizing:** Students note key points and restate them in summary form.

4. **Predicting:** Students make assumptions, generalizations, and predictions from what they have read and discussed. (Palincsar, 1986, in Gregory & Kuzmich, 2005)

These are referred to as the "fab four" by Lori Oczuks (2003), reading coach and author.

Reciprocal teaching is an amalgamation of reading strategies that effective readers are thought to use. These in-depth strategies vary from simply slowing down the rate of reading or decoding, to re-reading, to deliberately summarizing the material. Once the strategy (or strategies) has helped to restore meaning in the text, the successful reader can use this.

Strategy 1: Questioning

Readers monitor and assess their own understanding of the text by asking themselves questions. Through questioning students identify information, themes, and ideas that are key pieces of information. These are used to generate questions that are used as self-review for the reader. Questioning causes learners to go deeper and construct meaning (Doolittle, Hicks, Triplett, Nichols, & Young, 2006).

The *questioner* will pose questions related to unclear ideas or passages, confusing information, and connections to previously learned concepts.

Strategy 2: Clarifying

This step in the strategy focuses on specific steps to help with decoding (letter-sound correspondence, "chunking" or breaking down information into manageable pieces, spelling, etc.), as well as strategies to deal with difficult vocabulary.

Clarifying involves the learner identifying and clarifying confusing, difficult, or unfamiliar passages of a text. These passages may include unusual sentence structure, unfamiliar vocabulary, unclear references, or obscure concepts. Clarifying encourages the motivation to clear up confusion through re-reading, the use of context of the passage, and the use of other resources such as technology, a dictionary, or a thesaurus (Doolittle et al., 2006).

The *clarifier* in the group will identify the confusing parts and try to answer the questions that were posed.

Strategy 3: Summarizing

Summarization requires the reader to perform the task of selecting important and less important information in the passage. The student may delete extraneous information and organize key points (Palincsar & Brown, 1984).

Summarizing is identifying important information, themes, and ideas found in a text and condensing these into a clear and concise statement that communicates the essence of the text. Summarizing may be based on a single paragraph, a part of a passage, or an entire passage (Doolittle et al., 2006).

The *summarizer* restates in his or her own words the main idea of the text. This can happen at any time while reading the story, and it is key for those students who are at risk. It can happen first at paragraphs, then to the whole text.

Strategy 4: Predicting

The prediction phase is where readers actively combine their own prior knowledge with what they gathered from the text. Students imagine what might happen next in a narrative text. Students predict what they might learn or read about in next passages when reading an informational text. Predictions don't necessarily need to be accurate, but they need to be clear (Williams, 2010).

Predicting offers an overall rationale for reading—to validate or disconfirm self-generated hypotheses (Doolittle et al., 2006). The *predictor* can offer possibilities about what the author will share next or, if it's a literary piece, the predictor could suggest what the next events in the story will be.

The sequence of reading, questioning, clarifying, summarizing, and predicting is then repeated with subsequent sections of text (Slater & Horstman, 2002).

Instructional Format for Reciprocal Teaching

Reciprocal teaching follows a dialogic/dialectic process. Palincsar, Ransom, and Derber (1989) indicate that dialogue is a more familiar, natural method than writing, which is more labor intensive.

Reciprocal teaching illustrates a number of intriguing ideas for teaching and learning and is premised on both developmental and cognitive theories. The reciprocal teaching strategies represent those used by successful learners while interacting with the text. They tend to foster self-regulation, self-monitoring, and promoting intentional learning (Brown, 1980).

Reciprocal teaching follows a scaffolded curve, starting with high levels of teacher instruction, modeling, and input that is gradually withdrawn so that students eventually are able to use the strategies independently.

Reciprocal teaching begins with the students and teacher reading a short passage of text together. To begin the teacher models the "fab four" strategies that make up reciprocal teaching, and teacher and students share in conversation to come to a consensus about the text (Williams, 2010). The teacher then overtly models his or her thinking processes out loud, using each of the four reading strategies in turn. Students follow the teacher's model with their own strategies, also verbalizing their thought processes to their colleagues.

Over time, the teacher withdraws more and more as students become more adept and confident using the strategies. Over time, responsibility for leading the small-group discussions of the text and the strategies is transferred to the students. This gives the teacher or reading tutor the opportunity to observe the group and diagnose strengths, weaknesses, and misconceptions and to provide follow-up and interventions as needed.

Figure 3.8 chronicles the process of gradual release of teacher support when using reciprocal teaching.

Figure 3.8 Learning to Read Within Vygotsky's Zone of Proximal Development

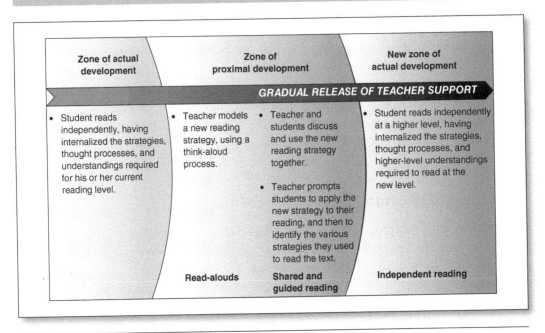

Source: © Queen's Printer for Ontario, 2003. Reproduced with permission.

Reciprocal teaching encompasses several techniques involving the who, what, and where of learning (Mayer, 2008):

- What are learned are cognitive strategies for reading comprehension. The process focuses on how to learn rather than what to learn.
- Learning of the cognitive strategies occurs within real reading comprehension tasks that are not taught in isolation.

These strategies can be used with any content area or subject discipline.

SUMMARY

The influence of peers cannot be denied. The social aspect of the brain as well as the safe environment where peers can interact plus the strategies to activate and facilitate discussion is key to increasing student achievement. Teachers who defer to "stand and deliver" as the way they've always done it are missing key opportunities to activate learning, engage students, and deepen understanding of new knowledge and skill development for all students.

In the next chapter we will look at cooperative group learning as a powerful way to activate thinking and increase student achievement through dialogue and social interaction.

DISCUSSION POINTS

- Read and discuss the research on peer influence.

- Discuss humans' innate social needs, how relationships are essential, and how classrooms do or do not support these needs. Brainstorm a list of how we might meet these needs.

- With your colleagues debate the pros and cons of monologue and dialogue. You might use a T chart for each.

Dialogue		Monologue	
Advantages	Disadvantages	Advantages	Disadvantages

- What are the advantages of waiting for students to think before answering and using strategies such as Think Pair Share?

- Consider the strategies to deal with quiet time while students think. How can teachers extend thinking? Take turns posing a question and extending thinking with suggested responses.

- Using Bloom's revised taxonomy, experiment with a recall question and restating a version at each level.

- Read and discuss the concept of cubing and create one that you might use with your students.

- Discuss using partners to foster dialogue and peer interaction to create more focused discussion. Consider ways for students to get a partner during partnered tasks. Consider some tips for ensuring productive dialogue.

- After reading the section on peer tutoring, discuss the concept and the benefits to both students and teachers.

- After reading the information about reciprocal teaching, plan a learning experience related to an upcoming reading. Conduct a mock reciprocal teaching experience.

4 Activating Cooperative Learning

Cooperative group learning (CGL) is the use of small student groups to allow students to research and debate together, teach each other, and present findings as a group. There have been over 600 studies since the 1980s that support the effectiveness of CGL (see, e.g., Johnson & Johnson, 1981; Johnson, Johnson, and Holubec, 1998; Marzano, Pickering, & Pollock 2001; Dean et al., 2012; Cawelti, 2004). Synthesizing the research on cooperative group learning has an effect size of 0.73 with an associated percentile gain on standardized assessments of 27. A study by Brady and Tsay (2010) supports that cooperative learning is an active pedagogy that fosters higher academic achievement.

Visible learning research from John Hattie's (2009) meta-analysis also places cooperative group learning on the list of impactful strategies for student achievement.

- Cooperation vs. individualistic learning: effect size of $d = 0.59$
- Cooperation vs. competitive learning: effect size of $d = 0.54$
- Small group learning: effect size of $d = 0.49$
- Cooperative learning: effect size of $d = 0.42$

Barkley et al. (2005, pp. 17–18) summed it up this way: "In extensive meta-analyses across hundreds of studies, cooperative arrangements were found superior to either competitive or individualistic structures on a variety of outcome measures, generally showing higher achievement, higher-level reasoning, more frequent generation of new ideas and solutions, and greater transfer of what is learned from one situation to another."

WHY TEACHERS CAN BE SKEPTICAL OF CGL

Given the clear benefits of CGL, why is it so seldom used in the classroom? Many teachers approach group work with optimism and hope, yet soon the wheels fall off and they retreat to other methods. Unfortunately it is one of the least understood or well-implemented strategies (Antil, Jenkins, Wayne, & Vadasy, 1998; Koutselini, 2009). Here are some of the reasons teachers give for pulling back from CGL:

- The students don't stay focused.
- Time is wasted.
- They get off task.
- Disagreements escalate.
- There are slackers.
- There are bossy students.
- I can tell them this information more quickly than it takes to set up group work.
- I'm not confident in their ability to learn without me.

In reality all these things can happen. But thoughtful planning and strategic orchestration can address many of these issues (see Figure 4.1).

This chapter addresses the benefits that students accrue from cooperative learning and provides some concrete methods for incorporating it into the classroom successfully.

WHY THE BRAIN LOVES CGL

The brain loves it when we collaborate. We have the innate need for social interaction. The release of dopamine is increased by cooperative tasks. Dopamine, a neurotransmitter that is responsible for attention, memory storage, and comprehension as well as executive functioning, is released increasingly in brain areas connected with memory and learning when we have positive experiences such as those in supportive groups. The brain also releases more dopamine when one is at play, laughing, exercising, and being acknowledged for success. Yet another feel-good neurotransmitter, oxytocin, is activated when trust is developed and social bonding occurs. There is diversity in all classrooms and thus there needs to be ongoing team building to foster trust and make connections and social bonds between and among students (Waelti, Dickinson, & Shultz, 2001).

Figure 4.1 Cooperative Group Learning Issues and Resolutions

Issue	Resolution
1. I can tell them faster. I only have so much time to teach this topic. It takes too much time to have them work in groups.	• Time is well spent if students are developing deep concepts and expanding their understanding.
2. They waste time and are often off task talking about other things.	• You must provide a clear target and goal for the group. • They need a realistic time frame. Use a timer. • Give short and irregular amounts of time such as 13 and a half minutes. This creates a sense of urgency and they get to the task quicker. If students are given too much time, they waste it.
3. Someone takes over and does all the work and you have hangers-on who take credit but coast.	• Start small and work in pairs. It's hard to get left out of a pair. Give them a specific job to do and make sure they are accountable when finished. • Have each person write a completion card at the end of the task: What did I do? What did I learn? • Select random reporters.
4. Disagreements occur.	• Teach social skills as needed, like how to disagree agreeably. • Appoint a peace maker. • Teach conflict resolution skills. • Focus on social skills.

The world depends on people collaborating in order to function (Johnson & Johnson, 2009). Cooperative group learning (CGL) helps foster collaboration skills as well as mastery of the subject matter at hand. Vocabulary, concept development, and higher-order thinking are built into the process and students use academic and domain vocabulary in context. Hattie suggests that from the research we get an effect size of $d = 0.82$ from dialogue, and group work gives all students a voice, whereas teacher monologue doesn't. Teachers activate and orchestrate learning between and among students.

CGL is not just a powerful strategy for student learning but also a vehicle for the valuable discussion to activate surface learning and deepen student understanding. It also helps develops the 21st century skills that are vital for students to succeed in life in a complex, ever-changing world (Figure 4.2). The category of Learning and Innovation Skills includes the 4 C's:

Communication

Collaboration

Critical thinking and problem solving

Creativity and innovation

All these can be fostered in cooperative group learning opportunities.

Figure 4.2 21st Century Skills

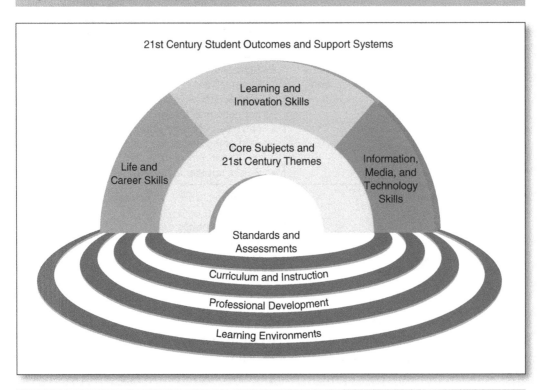

Source: P21, Framework for 21st Century Learning, http://www.p21.org.

As we have seen in previous chapters, brains flourish when there is safety and just the right amount of stimulation. CGL supports these brain needs in several ways:

- Students have more time to talk and share perspectives reconstructing their opinions and actively process learning. They develop the skills of summarizing, defending, explaining, elaborating, and exemplifying.

- Students learn to disagree constructively through clarification, and revisiting and rethinking information and opinions, leading to deeper understanding.
- Students are exposed to different perspectives and points of view of others that may provide comparative thinking.
- In a small safe group, there is less anxiety and risk of ridicule or embarrassment.
- Group interaction and discussion sparks new ideas not thought of on one's own. We tend to piggy-bank ideas suggested by others.
- Students achieve a stronger knowledge base and greater achievement when they explore concepts collaboratively (Hythecker, Dansereau, & Rocklin, 1988; Qin, Johnson, & Johnson, 1995).

When CGL is well implemented we can look forward to students developing:

- Greater achievement academically
- On-task behavior
- Increased social skills and empathy
- Greater retention of material through elaboration
- Higher levels of thinking and reasoning
- Higher levels of social support
- Higher self-esteem
- Higher motivation (intrinsic)
- Better attitude toward school, teachers, and peers
- Greater positive psychological well-being (Johnson, Johnson, & Holubec, 1998)

START SMALL

We know that teacher monologue prevails 85% of the time in many classrooms, more so every year as students progress through school. It can be useful in many instances but shouldn't be the most pervasive strategy. We want students to work independently at times to consolidate their ideas, apply knowledge and skills, pre- and self-assess, and reflect and set goals. The research shows that dialogue and social interaction fosters a higher impact on student achievement and thus more time spent in partners and small groups will yield greater success. Partners are certainly a place to start, as it is hard to get left out of a pair. There is less off-task behavior, more air time for equal dialogue, more of a safe environment, more participation, and less conflict with only two people involved. Given a class of 30 students, each one would have less than

30 seconds to speak every hour (Lie, 2008). So partner work would certainly be a great way to get every student talking, chewing, and digesting new information and skills.

The concept of group or partner work is simple enough, but the implementation is a process. Often CGL tasks don't go smoothly because we start in too grand a way. The tasks are too complex, the groups are too large, and students may lack the social skills to be successful. Often it's cognitive overload as they try to juggle interpersonal issues, including conflicts or differences of opinion, and the process of the task. Again, if one is starting out to foster dialogue and peer interaction, partners are the place to begin, not small groups. Until students have social skills and experience working with others it is better not to have groups where they can hide or escalate conflict. Lots of partner work with random partners give students lots of practice working with others and builds class community and support by developing familiarity with everyone in the class and practicing social skills in a controlled environment without the complexity of multiple personalities.

Figure 4.3 shows some possible classroom structure. In the figure, T stands for total group configuration, A for students working alone, P for partners, and S for small groups. All these are useful and appropriate if they are being used in disproportion to their impact and effect on student achievement.

There are many interpretations of CGL. The best described and most successful approach is the Johnsons' method, which gives specific techniques for designing group work and student interaction that gains both academic success and fosters the growth of interpersonal skills so important for success in life. Their model also includes group processing that helps students develop metacognition. The following sections provide concrete suggestions on how to implement CGL successfully using the Johnson method and other suggestions.

DESIGNING SMALL GROUPS

The first step in CGL is putting the students together in small groups. This may seem easy, but there are lots of issues to consider. Most importantly, on what basis should groups be formed? There are three main choices: ability groups, heterogeneous groups, and random groups.

Ability grouping is putting together learners of similar competence levels. Ability groups are structured based on student needs such as a gap in knowledge or skill identified in pre-assessment or as they work

Figure 4.3 TAPS Chart for Possible Classroom Structures

T: Total	A: Alone	P: Partners	S: Small Groups
Definition			
Whole-class instruction All students doing the same thing Often teacher directed	Students working independently by choice or as directed	Students are paired through random selection (counting off, numbering, etc.) Teacher designed Students' choice Task or interest oriented Teacher choice	Random or structured by teacher or students Interest or task oriented Heterogeneous for cooperative groups Homogeneous for skill development
Suggested Strategies for Each Grouping			
Pre-assessment Modeling new skills Guest speaker Providing new information Viewing a video Lecturette	Pre-assessment Self-assessment Independent study Note taking and summarizing Reflection Journal entry Portfolio assessing Tickets out Textbook(s) assignment Internet search	Brainstorming Processing information Checking for understanding Peer editing Peer evaluation Researching Interest in similar topic Planning for homework Checking homework	Group projects Learning centers Consensus building Cooperative group learning tasks Problem solving Portfolio conferences Group investigation Carousel brainstorming Graffiti brainstorming

Source: Adapted from Gregory and Chapman (2013), Figure 5.15.

on a task. The idea behind ability grouping is that students at the same competence level work together well because they will go at a similar pace, understand the same ideas, be familiar with the same resources, and so on. Here is how one teacher might use ability groups: After students completed an exit card at the end of class on Monday, Ms. Johnson examines the cards and finds that some students had a good understanding of the concept of navigating the Internet. As a result of this formative assessment, on Tuesday she divides the students into three groups: (1) students with independent skills completed an advanced search; (2) students with an average capability conducted a focused challenge to practice; and (3) those with limited ability worked with the teacher to review the steps and develop their skills.

Although ability grouping seems to offer obvious benefits, it has serious downsides. Grouping by ability can limit the knowledge and experience available to the group and lead to "group think." It can have negative effects on students' self-efficacy if they perceive that they have been placed in a group for which the teacher has low expectations (Johnson & Johnson, 2009). Also, ability grouping is not how the real world works. The real world is heterogeneous and people work and interact with people who are often different from themselves and who have a variety of experiences, interests, preferences, and competencies (Frey, Fisher, & Everlove, 2009).

Lou et al. (1996) have identified several problems with ability groupings:

- Low-ability learners usually perform worse in homogeneous groupings because of a lack of role models.
- Average-ability learners benefit more from homogeneous groups than do low-ability and high-ability learners.
- High-ability learners do not make much in the way of gains.

No one is suggesting that students should be tracked and left in the "ruts"; rather, they should be moved in and out of homogeneous and heterogeneous groups for specific tasks as needed. Ability grouping should only be used to bring a group of students together for a particular mini-lesson. They should not be groups that endure over time and are labeled (e.g., bluebirds, buzzards, and crows), and ability grouping should never be a teacher's only method (Lou et al., 1996). Hattie (2009) shows a low effect size of 0.12 for ability grouping having a negative effect.

Another type of grouping is heterogeneous groups. Heterogeneous grouping reflects a deliberately designed group of varying skill levels.

Let's look back to Ms. Johnson's class. Instead of ability grouping, she might have created groups of three students, one each at the advanced, average, and beginning levels. The mixed-level group would work together to, for instance, play a teams game tournament challenge.

This group design has several benefits. Diverse members of a group are more like groups that students will encounter in the real world. The diversity is often an advantage as we bring students together with different prior knowledge and perspectives. Their skill sets are complementary, and when the group is working together this is a plus. The groups vary in age, cultures, gender, and competencies (Lou, Abrami, & d'Apollonia, 2001). They learn together and teach each other activating learning through social interaction and complementary knowledge and skills.

Lastly, small groups can be put together randomly. Ultimately, there is never one way to configure groups. The teacher's discretion and the data available will influence the decisions concerning grouping. Not matter what conclusions are made, the groups should be fluid and not forever. For another skill a different configuration might have been used. We don't all learn in the same way on the same day.

ELEMENTS OF SUCCESSFUL GROUP WORK

The frustrations that teachers express about CGL make it clear that successful group work doesn't just happen. Many researchers have investigated the traits that make CGL function well. One of the clearest of these is the five elements of the Johnson method (Johnson, Johnson, & Holubec, 1998). These five elements are positive interdependence, individual accountability, group processing, social skills, and face-to-face interaction—denoted by the acronym PIGSF (see Figure 4.4). Guiding planning with PIGSF will help teachers in group and task design that will maximum efficiency, attention to task, and more equal participation of each group member.

Element 1: Positive Interdependence

Positive interdependence is essential to create a collaborate approach to the task. Roles should be appropriate to the task assigned: reader, writer, checker, project manager, resource manager, technology manager. One way this can be done is by giving students roles and tasks that will help facilitate the process. An environment conducive to the task should be structured. Sequencing the steps (chunking and scaffolding) help students progress. Sometimes competition between

Figure 4.4 Using Cooperative Group Learning

Element	Purpose	Implications
Positive interdependence	To allow students to work together and rely on one another for success.	Create a goal and conditions for relying on each other by sharing resources and roles to complete the task.
Individual accountability	To allow students to be responsible for learning and for demonstrating competence.	Create a manageable group of three or four and structure the task so that at the end each person demonstrates competence in some assessment task (quick write, random reporter, etc.).
Group processing	To allow students to reflect on their contributions to the task and the group function and use of social skills.	Assign checklists, journals, exit cards, and sentence stems to provide feedback for self and group.
Social skills	To have students use social skills to help group functioning.	Overtly teach what the social skill is and how to use it.
Face-to-face interaction	To have students use dialogue and questioning to achieve the task together.	Encourage dialogue and foster effort and recognition of contributions.

Source: Adapted from Johnson, Johnson, and Holubec (1998).

groups is suggested. Resources may be limited to each member so that they need to rely on one another.

Element 2: Individual Accountability

Johnson, Johnson, and Holubec (1998) define individual accountability as "the measurement of whether or not each group member has achieved the groups' goal. Assessing the quality and quantity of each member's contributions and giving the results to all group members."

In CGL, although students are learning together, ultimately they are responsible for the new learning individually. Thus they are responsible for completing their part of the group task and learning the skills and concepts set out as a goal. This is not passive learning but engaging opportunities for self directed and collaborative learning.

Ways students can be accountable are to demonstrate individually after the group task. They can complete a test at the end of the learning.

They can use an exit card explaining what they have learned. They might be called on as the reporter to explain what the group accomplished.

Element 3: Social Skills

Sometimes we need to teach students appropriate social skills so that they can increase the efficiency and productivity in their group. Older students don't necessarily have any better social skills than younger children. Middle and high school teachers may feel that they don't have time to teach social skills. But if they aren't taught at some point, how will they learn them? The number one reason people lose their jobs is not because they don't have information and skills but because they can't get along with others. We are trying to prepare students for success in life and not just passing the test. We do know that enduring social skills should become part of their repertoire for future success (Goleman, 1995).

Some children come to school with the ability to share and take turns and other social skills, but some don't. So explicitly teaching these skills is essential to successful group work.

There are some foundational social skills that would increase the quality of group interactions and on task behavior for successful task completion:

- Active listening
- Taking turns
- Encouraging language
- Speaking in a positive way
- Using appropriate voice volume
- Equal participation
- Persistence
- Offering and asking for help
- Polite, respectful language

Here are some skills for working in a group:

- Checking for clarity
- Following directions
- Asking for clarification
- Disagreeing in an agreeable way
- Managing conflicts
- Accepting others' opinions
- Encouraging others

Many of these skills (e.g., active listening, polite language) are addressed in previous chapters. The important thing is that teachers not assume that students know how to use these skills in small groups. How to interact in small groups is something that itself can be taught cooperatively. Here are some strategies that teachers can use to implement social skills learning:

- Sometimes the group breaks down when a social skill is lacking, and this can become a teachable moment. Through teacher facilitation the group discusses the situation and students identify what skill might be needed and a solution for the problem.

- To demonstrate the skill, it might be modeled or used in a role-play. It might be exaggerated to prove the point. A video, clip from YouTube, or story might clarify the skill.

- A T chart delineating what the skill "Looks Like" or "Sounds Like" can be constructed. A double T chart might be used to add the third aspect of what it "Feels Like" (Hill & Hancock, 1993). Self-reflection can be employed by thinking about how the skill feels. This evokes personal feelings and empathy for others. Students can brainstorm the indicators, contributing ideas for the chart in their own words so that as they use the indicators the language is comfortable and familiar to use as it is their own. What a first grader or eighth grader would say would be different. Figure 4.5 is an example of a chart that describes equal participation. Students created it during a discussion about the importance of equal participation. With very young children symbols may be used instead of words.

Figure 4.5 Social Skill Chart for Equal Participation

Looks Like	Feels Like	Sounds Like
Everyone has a turn.	We are a group.	Encouraging others to participate.
Everyone does some of the work.	Our goal was achieved together.	"Your turn, Jake . . ."
Everyone shares ideas and makes suggestions.	Everyone feels satisfied.	"Please give us your ideas."
		"What would you like to do to help us?"

Source: Adapted from Hill and Hancock (1993).

• An organizer can also be used to record information for any idea or concept that has three parts. It would work with the jigsaw technique. Each student reads and summarizes part of a topic. You could give students roles so that they rotate roles as they explain and record their part. The roles that might be used could be reporter, recorder, and clarifier. That way everyone is engaged at each step.

• Students can show that they understand the skill by drawing about it, role-playing a situation where the skill is used appropriately, using puppets to demonstrate the skill in a situation, or writing about themselves or others using this skill in real-life situations.

• Social skill selection should be appropriate for the task in which the students are engaged. Disagreeing in an agreeable way is suitable for a task such as academic controversy where opinions will differ. When students are generating ideas in an activity, the social skill most appropriate might be equal participation. Having generated a T chart, they will have some language prompts to use while working together.

• In a self-contained elementary classroom the teacher may sequence the social skills to be taught based on building competencies over time. In high school, teachers may decide as a faculty to have some teachers focus on a particular set of social skills so that all classes may use them but all teachers don't have to initiate them.

Element 4: Group Processing

Students improve their social skills and group interaction by targeting them as they work together. But they will improve even more with group processing. This step is sometimes omitted as time runs out after the task is completed. It does not have to be long and involved. Just a few minutes to consciously comment on how the group functioned, if they used the skill, and how they might improve next time. Thumbs up, sideways, or down will indicate what the level of competence the member think they achieved. They can also use raised fingers:

5 = We're great at this

4 = We did a good job

3 = We're average

2 = We need to practice

This reflection is a form of metacognition and develops self-awareness. Sometimes journal entries or checklists may be used, but of course they take more time.

Element 5: Face-to-Face Interaction

CGL is not individualistic. The group combines thoughts, debates, comes to a consensus, summarizes, and builds on each other's ideas. The dialogue leads to higher-order thinking, and taking surface learning to a deeper level through critical and creative processes. Skills of communication and collaboration are developed.

IMPLEMENTING CGL: JIGSAW, ACADEMIC CONTROVERSY, AND GROUP INVESTIGATION

The benefits of CGL for students are clear. And the Johnson method shows what elements must be incorporated for CGL to go well. The section presents three concrete methods for implementing CGL in the classroom: jigsaw, academic controversy, and group investigation.

Jigsaw

Jigsaw is a way of organizing group learning to process information, deepen understanding, and facilitate dialogue. The jigsaw (Aronson, 1978) helps students learn material more deeply. The focused discussion when teaching peers provides rehearsal and deepens understanding and retention.

Jigsaw taps peer teaching and sharing and offers students an active role in learning material that increases long-term memory and supports the use of active and social learning. Most important for the teacher, it offers clear steps around which he or she can structure lesson plans.

There are three types of jigsaw that might be used.

Simple Jigsaw

The simple jigsaw structure (Figure 4.6) has each member of the small group become become an expert on a part of the material. Each member then has the responsibility for teaching his or her portion to their group. The academic goal is for all members of the group to understand fully all the material. Here's how it works:

1. Arrange the cooperative groups of four and number or letter off. Assign a portion of the material or a task to each member of the group (e.g., A, B, C, D or 1, 2, 3, 4).

2. Have students read and learn their section and highlight key ideas. Students may record key content on an advance organizer or chart.

3. Then students teach their section to the members of their cooperative group, A, B, C, and D each in turn. Members are responsible for ensuring that all members of their group have learned all of the material (promoting individual accountability).

4. Assess mastery of the material using individual assignments or tests, whole-class debriefing, presentations or oral quizzes, or exit cards.

Figure 4.6   Simple Jigsaw

Source: Gregory and Kuzmich (2010).

Expert Jigsaw

The expert jigsaw (Figure 4.7) is a variant that has each student in a group work with their counterpart in other groups to ensure that the new material is well understood before they teach their home base partners. The discussion with their expert small group allows for all students to clarify ideas and check for understanding. This also allows the teacher to monitor the expert groups for accuracy so incorrect information isn't shared back in the base group. The opportunity to teach each other deepens student understanding and provides rehearsal that helps move the new learning into long-term memory. Here's how it works:

1. Select a passage or chapter and divide into segments.

2. Form small (base) groups of two, three, or four students.

3. Number students and assign each member a portion of the article or chapter.

4. Give students time to read their portion silently and to highlight key ideas. You may provide an advance organizer for students to record key ideas.

5. Create new expert groups from the individuals who have read the same material (all the 1, 2, 3, and 4's meet up and become experts on their material). Allow them time to discuss what they have read. Monitor the expert groups for accuracy and clarity.

6. Recreate the original base groups and have students teach the rest of their base group about the information from their readings.

7. Have students discuss the implications of the reading or summarize key themes.

8. Assess through whole-class debriefing, quizzes, individual tests, oral reports, or presentations.

Figure 4.7 Expert Jigsaw

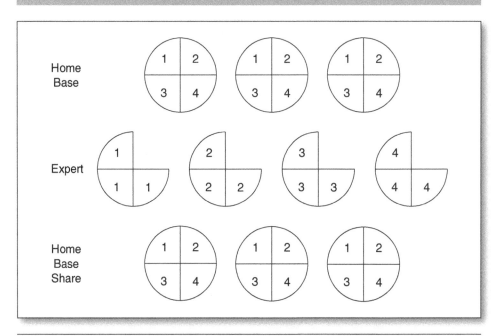

Source: Gregory and Chapman (2013).

Table Jigsaw

In the table jigsaw variant (Figure 4.8), each group is responsible for a different piece of content. Each table studies the material and decides how to teach or present it to the large group.

Students remain in their home group and are perhaps assigned roles and resources related to the task. They are the expert group, as the entire group becomes an expert as an aspect of the topic or issue and presents their part to the whole class.

Figure 4.8 Table Jigsaw

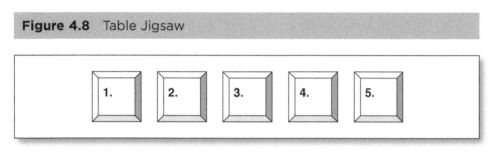

Source: Gregory and Kuzmich (2010).

Academic Controversy

Controversy exists when one person's ideas, information, conclusions, theories, and opinions are incompatible with those of another, and the two seek to reach an agreement (Johnson, Johnson, & Smith, 1996). Controversies are inherent in both academic content (intellectual issues exist in every academic discipline and subject area) and cooperative groups (members have different ideas, opinions, and conclusions as they are working together to complete assignments and master learning).

Academic controversy is the instructional use of intellectual conflict to promote higher achievement and increase the quality of problem solving, psychological health, and well-being. In an academic controversy activity, students refute opposing positions, rebut attacks on their own position, reverse perspectives, and create a synthesis on which group members can come to consensus.

Structured academic controversy is most often contrasted with concurrence seeking, debate, and individualistic learning. To resolve an issue through concurrence, students inhibit discussion to avoid any disagreement and compromise quickly to reach a consensus. In a debate, students present and defend only one position before a judge who ultimately determines who presented the best position. In individualistic learning students consider issues independently, working on their own with their own set of materials at their own pace. Academic controversy results in more positive outcomes for students compared to concurrence seeking, debate, or individualistic learning.

There is considerable research evidence validating the use of academic controversy (Johnson & Johnson, 1989; Johnson, Johnson, & Smith, 1996). To create a successful academic controversy lesson teachers should focus on the following:

1. Be sure about instructional objectives, group size, group formation, room arrangements, materials, and student roles.

2. Orchestrate the academic task: Explain the task, and structure positive interdependence, controversy, accountability, criteria for success, and desired behaviors.

3. Observe and intervene: Monitor and provide assistance, and help resolve any conflict that may arise.

4. Evaluate and process: Provide closure, assess and evaluate student learning, and provide group processing and celebration.

The Steps of Academic Controversy

Here are the step-by-step instructions that students should follow to complete an academic controversy assignment.

1. **Create the best case for your position**.
   a. Research the text or multiple sources related to the issue.
   b. Organize and frame logical, compelling, well-reasoned arguments.

2. **Present the best case for both positions.** While each side presents, the other listens and take notes without comment.
   a. Pair A students present arguments for Position A.
   b. Pair B students present arguments for Position B.

3. **Engage in open discussion**. Students engage in conversation about the issue, continuing to advocate their positions and refute the evidence and reasoning of the other side.

4. **Reverse perspectives.** Pairs switch sides, adopting the point of view they earlier refuted. The job of each pair is now to present the best case for what was previously the opposing position. In turn, they listen to the other side present the best case for what used to be their position.

    a. Pair A students present arguments for Position B.

    b. Pair B students present arguments for Position A.

5. **Synthesize and come to consensus.** Opposing pairs work together to integrate the most powerful arguments from both positions and meld them into a new position that all can agree to.

6. **Prepare a report.** The entire group writes a joint report explaining the synthesis. The report may be presented orally to the class.

Research Note-Taking Form for Academic Controversy

As you research your position, you can use the form in Figure 4.9 to take notes. In the left-hand column, write down the name of your source. In the second column, write down your notes. In the third, write your comments, questions, interpretations, and reactions.

Figure 4.9 Research Note-Taking Form

Source	Notes	Comments

Reaching Consensus: Synthesis/Resolution Form

Your goal is to come up with a solution that represents a synthesis of the reasoning behind both positions—a solution that all four of you can agree to. To begin, note what you consider to be the key points from both arguments. Then use the middle column to brainstorm ideas for solutions (see Figure 4.10).

Rules for Academic Controversy

1. I am critical of ideas, not people. I challenge and refute ideas.

2. I remember that we are all in this together. We are looking for the best decision.

3. I encourage everyone to participate and to master all the relevant information.

4. I listen to everyone's ideas, even if I don't agree.

5. I restate what someone has said if it is not clear.

6. I first bring out all ideas and facts supporting both sides, and then I try to put them together in a way that makes sense.

7. I try to understand both sides of the issue. I change my mind when evidence clearly indicates that I should do so.

Figure 4.10 Synthesis/Resolution Form

Position A: Key Points	Ideas That Might Work for Both	Position B: Key Points

Group Investigation

Group investigation (Sharan & Sharan, 1990) is a cooperative structure that enables students to plan and carry out a course of study. This structure is complex because students are involved in multifaceted learning tasks that demand greater student autonomy and group self-direction.

Six stages are involved:

1. Grouping
2. Planning
3. Investigating
4. Organizing
5. Presenting
6. Evaluating

Stage 1: Grouping

1. **Present the topic:** Select a multifaceted topic and use the question to set the tone and define the scope of the inquiry. Students may scan a variety of resources to activate prior learning and stimulate inquiry.

2. **Clarify the topic:** Develop a list of questions that the students would like to investigate. You may have the whole class brainstorm together, small groups may brainstorm and report their list, or individuals can write questions and use a snowball technique to combine answers into one list.

3. **Classify questions to create sub-topics.**

4. **Form investigation groups:** Students select subtopics of interest and form cooperative groups. Teachers will want to monitor or assign students to ensure heterogeneity of groups.

Stage 2: Planning

1. **Clarify the task:** Each group explores their subtopic and formulates a researchable problem. Focus questions are developed to outline the scope of the inquiry.

2. **Develop an action plan:** The group decides aspects to investigate, deadlines for reporting back, and resources needed.

3. **Assign or have students select job responsibilities:** Some jobs might be materials manager, discussion coordinator, recorder, or progress monitor.

Stage 3: Investigating

1. **Prepare a daily plan:** Group members complete an action plan for each investigation day (Figure 4.11).

2. **Research the subtopic:** Gather data from a variety of resources, print, media, and Internet.

3. **Analyze and evaluate data:** Assess the relevance of the data related to the question.

4. **Apply the data:** Members share their data to solve the group problem.

Figure 4.11 Daily Investigation Plan

Date:	
Group:	
Plan:	
ACTION	NAME
1. _____	_____
2. _____	_____
3. _____	_____
4. _____	_____

Stage 4: Organizing

1. **Select the reporting method:** Determine the presentation format. It may be common to all groups or groups may select (e.g., exhibition, display, learning center, model, written reports, PowerPoint, multimedia).

2. **Plan the report:** Members discuss individual roles for the presentation and complete a presentation plan.

3. **Construct the report:** Individual assignments are completed.

Stage 5: Presenting

1. **Present the reports:** Groups present according to the schedule.

2. **Respond to the report:** Other groups may seek clarification or give feedback.

Stage 6: Evaluating

The assessment when using group investigation is ongoing and visible as the students process their thinking through dialogue that shows their grasp of concepts. The teacher is able to monitor the progress, give feedback and guidance, and offer probing questions to extend thinking and actions. Often students can create their own criteria for success and self-evaluate at the end of the investigation. This is a highly effective instructional model as it is very student-directed, building an investigation around their interests.

A well-rehearsed process and communication are necessary for optimal cooperative group interaction. By thoughtful structuring of cooperative groups, students will be more successful, learn at deeper levels, and use higher levels of creative and critical thinking as they have an opportunity to practice some of these skills:

- Apply knowledge
- Set learning and goals
- Use strategies and study skills that will promote long-term memory
- Generalize and use critical thinking skills
- Generate and test hypothesis and justify conclusions
- Develop problem-solving strategies
- Analyze data, issues, problems, processes, and products and determine next steps
- Demonstrate creativity
- Make contributions to the team when challenged

SUMMARY

Considering the impact of cooperative group learning on student achievement, it is imperative that everything possible be done for the implementation in all classrooms. Not only does it have its own impact, but it also fosters dialogue, and critical and creative thinking, and builds collaborative skills. CGL is indeed a powerful strategy that teachers can use that activates students' minds and thinking.

DISCUSSION POINTS

- Read the research and benefits for CGL. Discuss the implications for your classroom and students.

- Read and discuss ability and heterogeneous groups and the research regarding their advantages and disadvantages. Which are used more in your classroom and why?

- Brainstorm with colleagues why CGL sometimes goes poorly and teachers abandon the strategy.

- Using Figure 4.1, discuss the issues teachers face and the suggested resolutions.

- Consider the five elements of the Johnson method and how they might help keep students focused and working successfully together.

- Discuss the social skills your students might need to be successful. How would you teach the skills? Create a T or Y chart to help students use the skills.

- Plan a cooperative lesson making sure the five elements are included.

- Discuss the different types of jigsaws. Create a lesson with one of them. Come back and discuss how it went and what you would do differently.

- Use the academic controversy strategy to debate the notion of CGL itself. Why is or why isn't it a valuable strategy to activate student learning?

- Create a lesson plan based on the method of group investigation.

5 Activating the Power of Goals and Standards

Alice: "Would you tell me, please, which way I ought to go from here?"

Cheshire Cat: "That depends a good deal on where you want to get to."

Alice: "I don't much care where—"

Cheshire Cat: "Then it doesn't matter which way you go."

—Lewis Carroll, *Alice's Adventures in Wonderland*

People banter around many terms such as standards, goals, instructional and behavioral objectives, intentions, targets, and progressions with similar or different understandings. All in all it comes down to what students should know and be able to do in terms of knowledge, understandings, and skills. People need to know where they are going, both the planners and the travellers. The Cheshire cat in *Alice's Adventures in Wonderland* responds somewhat with the obvious.

Perhaps some students feel this way when an assignment is given. Clearly some things matter in terms of "where you want to go." David Perkins (1995) often said that we taught by the Bo Peep method . . . Leave them alone and they will come home, allowing them to make their own connections—but often they don't. He cautioned we should be more like a good shepherd, knowing the destination and guiding them to it as well as connecting the dots and ideas and concepts.

Back when the Earth was cooling and I began teaching, there were no real goals set forth for my third- and fourth-grade split class of thirty-eight children. There was a vague list of content topics in a little grey booklet, but what I was to do with them as a teacher or what the students should know at the end of the lesson or unit of study was not clear. I backward mapped, all right. At the end I figured out what they learned and reported somewhat on the findings. There also was not a consistent measure to judge my performance or that of my students. There was total autonomy (also known for some as isolation) in your classroom. Fortunately, through the kindness of other third- and fourth-grade teachers, I learned what I should be teaching and how to help my students learn. I formed my own professional learning community, out of naiveté and desperation, with experienced teachers that certainly improved my teaching and increased my instructional repertoire. We planned over a casserole or pizza on Thursday nights for a few hours at the school. I have always been grateful for the mentoring of these wonderful colleagues.

Hattie (2009) reports that setting challenging goals has an effect size of $d = 0.56$, 0.16 over the hinge point of 0.40. Marzano (2009) assigns even more impact to specifying goals: $d = 0.97$. Being clear about the goals and intentions of the learning task can actually show achievement gains one or two grades higher than tasks that don't have clear, specified, challenging goals. Setting goals also helps students become assessment capable learners and become more competent as self-reported grades, which have an effect size of 1.44.

This chapter examines the importance of goals for activating student learning and also the ways in which teachers can incorporate effective goal-setting in their classrooms.

THE POWER OF GOALS: TAPPING THE UNCONSCIOUS MIND

As we have seen in the previous chapters, neuroscience is unearthing some incredible insights into the way our brains work. One thing we've learned is that the brain is a parallel processor: it works simultaneously on the conscious and subconscious levels. Think of a time when you couldn't remember someone's name or the name of a restaurant in a city you visited. Your conscious mind couldn't come up with it, but once the goal of finding that name was planted in your head, the subconscious mind got to work. While you were carrying on with your conversation, the brain, being goal oriented, was searching your stored mental files until the answer was found.

The subconscious mind is responsible for about 90% of the decisions we make, and it's also in charge of performing creative tasks and navigating the unknown (Peterson, 2007). The Princeton Neuroscience Institute (PNI), using brain scans of human volunteers, found that updating goals takes place in the prefrontal cortex; and evidence points to the fact that the neurotransmitter dopamine is associated with the signals. It is also dopamine that is responsible for tagging new information, updating working memory, and adjusting goals when it enters the prefrontal cortex. Dopamine is known to play a key role in mental processes, and dopamine release is an intrinsic form of motivation. There is strong evidence that the dopaminergic nuclei enable the prefrontal cortex to save information that is relevant for updating behavior and discarding that which is not (Cohen et al., 2011).

The subconscious mind will be working on problems no matter what we do, but its power can also be directed. Coaches may ask athletes to visualize success before a match or competition for this very reason. Why can't teachers do the same?

It seems they can. The same mental instructions for actions or mental images can impact processes in the brain, including attention, motor control, perception, planning, and memory. Electromyography (EMG) shows that according to the brain there is no difference between a thought about an action or the real thing (McTaggart, 2008; Pillay, 2011). Thanks to neuroimaging, scientists have discovered that visualization works because excited neurons in our brains transmit information and treat imagery as equivalent to real-life situations. New neural pathways (clusters of cells in our brain that work together) form memories or learned behaviors that are created when we visualize an act or process. These neural pathways prime our body to act to conform to what we imagined. We don't actually perform the physical activity, but visualizing it is the same as real practice to the brain. Our mirror neurons also play a role, as when we experience a demonstration or observation, we are able to replicate the process or skill.

Asking students to visualize how it will feel or look when they are successful creates a portrait for their subconscious mind and helps it get to work on the right goal. If the brain knows what is expected and the goal is clear, it will ultimately work progressively toward the goal even when it is not consciously focused on it.

Before getting students to focus on specific goals, teachers and schools need to be crystal clear themselves about what those goals will be. Marzano (2009) defines two types of objectives. Declarative objectives are related to content—information and facts like who, what, where, and when (e.g., students can identify the causes of the Second World War). Procedural objectives are related to the processes and skills that students should acquire by the end of the learning process (e.g., students can create a timeline of events that chronicle the Second World War). Goals for students tend to include both of these types of objectives, but many other elements have to be taken into account.

There are other ways of stating these different types of knowledge or objectives. Some different categories of knowledge might be the following:

- About a topic (know about different steps in the water cycle)
- About how something is produced (how to construct a bar graph)
- About why something happens (why weather conditions are changing)
- About what causes things to happen (causes of a tsunami)

Objectives may also be the development of a certain skill rather than a piece of knowledge. These objectives often start with "to be able to":

- To be able to write a compare-and-contrast paragraph
- To be able to solve a two-step problem
- To be able to work with a cooperative group
- To be able to build an argument for a debate
- To be able to use media for a positive or negative effect

Skills and knowledge objectives are often combined. For example a compare-and-contrast paragraph requires declarative knowledge to develop the comparison.

There are also objectives that focus on building understanding and deepening surface knowledge. Considering new information at a variety of levels of thinking will help students make sense of new content and help store it in long-term memory. First students must be able to recall the content, but understanding requires analysis and perhaps comparison with something else. So if they are asked to compare and contrast, they first recall a historical issue and then analyze the elements for comparison's sake. Understanding is a higher cognitive order but requires content to begin with.

Objectives related to understanding might be stated in this way:

- Understand the elements related to a historical issue
- Understand how exercise affects health
- Understand how persuasive language influences the reader
- Understand how to run a search engine for research
- Understand the effect of excessive sodium on your health

A challenge for teachers is translating the goals from the curriculum guide into clear learning objectives in the classroom. Unpacking the curriculum can be a focus of meetings so that teachers truly internalize the expectations into language that teachers and students understand, and increase a shared understanding between and among teachers as they develop successful criteria and transparent goals for students and consistency across the school.

Setting Broad Goals With Learning Progressions

When devising goals for students, one of the most important issues to keep in mind is learning progressions. Learning progressions are the steps required to fully develop the objective, the purposeful sequencing of teaching and learning targets across multiple developmental stages, ages, or grade levels. The term relates to learning standards—clear, concise, articulated descriptions of what students should know and be able to do at a specific stage or level.

The following reading standards, taken from the Common Core State Standards (CCSS), show an example of how learning progressions work and how each standard builds on the previous one, increasingly complex as students progress from one grade to the next:

1. **Kindergarten:** Identify the front cover, back cover, and title page of a book.

2. **Grade 1:** Know and use various text features (e.g., headings, tables of contents, glossaries, electronic menus, icons) to locate facts or information in a text.

3. **Grade 2:** Know and use various text features (e.g., captions, bold print, subheadings, glossaries, indexes, electronic menus, icons) to locate key facts or information in a text efficiently.

4. **Grade 3:** Use text features and search tools (e.g., key words, sidebars, hyperlinks) to locate information relevant to a given topic efficiently.

5. **Grade 4:** Describe the overall structure (e.g., chronology, comparison, cause/effect, problem/solution) of events, ideas, concepts, or information in a text or part of a text.

6. **Grade 5:** Compare and contrast the overall structure (e.g., chronology, comparison, cause/effect, problem/solution) of events, ideas, concepts, or information in two or more texts.

7. **Grades 6–8:** Analyze the structure an author uses to organize a text, including how the major sections contribute to the whole and to an understanding of the topic.

8. **Grades 9–10:** Analyze the structure of the relationships among concepts in the text, including relationships among key terms (e.g., force, friction, reaction force, energy).

9. **Grades 11–12:** Analyze how the text structures information or ideas into categories or hierarchies, demonstrating understanding of the information or ideas.

Figure 5.1 on the next page shows the grade progressions for Number and Operations in Base Ten in Mathematics CCSS.

Learning progressions are key to setting up realistic and brain-friendly Goldilocks goals (not too easy, not too hard) for students. Heritage, Kim, and Vendlinski (2008) stress the importance of taking standards from the CCSS or other targeted standards so that teachers understand what comes before or after a particular learning standard or goal. This is very helpful for teachers because they can better assess a student's current knowledge and skill if they are clear about what they were expected to do the preceding year and what the next levels of competency are. This can help teachers adjust the learning goals so that they are just beyond the skill level and students will more likely engage in a task that seems doable and within their reach. It also informs the teacher as to missing skills or knowledge that needs to be addressed before the student can be successful with the new goals and expectations. One high school assessed ninth-grade students to determine their basic math skills at the beginning of the year. They then provided a concentrated effort to reteach and help students hone their basic skills quickly in the first month so that they could master the ninth-grade standards. At the end of the first marking period, these students were more on track than ninth-grade students in other years. This was a diagnostic effort and remediation that paid off for everyone.

Another example of a learning progression is the focal points devised by the National Council of Teachers of Mathematics (NCTM, 2007). These outline the core mathematical ideas that need to be learned at each grade level. It would be possible to develop a learning progression for these ideas. In the case of algebra, for example, here is the learning progression for several grades, including earlier grades that had antecedent goals:

- **Grade 3:** "Use properties of addition and multiplication to multiply whole numbers and apply increasingly sophisticated strategies based on these properties to solve multiplication and division problems involving basic facts."
- **Grade 4:** "Identify, describe and extend numeric patterns involving all operations and nonnumeric growing or repeating patterns."

Figure 5.1 Common Core State Standards: Mathematics Learning Progressions, Number and Operations in Base Ten

Kindergarten	Grade 1	Grade 2	Grade 3	Grade 4	Grade 5
Work with numbers 11–19 to gain foundations for place value.	**Extend the counting sequence.**	**Understand place value.**	**Use place value understanding and properties of operations to perform multi-digit arithmetic.**	**Generalize place value understanding for multi-digit whole numbers.**	**Understand the place value system.**
1. Compose and decompose numbers from 11 to 19 into ten ones and some further ones, e.g., by using objects or drawings, and record each composition or decomposition by a drawing or equation (e.g., $18 = 10 + 8$); understand that these numbers are composed of ten ones and one, two, three, four, five, six, seven, eight, or nine ones.	1. Count to 120, starting at any number less than 120. In this range, read and write numerals and represent a number of objects with a written numeral.	1. Understand that the three digits of a three-digit number represent amounts of hundreds, tens, and ones; e.g., 706 equals 7 hundreds, 0 tens, and 6 ones. Understand the following as special cases:	1. Use place value understanding to round whole numbers to the nearest 10 or 100.	1. Recognize that in a multi-digit whole number, a digit in one place represents ten times what it represents in the place to its right. *For example, recognize that $700 \div 70 = 10$ by applying concepts of place value and division.*	1. Recognize that in a multi-digit number, a digit in one place represents 10 times as much as it represents in the place to its right and $\frac{1}{10}$ of what it represents in the place to its left.
	Understand place value.	a. 100 can be thought of as a bundle of ten tens—called a "hundred."	2. Fluently add and subtract within 1000 using strategies and algorithms based on place value, properties of operations, and/or the relationship between addition and subtraction.	2. Read and write multi-digit whole numbers using base-ten numerals, number names, and expanded form. Compare two multi-digit numbers based on meanings of the digits in each place, using >, =, and < symbols to record the results of comparisons.	2. Explain patterns in the number of zeros of the product when multiplying a number by powers of 10, and explain patterns in the placement of the decimal point when a decimal is multiplied or divided by a power of 10. Use whole-number exponents to denote powers of 10.
	2. Understand that the two digits of a two-digit number represent amounts of tens and ones. Understand the following as special cases:	b. The numbers 100, 200, 300, 400, 500, 600, 700, 800, 900 refer to one, two, three, four, five, six, seven, eight, or nine hundreds (and 0 tens and 0 ones).	3. Multiply one-digit whole numbers by multiples of 10 in the range 10–90 (e.g., 9×80, 5×60) using strategies based on place value and properties of operations.	3. Use place value understanding to round multi-digit whole numbers to any place.	3. Read, write, and compare decimals to thousandths.
	a. 10 can be thought of as a bundle of ten ones—called a "ten."	2. Count within 1000; skip-count by 5s, 10s, and 100s.		**Use place value understanding and properties of operations to perform multi-digit arithmetic.**	a. Read and write decimals to thousandths using base-ten numerals, number names, and expanded form, e.g., $347.392 = 3 \times 100 + 4 \times 10 + 7 \times 1 + 3 \times \frac{1}{10} + 9 \times \frac{1}{100} + 2 \times \frac{1}{1000}$.
	b. The numbers from 11 to 19 are composed of a ten and one, two, three, four, five, six, seven, eight, or nine ones.	3. Read and write numbers to 1000 using base-ten numerals, number names, and expanded form.		4. Fluently add and subtract multi-digit whole numbers using the standard algorithm.	
	c. The numbers 10, 20, 30, 40, 50, 60, 70, 80, 90 refer to one, two, three, four, five, six, seven, eight, or nine tens (and 0 ones).	4. Compare two three-digit numbers based on meanings of the hundreds, tens, and ones digits, using >, =, and < symbols to record the results of comparisons.			

Kindergarten	Grade 1	Grade 2	Grade 3	Grade 4	Grade 5
	3. Compare two two-digit numbers based on meanings of the tens and ones digits, recording the results of comparisons with the symbols >, =, and <.

Use place value understanding and properties of operations to add and subtract.

4. Add within 100, including adding a two-digit number and a one-digit number, and adding a two-digit number and a multiple of 10, using concrete models or drawings and strategies based on place value, properties of operations, and/or the relationship between addition and subtraction.

5. Given a two-digit number, mentally find 10 more or 10 less than the number, without having to count; explain the reasoning used. | **Use place value understanding and properties of operations to add and subtract.**

5. Fluently add and subtract within 100 using strategies based on place value, properties of operations, and/or the relationship between addition and subtraction.

6. Add up to four two-digit numbers using strategies based on place value and properties of operations.

7. Add and subtract within 1000, using concrete models or drawings and strategies based on place value, properties of operations, and/or the relationship between addition and subtraction; relate the strategy to a written method. Understand that in adding or subtracting three-digit numbers, one adds or subtracts hundreds and hundreds, tens and tens, ones and ones; and sometimes it is necessary to compose or decompose tens or hundreds. | | 5. Multiply a whole number of up to four digits by a one-digit whole number, and multiply two two-digit numbers, using strategies based on place value and the properties of operations. Illustrate and explain the calculation by using equations, rectangular arrays, and/or area models.

6. Find whole-number quotients and remainders with up to four-digit dividends and one-digit divisors, using strategies based on place value, the properties of operations, and/or the relationship between multiplication and division. Illustrate and explain the calculation by using equations, rectangular arrays, and/or area models. | b. Compare two decimals to thousandths based on meanings of the digits in each place, using >, =, and < symbols to record the results of comparisons.

4. Use place value understanding to round decimals to any place.

Perform operations with multi-digit whole numbers and with decimals to hundredths.

5. Fluently multiply multi-digit whole numbers using the standard algorithm.

6. Find whole-number quotients of whole numbers with up to four-digit dividends and two-digit divisors, using strategies based on place value, the properties of operations, and/or the relationship between multiplication and division. Illustrate and explain the calculation by using equations, rectangular arrays, and/or area models. |

- **Grade 5:** "Use patterns, models, and relationships as contexts for writing and solving simple equations and inequalities."
- **Grade 6:** "Solve simple one-step equations by using number sense, properties of operations, and the idea of maintaining equality on both sides of an equation."
- **Grade 7:** "Understand that when the properties of equality to express an equation in a new way are used, solutions obtained for the new equation also solve the original equation."

With this information, a teacher can pre-assess the preceding year's progressions to know where there is competency or gaps that need to be reviewed or filled. A sixth-grade teacher whose students need help solving simple one-step equations by using properties of operations might decide that she needs to focus on developing a better understanding of some basic concepts with which students might need reinforcement, for example, that division reverses multiplication and that subtraction reverses addition. It may be that for some students she needs to revisit skills that should have been mastered previously in earlier grades. For students who have grasped the sixth-grade concepts, the teacher might move them forward toward the seventh-grade idea of working on two-step equations.

This process could be referred to as a form of acceleration. This technique is often ignored in order to keep the class together and not infringe on the next grade's content. But this holds back quicker learners and bores them as they mark time waiting for the others. When I attended grade school, the year's learning was divided into units. There were three units at each grade level: units 1–3 for first grade, units 4–6 at second grade, and so on. Students could progress through the units at their own pace. Learners who had grasped and learned concepts and skills more quickly and thoroughly could, after three years, actually be a whole year ahead academically and not have neglected or skipped any knowledge or skills. This acceleration had some social implications, as by ninth grade I was much younger than my cohort group. As a young high school student I was not allowed the same independence as my classmates, students a year or two older. However, there are no studies supporting lack of social or emotional acceptance of accelerated students. In fact, Hattie's findings related to acceleration are more than promising; he finds an effect size for acceleration of $d = 0.88$.

Accelerating students through the curricula is an alternative to special classes for gifted children, although it could certainly be used with regular students whose grasp of content and skills in a particular area warrants acceleration. When we accelerate instruction for gifted, bright students, allowing them to work with like minds and move at an appropriate pace not waiting for classmates to catch up, we find significant gains in achievement and that acceleration outperforms enrichment (Kulik & Kulik, 1984). Kulik and Kulik also found that accelerated students had higher ambitions educationally and still participated well in school activities outside the classroom. Often more able learners are offered enriched learning activities (activities meant to broaden the educational life of a student), but these did not show significant gains in student achievement with only an effect of $d = 0.39$ (Hattie, 2009). George, Cohn, and Stanley (1979) found that at best enrichment might only help with the issue of boredom. The impact was different depending on the teacher's ability and experience with gifted students (more impact) from experienced teachers and less impact with teachers who had limited experience with gifted students.

Figure 5.2 shows some ideas for teachers' consideration in developing learning progressions.

Learning progressions are the building blocks of instruction. They indicate the sequence of the instructional tasks toward the learning intentions. They convey the stepping stones to success including the sub-skills and the enabling knowledge needed. Sometimes we as educators know a skill so well that we take the steps involved for granted. It can be helpful to break down the skill into a task analysis to find gaps or vague areas in our instructions. It helps to analyze the task so that it is not only clear to the teacher but also can be conveyed clearly to the students and seen as manageable and achievable. The University of California at Berkeley provides some solid advice on setting goals for classes with mixed levels of mastery (University of California, Berkeley, n.d.).

Figure 5.2 Developing Learning Progressions

Consider an essential topic in your curriculum and the standards.

1. What would you like student thinking to look like (the upper criteria)?

2. What basic understanding do your most struggling students have about this topic before instruction (the lower criteria)?

3. What is challenging for students about this topic?

4. What roadblocks do students typically meet as they move from their initial thoughts to targeted thinking about the topic?

5. What assessment strategies might you use to learn more about student thinking in this middle ground?

SETTING DAILY LEARNING GOALS

Learning progressions address the broad goals for students over the course of a unit or year. Daily goals are much smaller. They refer to the goals that students are intended to reach during a single day, single assignment, or, at most, single unit. Whereas learning progressions are helpful specifically to the teacher for assessment and planning purposes, daily goals are equally important to teachers and students. They help the learners identify what success would look like and understand how that would work (Moss & Brookhart, 2012). Students have a greater chance of accomplishing the learning goal if it is specific, measurable, and attainable. This section will discuss some of the ways that teachers can harness the power of daily goal-setting for their students.

Clarity

The first key to effective goal-setting is clarity. The teacher may know exactly what the goal is, but do the students? The greater transparency in sharing learning goals, the greater commitment students have to engaging in the work to achieve it. When goals are transparent at the beginning of learning, the conscious and the subconscious brains are activated.

The three big questions for learners, according to Professor Hattie, should be:

- **Where am I going?** Intentions, success criteria, and goal setting
- **How am I going?** Ongoing assessment from self, peer, and teacher
- **Where to next?** Progressions, next steps, feed forward

There are numerous ways to communicate the answers to these questions to students and communicate daily goals: bulletin boards, hand-outs, blackboard, and so on. Teachers can tap into the power of flipping the classroom, for example stating goals on a website that students can check during off-hours. Teachers might also verbally describe the goals and ask students to write them down in their own words so that the goals are clear and meaningful to them. A learning intentions chart communicates goals through three statements: "Today We Will," Today I Will," and "Right Now I Am":

- **Today we will:** Model and solve one-variable, one-step inequalities that represent problems including number lines.
- **Today I will:** Learn how symbols <, >, and = are useful
- **Right now I am:** Relating my knowledge of inequalities to number lines.

A chart may be used to outline the intentions for students (see Figure 5.3). This may also be a white board posting or a pocket chart where the objectives or goals are posted. A chart may also be used to outline the intentions for students for the week (see Figure 5.4). Other ways to share goals are by laminating a poster board and writing the weekly or daily objectives with dry erase marker. Some teachers put the language arts objectives, one on each page in plastic covers, in a three-ring binder and display the page related to the daily focus. Teachers have shared multiple ways to post goals on websites and blogs like theorganizedclassroomblog.com. Or search online for "posting goals in your classroom."

Specificity

Specificity is another key to successful goal-setting. For example, the learning goal may be to use color effectively in creating mood in a painting.

Figure 5.3 Student Learning Intentions Chart

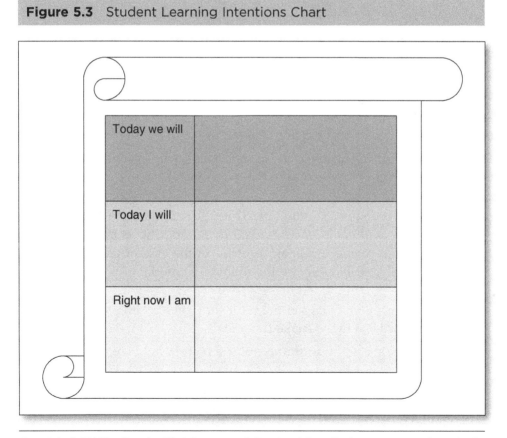

Today we will	
Today I will	
Right now I am	

Figure 5.4 Goals for the Week Chart

Goals for This Week	
Language Arts	
Reading	
Social Studies	
Math	

What might that mean to students? Does that mean use a lot of color, as much color as you can? Teachers need to get specific as to what they are looking for that would designate success. In the case of using color effectively the teacher might suggest the following criteria:

- When someone looks at the color they get a feeling and understand that I was trying to make them feel _____.
- The color used in four areas of the picture help create the mood of _____.
- The color I used creates the overall mood of _____.
- I used _____ because I want people to _____.

Specificity can also be conveyed to students in the form of "success criteria." Here is an example from a social studies class:

- **Sample:** A world history class is studying a unit on the first explorers of America who landed on the Atlantic coast. The expectation is that they write a historical paper chronicling the travel and accomplishments of one of the explorers.
- **Learning Intentions:** Students will be able to write a detailed historical paper.
- **Success Criteria:** Students will write a historical paper about one of the Atlantic coast explorers. There will be an introduction, content, and conclusion. It will include the who, what, where, and when information as well as the reasons for (the why) and accomplishments of the exploration.

Rubrics

Another important technique to help students hit the mark and achieve success is creating a rubric. With carefully selected criteria that reflect the attributes of the overall goal, we can delineate the indicators at each of three or four levels so that students can examine their work and both know where they are and what they need to work on next to improve their work or performance. This will ultimately increase the quality of the task, help students focus on what matters related to details and quality, and enable student progress toward the completion of the task.

Giving students the rubric and discussing the criteria and aspects of quality required of the assignment at the beginning of the project or assignment helps ensure their clarity and success. Precision of language is important as vague or qualitative language such as "few," "a couple," or even "adequate" or "excellent" is not very helpful, as students may have limited or a different understanding of these. Students can use rubrics for self-assessment and goal-setting or with peer collaboration and dialogue regarding quality of the task and next steps.

Rubrics, if time permits, can be built with the students as the discussion and selection of terms help with clarity and understanding. After they have been used they may need modifications if areas could be better stated to avoid confusion.

There are numerous online resources to help teachers built rubrics, such as edudemic.com and rubistar.4teachers.org. An example for a speech is given in Figure 5.5. You may want to add criteria for visual arts. Check rubistar.4teachers.org.

Flexibility

Flexibility is a third key to goal-setting. Flexibility may be needed for several reasons: Students in the same class may be starting from very

Figure 5.5 Rubric for a Speech

Purposes:

Use during the design and practice phase to give peer feedback or to self-assess.
Use as a grading or evaluation device.
Use up front as a clear target.

Criteria	Indicators			
	1	2	3	4
Originality	Only the facts are presented.	Moments of creativity but mostly facts are presented.	Unique and creative ideas were presented.	Sparkling, creative elements of surprise and intrigue were presented.
Organization	Need to work at clarifying the message.	Topic is clear and somewhat engaging.	Focused topic engages the audience.	Topic is motivating, clear, and expands on ideas.
Coherency and Flow	Need to connect ideas to have a flow.	Most ideas linked, some flawed, but pauses are distracting.	Flow from idea to idea. Linked well. Connected.	Extremely clear with purpose, and logical flow.
Voice	Monotone and lacks expression.	Some expression and volume control.	Easily heard, appropriate, and varied expression.	Clear, varied volume with creative expression.
Eye Contact	Mostly read from notes.	Occasionally glanced at audience.	Familiar with presentation and confident to make eye contact.	Obviously knowledgeable and used eye contact to engage the audience.
Visual Aids				

Source: Robbins, Gregory, and Herndon (2000).

different skill levels. Students may progress at different rates, with some getting stuck on a single (but key) point and others finding an unexpected affinity for the lesson.

Clarke, Timperley, and Hattie (2001) list some ways that teachers can incorporate flexibility into their goal-setting:

- Adjust assignments for students who begin and progress at different places. Differentiation by readiness will help keep students positive and motivated toward the task.
- Remember that the journey is not linear or precise but can be recursive and adjusted.
- Realize that one activity may contribute to several learning intentions, and one learning activity may need several tasks to accomplish it.
- Appreciate the incidental learning that takes place alongside learning geared toward stated goals. Students can reflect and consider what else they learned in addition to the targeted knowledge and skills.
- Track the learning intentions and help students see growth through effort. Students' progress can be chronicled in journals or logs.

Personalization

We know that in education, one size never fits all. The section on flexibility above provides some suggestions for accommodating different rates of learning. But differences among students go far beyond learning rates. For goal-setting to be challenging and accurate to particular students, teachers must know their learners—their readiness, interests, and preferences. Teachers need to devise ways to collect information about their students. Then they can incorporate that data in their instructional process. Many strategies and surveys were shared in Chapter 1 that help teachers get to know the whole student. But remember—no labels!

Another important aspect in personalizing goals is including the student and the parents into the goal-setting process. We've noted above the importance of having students restate goals in their own words. Students should feel that they are active participants, and, ideally, parents would be part of the process as well. Some items for students, parents, and teachers alike should consider include the following:

- What is the current level of achievement?
- What level of challenge would be appropriate?

- What support would the student need?
- How will progression toward the goal be monitored?

With this information the teacher designs the learning tasks that the student will engage with to learn, practice, and develop the skills. It's important that both students and parents understand that the goal is not simply to complete the goal quickly. Hastie (2011) notes that often students see goals only in terms of completion in time, in which faster is better. But fast completion doesn't always allow students to understand the goal more comprehensively and set a personal goal.

THE GOAL OF GOALS: FLOW

Flow is a term coined by Hungarian psychologist Mihaly Csikszentmihalyi in his seminal book *Flow: The Psychology of Optimal Experience.* Flow is defined as a state of happy absorption in a task that is so engaging that the person hardly notices the passage of time. The joy of being immersed in a just-difficult-enough task that interests the person is what is called *intrinsic motivation.* That joy is reward enough for pressing on, overcoming obstacles, and becoming better at the task. This is evident in anything we enjoy doing and want to get better at, from video games to skateboarding to ballroom dancing.

Six factors characterize an experience of flow:

- Concentration that is intense and focused
- Awareness followed by quick action
- Being unaware of the passage of time
- A sense of control and autonomy
- Being un-self-conscious
- A task that is intrinsically rewarding

There are three conditions that have to be met in order to be able to get into flow:

1. There needs to be a clear set of goals and progress steps created.

2. The expectations should be clear and immediate feedback should be available by whatever means is best so that approach, strategies, and performance can be modified to changing demands.

3. One must be confident that the task is doable (growth mindset) and believe that although the perceived challenge is somewhat

greater than one's perceived skill level, it can be attained with effort and persistence.

Schaffer (2013) developed the Flow Condition Questionnaire (FCQ), which measures what he considers to be the seven key conditions that allow flow when used with open-ended, qualitative, follow-up questions such as "What led to your answer?" The FCQ is reproduced in Figure 5.6.

Flow is the goal of all our other goals, whether broad goals or daily tasks. It allows learning in the present and provides students with a positive experience of learning that will accompany them for the rest of the lives and turn them into lifelong learners. So how, specifically, do we

Figure 5.6 Flow Condition Questionnaire (FCQ)

Please indicate how much of the time you knew each of the following **while you were doing the activity** by marking one circle for each question.

How much of the time did you know . . . ?	Never		About half of the time		Always
What to do next	○	○	○	○	○
How to do what you were doing	○	○	○	○	○
How well you were doing	○	○	○	○	○
Where to go next	○	○	○	○	○

Please answer the following questions about how you felt **while you were doing the activity** by marking one circle for each question.

	Not at all				Very much
How challenging did this activity feel?	○	○	○	○	○
How much did you feel able to overcome the challenges you faced?	○	○	○	○	○
How distracted were you from what you were doing?	○	○	○	○	○

Reverse the score of the last question to get Freedom From Distractions. The items above are in the following order: Clear What to Do, Clear How to Do It, Clear How Well Doing, Clear Where to Go, Challenge, Skill, and Freedom From Distractions.

Source: Schaffer (2013).

get them to a state of flow? Some of the most useful things teachers can incorporate into their repertoire of teaching approaches are the zone of proximal development, Piagetian stages, strong support tools, and an attention to conceptual understanding.

The Zone of Proximal Development

One of Schaffer's conditions for flow is that the task must be perceived as doable. This does not mean easy. The best learning takes place when the task at hand is just beyond the current abilities of the learner—too easy and the student will be bored; too hard and the student will be discouraged.

The early-20th-century Soviet psychologist Lev Vygotsky described this ideal task as the zone of proximal development. For Vygotsky, giving students tasks that are just beyond their current skill or knowledge level not only gives them a positive experience of learning but helps them to become independent learners by demonstrating that they can get from point A to point B on their own steam if the steps are manageable enough.

There is a fine balance between the complexity of the challenge and the skill level of the student. This is why differentiation is so important and tasks should be adjusted for students reflective of their current competencies. To develop the appropriate level of challenge, teachers should conduct pre-assessments regarding the student's prior knowledge and skill level. Students are less liking to activate thinking and learning if they are overwhelmed or under-challenged. So like Goldilocks, tasks work best when they are "just right."

Wood and Lock (1987), quoted in Hattie (2009), note that if the goals are challenging, student performance is 250% higher than if goals are easy. Challenging is not to say that the goals should be unattainable or out of reach as that will result in self-defeating attitude and disappointment. If this happens students need to recalibrate their aspirations to be more in line with their current skill level. One's behavior and motivation will be greater if the expectations and aspirations are just beyond the ability or skill level. This is perceived as attainable and will trigger the release of dopamine (the feel-good neurotransmitter).

Learning takes effort and challenging goals require effort rather than "do your best" goals. "Do your best" is not a lofty quest and seems to allow for low-level effort and lack of stretch. Challenging appropriate goals are energizing for the student and activate their thinking and commitment to the task.

Andrew Martin (2006) suggests that a way of setting worthwhile goals is through personal bests. Personal bests can increase enjoyment of learning as well as participation and persistence regarding the task. They focus on having the learners compete against themselves and their last personal best and thus sustain motivation and continuous improvement (Absolum et al., 2009).

Hattie (2009, p. 165) puts it this way:

> The scenario is that effective teachers set appropriately challenging goals and then structure situations so that students can reach these goals. If teachers can encourage students to share commitment to these challenging goals, and if they provide feedback on how to be successful in learning as one is working to achieve the goals, then goals are more likely to be attained.

Piaget's Stages

Vygotsky drew on the work of Jean Piaget in developing his idea of the zone of proximal development. Piaget was a Swiss developmental psychologist who developed a model of child development. Piaget (1970) divided children's development into four stages:

1. Sensorimotor is the first stage (birth to 2 years). The infant is focused on the relationship between their body and the environment. One of the important concepts children learn at the sensorimotor stage is object permanence (the idea that an object still exists even if it is not in sight).

2. Preoperational is the second stage (2–7 years). In this stage youngsters think their point of view is everyone's point of view. They are developing concepts and language. Thinking is concrete and stable.

3. Logical thinking emerges in the concrete operational stage (7–12 years). One can change their mind and children begin to examine concepts more thoroughly.

4. In the formal operational stage (12 to adult) students are able to think in the abstract and in hypothetical terms. They are able to suggest hypotheses and show reasoning by being about to understand analogy and metaphor.

Jean Piaget's four developmental stages can give teachers insight into student thinking and help with crafting precise feedback. Hattie found that teachers' consideration of their students' Piagetian stage had a profound impact on the materials and tasks they offered learners and how the concept of difficulty and challenge applied to different of the tasks (Naglieri & Das, 1997b; Sweller, 2008). Attending to Piagetian stages has an effect size of 1.28, the second-highest ranking in Hattie's (2009) study, second only to students being able to estimate their own grades (ES 1.44), often referred to as being assessment-capable learners.

Attending to Piagetian stages means that teachers incorporate stage-appropriate techniques in their teaching, for example the use of objects or "manipulatives." In social studies, for instance, students can examine memorabilia from pioneer days, guess their uses, and discuss what we use today for the same tasks. If we pay attention to Piagetian stages of development we sometimes forget that it is not just 7- to 11-year-olds who need to have concrete representation of concepts or ideas. Even into adulthood the concrete stage can be a good beginning. Knowing students' Piagetian stages will help in setting goals and levels of complexity for students and help them achieve optimal flow.

Support

As we've seen in the previous chapters, social support is key to learning. Teachers who tap into students' motivational drives will foster their sense of autonomy and competency. Learners should be encouraged to make good choices that will stretch their learning. Teachers should offer feedback on students' effort and learning progression—not simply their intelligence—to encourage and propel students forward. Support is necessary, as it won't make a difference to student learning to have challenging tasks without balancing the challenge with support with both personnel and resources. It is the support that will keep students in flow. Without support, anxiety will lead to frustration. Constructive feedback in a timely fashion is key to progress and a continued quest for success.

This need for support was something that Vygotsky also recognized. One of the three major components of his social development theory is that social interaction plays a critical role in learning and cognition. The benefits that accrue from social interaction in the classroom are discussed in Chapters 1 and 2: multiple social interactions help deepen students' attachment to the material; a brain-friendly environment free of punishment, ridicule, and threat allows complex thinking by the prefrontal cortex; and interacting with more knowledgeable others and collaboration with peers allows for risk-taking and social bonding.

Although social support is important, students also need academic support. The tools used for academic support are often referred to as *scaffolding.* The *Glossary of Educational Reform* defines scaffolding as "a variety of instructional tactics used to move students toward greater understanding and independence in their learning. Becoming more self-directed is essential for life-long learners. It is a relevant descriptive metaphor: teachers provide successive levels of temporary support (as in a building support structure) that facilitates students reaching higher levels of comprehension and skill acquisition than they would be able to achieve without assistance."

If we are asking students to respond to challenging goals, scaffolding is essential. Extra-challenging tasks require that students may need some support to keep them engaged—activated, not discouraged. Students with an individualized education program (IEP) generally require scaffolding to support learning new skills and concepts. This extra assistance should be temporary and removed gradually as students become able to navigate on their own. As Vygotsky wrote, "what the child is able to do in collaboration today he will be able to do independently tomorrow" (Vygotsky, 1987, p. 211).

Scaffolding is implicit in many of the techniques that we've discussed so far, including flipping the classroom and communicating clear goals. Here are some common strategies for scaffolding:

- Posting a set of directions that give step-by-step guidance for referral
- Providing visual cues or graphic organizers
- Providing a "more knowledgeable other" for collaboration
- Using icons in illustrations for clarity
- Offering technology for assistance
- Offering webcasts and podcasts so students can review material and work at their own pace
- Adjusting the reading and resource material for struggling readers
- Monitoring and provide specific feedback.
- Helping students plan and monitor pacing so task can be completed

Conceptual Understanding

In *Visible Learning* Hattie (2009) asserts that there are five components of successful learning, what he calls the 5 C's: challenge, commitment, confidence, challenge of high expectations, and conceptual understanding. Many of these we have already discussed: challenge is much like the zone of proximal development, commitment is the principle of perseverance, confidence is having a growth mindset, and expectations are related to issues of grouping and messages that students receive about their potential. All of these are important to activating learning, but here we will focus on the last "C": conceptual understanding.

Conceptual understanding is what results when a student has mastered both the surface and deep types of understanding (Hattie, 2009).

Surface understanding is understanding an idea (or multiple ideas), and deep understanding is being able to extend ideas and relate them one to another.

The SOLO taxonomy stands for Structure of Observed Learning Outcomes (Biggs and Collis, 1982; Biggs and Tang, 2007). SOLO identifies five stages of increasing complexity of a students' understanding of a subject topic. Similarly to Bloom's taxonomy it is a progression where each level adds to the previous. Figure 5.7 defines the five stages of the SOLO taxonomy, description, verbs at each stage, and an example. You may use Figure 5.8 for recording prompts related to a unit of study.

Figure 5.7 SOLO Taxonomy Employed for a Unit on *Romeo and Juliet*

	Stage	Description	Verbs	Example
	1. Pre-structural: I'm not sure about . . .	Bits of unconnected information		
	2. Unistructural: I have one idea	Limited connections are made but not interpreted	Define, explain, identify	Who wrote *Romeo and Juliet*?
	3. Multistructural: I have a couple of ideas	Number of connections but not meta-connections	Define, identify, explain, list, combine	Define two themes that emerge from the play.
	4. Relational: I have a few ideas; I can link a few ideas together	Relationship of parts to the whole	Compare, contrast, explain, sequence, classify, relate, analyze, apply, parts to whole, create questions	Relate the theme of *Romeo and Juliet* to a modern-day issue.
	5. Extended abstract: I have a few ideas; I can link them to the big idea; I can see these ideas in a different and new way	Connections within and beyond to generalize and transfer principles	Evaluate, generalize, predict, create, imagine, hypothesize, reflect, theorize	What is the message that the playwright is trying to convey?

Figure 5.8 Surface and Deep Understanding

Surface		
 ▮	Unistructural (one idea)	
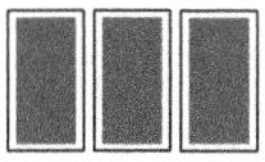 ▮▮▮	Multistructural (several ideas)	
Deep		
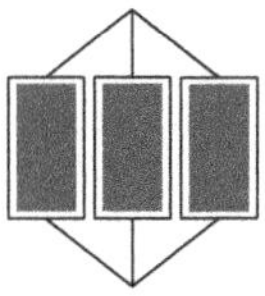 ▮▮▮	Relational (relating two or more ideas)	
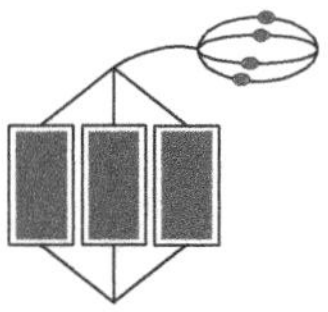 ▮▮▮	Extended abstract (extending an idea)	

If we use both surface and deep learning, it will lead the student to conceptual understanding as each step in the process develops the understanding further. Surface learning is acquiring and beginning to understand concepts and skills. Deep learning is when content and skills are understood and can be used to solve problems and complete projects. A teacher may use the framework in Figure 5.8 and adapt it to any number of subject areas.

The tertiary processing level of the SEEKING system is when conscious learning moves from appetitive to higher-order thinking. Students engage in project and problem based learning using the surface knowledge they have acquired at the secondary SEEKING level to develop concepts more deeply and be able to select and apply knowledge and skills in real situations.

Conceptual understanding is important to flow because it engages students on so many different levels. No one wants to learn just dry facts all day, just as students won't benefit from generic statements that lack empirical backup. Conceptual understanding unites *all* the types of understanding, keeping multiple aspects of students' intelligence engaged. This engagement is the key to flow, and flow really is our ultimate goal.

SUMMARY

Communicating clear goals and standards to students is essential for activating learning. It allows students to visualize success and allows their unconscious minds to work on goals in the background. Strategies like scaffolding and taxonomies can help students focus and experience flow.

DISCUSSION POINTS

- Read and discuss the power of setting goals and identifying standards. How do you share goals with your students?

- Do a web search and consider different, novel ways to display goals for students.

- How might teachers and students differ in the way they express goals? Write up a series of goals that might be in a teacher's voice and then rewrite them in language that might be used by students.

- Discuss Csikszentmihalyi's concept of flow. Talk about an experience in your life in which you've experienced flow. Take the flow questionnaire and discuss your results.

- The zone of proximal development targets learning just at the right degree of complexity to challenge the learner and activate their quest for learning. Discuss how you might adjust a lesson to accommodate the zones of proximal development for several students at different levels of mastery.

- Explore the websites for rubrics (edudemic.com and rubistar.4teachers. org). With your colleagues create a rubric for an upcoming assignment or task.

- In the pursuit of conceptual understanding, create surface learning and deep learning prompts for a unit of study.

6 Activating Assessment

Students cannot succeed in any subject, including math and science, without attention to all their learning and developmental needs. ASCD supports challenging goals and accountability that encompass the education of the whole child. In doing so, we advocate a more complete definition of a student achievement that supports the development of the child who is healthy, knowledgeable, motivated and engaged.

— Gene Carter of ASCD,
response to George W. Bush's State
of the Union address, February 1, 2006

Our modern world is suffering from what Robert Waterman (1987) dubbed the DRIP syndrome: we are data rich but information poor. We are expert at collecting data but not nearly as good at extracting meaningful information from that data.

Sadly, the DRIP syndrome has spread to schools (DuFour et al., 2010, p. 184). Teachers learn how students are doing through the tool of *assessment*. But too many times assessment is narrowly focused on grades and tests scores. Schools are expected to examine the district assessment data and teachers are mandated to collect and examine classroom data. It becomes a tedious task of documenting and maintaining records of student success or failure. But data alone is not the answer. Data only becomes meaningful when it is sifted through and analyzed to find the story that the data reveals (Hattie, 2012).

And data is not just scores and grades. Data that is helpful should include all sorts of information that informs us and students of their successes, needs, progress, and shortcomings. Stiggins suggests that any analysis requires "triangulation"—looking at at least three pieces of information to avoid false assumptions and ensure more accurate conclusions. Clearly, standardized test scores are not enough. Beyond test scores and printouts we really need to see how learners think, learn what is working and what is not, and plan instructional strategies and tasks accordingly.

So how can teachers "triangulate" their assessments? What can teachers do on a day-by-day basis in their classroom to accurately measure their students' progress and needs? This chapter examines some of the elements necessary for rich assessments that tell the story of students' progress and activate learning.

ASSESSMENT BASICS

Effective assessments start with some basic elements: encouragement, learner participation, and the use of formative assessment in addition to summative assessment.

Encouragement

The first element necessary for successful assessment is remembering that its purpose is encouragement. Assessments should not render students hopeless, intimidate them, or create anxiety, and we shouldn't use a baseball bat to provide feedback. Assessments help students see what success they have had, develop confidence in even the small steps, and make them hopeful about seeking more learning. Its purpose is motivational, not punitive (Stiggins, 2014). It should get students on a winning streak and keep them there. If we don't continually check for understanding, we won't keep them on that winning streak. Chronic failure will leave the learner helpless.

Grades alone are not motivating, as they only rank students and don't provide any constructive information related to improvement. But a varied, positive array of assessments can be the foundation of universal competence. By allowing students to understand their own needs and progress, it shows them how far they have come and provides them with a roadmap to get to the next level. Assessment can foster hope, and hope fosters engagement and persistence.

Learner Participation

We want sensitive, thoughtful, analytical independent scholars, then treat [students] like Belgian geese being stuffed for pate de foie gras. We reward them for compliance, rather than independence; for giving the answer we have taught them rather than for challenging the conclusions we have reached. (Crooks, 1988 p. 1)

We will never develop assessment-capable learners if we leave them out of the process. Having students identify quality work and create success criteria and rubrics helps them get clear about the intentions and makes the expectations transparent. Once clear on these counts, students are empowered and activated to move forward in the learning with confidence. Both the learning and the assessment should be student centered and teacher directed. It is a partnership enabling success. We don't want students to simply *be* assessed; we want them to become capable of assessing themselves.

Assessment-capable learners are clear about the learning objectives, can step back and compare their progress with the objective, can identify problem spots, and know how to communicate those stumbling blocks to the teacher. The teacher needs to be able to do these things as well, of course. But teaching students the elements of self-assessment makes students feel empowered and engaged with their own learning. It gives them a sense of autonomy and self-direction that is highly motivational.

This plays into the so-called learning laws developed by Thorndike (1932)—in particular the "law of readiness" that states that motivation is necessary so that a student is ready to learn and that the readiness to learn extends to physical, mental, and emotional readiness. Implicit in the law of readiness is feedback, repetition, and practice (required by Thorndike's "law of exercise"). Any new content or skill requires specific feedback and multiple exposures to develop competence. Learning is strengthened through pleasant and positive conditions with relevance and meaning built-in. Having students participate in their own assessment provides additional opportunities for feedback and practice, and it gives students' the positive experience of competency when they can direct and assess their own learning.

Formative Assessment

Assessment can be one of two types: summative and formative. Summative assessment measures the sum of learning that has been accomplished at the *end* of a unit. Formative assessment (assessment for learning) refers to all the tasks that provide information about student progress *during* a unit for the purpose of adjusting both teaching and learning (Black & Wiliam, 1998a; Cowie & Bell, 1999). Summative assessment recaps students' progress and helps teachers identify any need to backfill missing information or weak skills in preparation for the next unit. Formative assessment helps students identify strengths and weaknesses and set goals for further learning, and it helps teachers use to improve and adjust learning and identify students who are struggling. Summative assessment includes grading against a standard or benchmark, like standardized tests, an examination, or a final paper, project, or exhibition. Formative assessments should not be graded; students are assessed for the accuracy of their learning, to provide them with correction and inform them of their progress. Both are needed: formative assessment *for* learning and summative assessment *of* learning (Ainsworth & Viegut, 2006, p. 23). Sometimes the two can use the same tools (like tests), but their purpose is different (Wiliam, 2006).

Summative assessment is well established in schools, formative assessment less so. But formative assessments are powerful. Five reviews of over 4,000 research studies over 40 years show that well-implemented formative assessments can double the speed of student learning (Wiliam, 2007, p. 36). Hattie's meta-analysis shows that the effect size for formative evaluation is 0.90, fourth in the ranking and yielding almost two years of student gains in one academic year. The impact of various types of teacher, student, and peer feedback is $d = 0.73$. Other meta-analyses of hundreds of studies across all content areas, both knowledge and skills and levels of education, shows that formative assessment has a more positive impact than summative (Black & Wiliam, 1998b; Crooks 1988).

Benefits of Formative Assessment for Teachers

Formative assessment benefits teachers because it empowers them with information to better tune their instructional practices to where students are. Thus the learning is more targeted and time is better used. Teachers are more able to focus on growth from wherever the students begin the learning journey. They can tweak instruction to better activate thinking. Formative assessments also help teachers use flexible grouping appropriately, depending on whether some students need a homogeneous group for a focused instruction or heterogeneous groups for tasks.

Benefits of Formative Assessment for Students

Formative assessment allows students to take responsibility for their own learning, making them much more motivated to learn. As students monitor their own progress and receive corrective feedback, they are developing skills of self-assessment, self-regulation, and goal-setting that will benefit them throughout their educational journey.

Formative Assessment Principles

The following five strategies from Dylan Wiliam are the core of formative assessment and should guide us in building assessment capable learners.

1. **A deep understanding of learning intentions and success criteria.** It is imperative that students deeply internalize what is expected of them for their learning and their successful demonstration of their learning. Students need to be an integral part of the process. Teachers' knowledge of the learning progression is also necessary for accurate student diagnostic assessment and helping students stay actively involved with their learning.

2. **Quality classroom discussions, activities, and learning tasks that demonstrate students' learning.** Teachers need to develop effective instructional strategies that will allow students to develop the knowledge and skills and also provide a measure of success. Usually teacher driven, there is no reason that students should be left out of the process; students can provide feedback to teachers about their perceptions regarding learning tasks and progress.

3. **A feedback loop.** With a continual feedback loop, students have information about what and how they are doing. Peer, self, and teacher feedback using clear, transparent criteria and rubrics can facilitate this "feed-forward" loop, as can discussions about criteria and progress. The feedback needs to timely and specific to be helpful for students.

4. **Activating learners as resources for each other.** Students should interact with each other through discussions about the usefulness of classroom tasks and their own progress.

5. **Activating learners as teachers of their own learning.** Self-awareness and self-regulation should play a major role in many classrooms. A strong supportive community of trusting learners will activate students' ability to become more metacognitive.

HOW TO INCORPORATE ASSESSMENT IN THE CLASSROOM

Classroom assessment is key to the learning process. The following figure shows the cycle of learning and how assessment is evident at every step of student learning.

Just as the good cook tastes the soup continually as it simmers and decides what is needed to improve the quality and flavor, so the good teacher checks on the progress, clarity, and thoroughness of the learning and decides next steps. It is a thoughtful, conscious endeavor for the teacher and every learner. Figure 6.1 shows a typical process of teaching and learning with assessment built in. Assessment drives learning and helps the teacher plan and adjust instruction.

Figure 6.1 Teaching Learning Assessment Cycles

Identify standards, learning intentions

Design pre- and summative assessment tasks

Create rubrics or criteria for success

Give pre-assessment task and interpret data

Select instructional strategies and groups, and adjust complexity

Formative assessment interpreted and instruction adjusted

Continual formative assessment, feedback, reteaching

Culminating assessment task

Summative assessment, evaluate, next steps

Effective Teaching Learning Cycle

Prior Knowledge Assessment (Pre-Assessment)

What students can learn depends partly on what they already know. In the grand scheme, students' prior knowledge has helped them form what Jean Piaget (1970) called schematas—cognitive structures based on their experiences with the real world. These schematas are constantly changing as new learning takes place. New ideas trigger past experiences, and the learner will attempt to assimilate the new to fit in with the prior knowledge. If the new ideas or information simply don't fit with their current schemata, students will modify the schemata accordingly. The brain seeks equilibrium by balancing assimilation and accommodation to reduce cognitive tension.

In the more basic scheme of things, prior knowledge also determines what facts and skills students have. Knowing what students already know helps teachers backfill learning for those with missing knowledge and accelerate those students who are ahead of the curve. Graham Nuthall (2007) found that students already knew at least 40% to 60% of what was being taught, that a third of what each learned was different from their classmates, and that one-quarter of what they learned was dependent on their interactions with peers. They don't all start in the same place, know the same things, or need the same things. Each has different genes and their natural traits may or may not have been nurtured; but also each has had different experiences and opportunities (or lack of them). Prior knowledge is greater in some students because of personal interests or unique experiences as well as their socioeconomic situation. One size doesn't fit all.

Because prior knowledge is so important to students' learning, teachers need to find ways to assess it. Hattie (2009) maintains that accessing prior knowledge would have an effect size of 0.67; it gives the teacher the chance to adjust the learning and bridge the gap to meet the learner where they are. In fact, prior knowledge beats IQ as a predictor of success (Hattie, 2012). Misconceptions create interference for learners and need to be clarified or retaught to pave the way for a smoother learning experience. Reflection and metacognition will help students to construct a deeper understanding of material by becoming aware of their misunderstandings and wrong conclusions (Atkinson & Renkl, 2007).

Connectedness and organization (relationship of ideas) is essential and often stems from prior knowledge. Teachers need to help students with the connections and organization of ideas to form stronger schemas—what Perkins (1991) calls the shepherding principle.

Pre-assessing students about a new topic, skill, or standard they are about to learn lets teachers know what they already know or are capable of related to the new learning. Pre-assessment can give teachers information on many topics:

- Declarative knowledge: What each student already knows
- Procedural knowledge: What each student is able to do
- What skills and information are absent or underdeveloped that are needed in order to capitalize on new concepts or skills
- Student interests to tap motivation
- Misconceptions that need to be addressed

Pre-assessments draw on the power of memory as revealed by neuroscience. All long-term memory or prior knowledge is stored in unconscious mental files throughout the neocortex. When the concept is triggered in the brain, the brain accesses the long-term memory files and draws together in short-term memory all that it knows. For example, if you were asked to think about beaches, in about 4 to 7 seconds you would pull out all the information about beaches that was residing unconsciously in long-term memory files throughout the neo-cortex about a minute ago. Asking students to jot down a few things that come to mind about beaches would give the teacher insight into the experience, interests, and conceptual knowledge the student already has.

The hippocampus, located in the mid-brain limbic area, acts as a memory sorter and sends memories out for long-term storage to the appropriate area of the neocortex. Unconscious while stored, they can be retrieved to conscious memory as needed. Anything that is stored in long-term memory is in networks of association all over the neocortex, not in one file. For example, the concept of oceans is stored in occipital, temporal, cerebellum, spatial, and olfactory areas of the brain as there are memories of sights, sounds, movements, touch, and smells that are triggered. This schema may be used in a geography class about the world's oceans or to set a context for a setting in a story. There may be a lot in the file if you live in California or Maine but little if you have never seen an ocean. If you have ocean knowledge, the hippocampus spends time comparing the new information in class to what has been accessed from prior knowledge. It compares and contrasts new to established patterns.

The hippocampus works at turning short-term working memory into long-term memory, reorganizing and storing during REM (rapid eye movement) sleep. This is done by comparing and contrasting new information with that previously stored. Then the files are updated. Dopamine helps in this process. The hippocampus tries to integrate new information with existing information (Geake, 2009). Facilitating pre-assessment not only helps the teacher plan lessons but also activates these memory banks, priming students to think about the topic and promoting readiness.

The issue for teachers is the heavy curriculum and the crunch of time constraints that they feel when they weigh the use of assessments and the teaching of content and skills. They feel that there are so many concepts, skills, and standards to achieve and so little time that teachers are reluctant to "waste" time on preassessing. Yet pre- and formative assessment is time well spent when we are able to tailor the learning, omit things the students already know, and build background that they need to succeed. The trick is to focus on rapid formative assessment, which is more cost-effective (Yeh, 2011) and that quickly gets the information needed to plan more precisely and provide feedback to students about their progress.

There are many ways that skillful teachers can help students recall past information and experiences. It may be as simple as asking a few questions informally of students as they open a new topic. Teachers can insert comparisons into topic discussions, asking questions like:

- How is this like what we examined last week?
- Is this like something you have seen before?
- How is this like a ____?

Eliciting comparisons through like statements ("How is this like ____?") can help students identify with new information. Trying to make connections to prior knowledge or things they know about will build some connections to new concepts and ideas.

Beyond these simple off-the-cuff questions, teachers can use more formal types of pre-assessments. Here are some possible methods for assessing and activating students' prior knowledge.

Pre-Test

Give students a pre-test of multiple choice, true and false, or cloze statements to check on prior knowledge. Cloze statements (or fill-in-the-blanks) and tests omit key words in the text to assess students' knowledge of a topic. Many websites can help teachers create these more easily (see, for example, www.schoolhousetech.com).

Alphabet Brainstorm

The students are given a sheet with 26 sections (one for each alphabet letter; see Figure 6.2). They brainstorm something about the topic that begins with that letter. This may be done independently or with a partner.

Advance Organizers and Graphic Organizers

Advance organizers are activities that students do right before the start of a new unit to prime their brains to learn the new material (Ausubel, 1968). They improve students' readiness not only by focusing their attention on the topic and engaging their prior knowledge, but also by providing the opportunity to students to backfill or front-end load information that they may be missing to begin approaching a new unit of study. Marzano, Pickering, & Pollock (2001) and Dean et al. (2012) report an effect size of 0.74 by using advance organizers.

Figure 6.2 Alphabet Brainstorm

A		N
B		O
C		P
D		Q
E		R
F		S
G		T
H		U
I		V
J		W
K		X
L		Y
M		Z

There are several types of advance organizers that can provide information prior to the new unit to provide hooks for the learning:

- **Narrative:** Information in story form
- **Skimming:** Reading or participating in a jigsaw with peers
- **Graphic organizers:** Using concept webs or fishbones (see Figures 6.3 and 6.4)
- **Technology:** Searching online for background information (check the Khan Academy or http://flippedlearning.org) or using a teacher-made video

The pre-assessments that teachers use should gather information about student readiness to learn the new information or skill, their prior level of expertise, mindset, interests, or predisposition to the new unit of study. Even the questions they might have related to the topic are of importance. But don't take the time to pre-assess if you aren't going to really look at what you find and teach the same old "laminated lesson" you have always taught. Don't fall victim to DRIP syndrome! Use the data you gather to tailor your lesson plans to what you learn about students' prior knowledge.

Pre-assessment activities should be presented at least a few days before the new unit to give teachers the time to look at this data and make instructional decisions prior to the unit beginning. If students are already knowledgeable or proficient, there is time to develop a deeper or more rigorous task that will challenge them. This also gives teachers time to fill in some gaps for students who have misconceptions or are missing prior

Figure 6.3 Fishbone

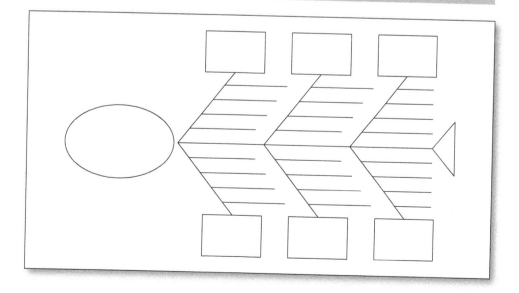

Figure 6.4 Concept Web

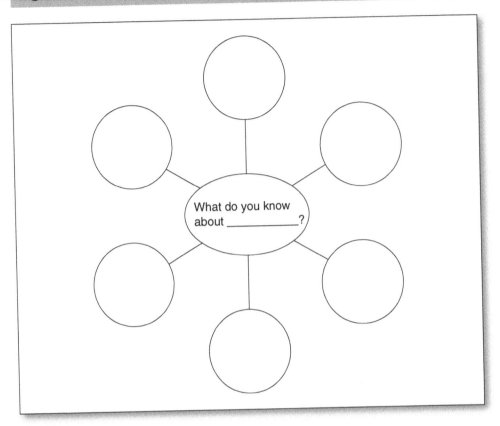

What do you know about _____?

knowledge or skills by using strategies such as flipping the classroom (using videos or information on websites sometimes outside of class so students can catch up). These types of activities announce the coming attraction and activate students' thinking about the new topic.

Current Progress Assessment (Formative Assessment)

Pre-assessment is invaluable to lesson planning. But once lessons are underway, formative assessment takes over, giving teachers feedback on the effectiveness of the instructional approaches and engaging students by developing their self-assessment skills. As with prior knowledge assessment, formative assessment can sometimes be very informal. It may be simply circulating around the classroom as students do pair work and eavesdropping. It could be playing 20 Questions with a word or object related to the lesson topic. But there are some more structured formative assessments as well.

KWL: Know, Want to Learn, Learned

KWL charts (Ogle, 1986) ask students to self-report on what they know about a topic, what they want or wanted to learn, and what they think they actually have learned (a modified form of the KWL can also be used for pre-assessment). These charts activate prior knowledge, which forms connections to their current learning. And the variations in Figure 6.5 also provide an opportunity for students to self-assess and for teachers to learn about students' interests as well as their progress. The GEL chart asks the students what have they GOT at the moment, what do they EXPECT they might learn related to this topic, and what they have LEARNED so eventually things will GEL for them. The last one sets students up for planning a task. What do I know? What do I need to know? It asks students to brainstorm strategies of what to do and then to prioritize those steps.

W-5 Charts

W-5 charts (Figure 6.6) ask students the five big W questions: Who? What? When? Where? Why? Students can write down any key points, and they can use illustrations, diagrams, and symbols as well. As the teacher scans these, she can decide what to teach, choose strategies to use, remind herself of student expertise and resources, and decide how to group students. It also may be necessary to reteach or fill in the blanks for students, depending on gaps noted.

Anticipation Guides

Anticipation guides are useful to compare what students knew before a lesson versus after. It helps answers the question, Where are we now? Students also become aware of what they bring to the learning or the deficits in their prior knowledge. This awareness becomes part of the metacognitive process as they see the beginning of the learning and can note progress as they reflect on the learning journey. Figure 6.7 provides a sample of an anticipation guide for a segment on mammals. Although this is a science topic, anticipation guides also can access prior opinions related to a new topic such as moral issues related to literacy characters or situations or opinions such as historical or political issues. Figure 6.8 can be used to develop any anticipation guide for students.

Rubrics

Teachers give students a rubric with the four levels of proficiency for each criterion for a task or project. Students conduct self- and peer

Figure 6.5 KWL and Variations

Know or think I know	Want to know or wonder about	Learned

Got	Expect	Learned

Know or think I know	Want to know or wonder about	Learned	Know more

Know	Need	Do

Figure 6.6 W-5 Chart

Criteria	Key Points	Illustrations/Diagrams
Who?		
What?		
Where?		
When?		
Why?		

Figure 6.7 Anticipation Guide for Mammals

Before the Reading			After the Reading		
Agree	Disagree	Consider these:	Yes	No	Evidence
		Mammals have two legs.			
		All mammals have live young.			
		Mammals hibernate.			
		Mammals eat meat.			
		Mammals breathe with lungs.			
		Mammals have warm blood.			

Figure 6.8 Anticipation Guide

Before the Reading		Consider these:	After the Reading		Evidence
Agree	Disagree		Yes	No	

assessments to plot where they see their capabilities at the beginning of the task and identify the level they predict they can achieve for each criterion. Assessment-capable learners develop a high level of expertise at plotting and predicting their progress. Peer assessment and feedback is more accurate when using a rubric to identify the level of expertise based on criteria and not just opinion.

Graffiti Placemat

Placemats were introduced in Chapter 1, and here is a great way to use them. Students can work in groups of three or four on a placemat (see Figures 6.9 and 6.10). Ask each student to jot down everything (words or symbols like wall graffiti) that they know about the topic (i.e., the Civil War). Give the students a limited amount of time to do this with a colored marker. After the brainstorming have students share their ideas and create a "big question" (beyond simple recall that might be investigated in

Figure 6.9 Graffiti Placemat for Three Students

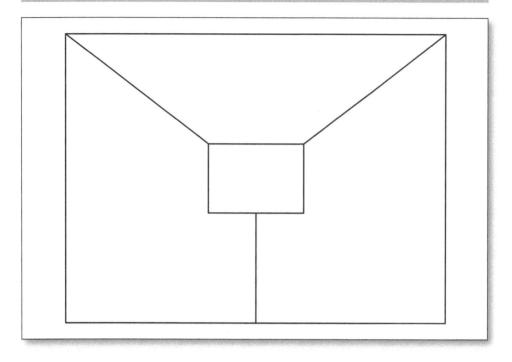

Figure 6.10 Graffiti Placemat for Four Students

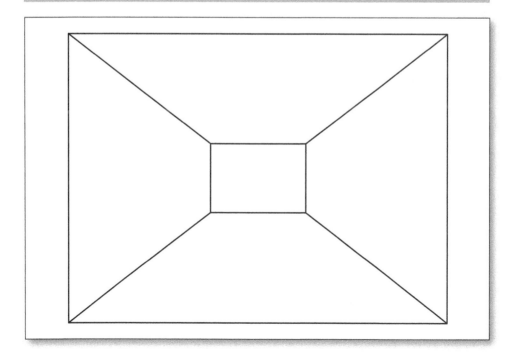

the unit). The big question can be built into the unit so students see relevance and meaning (Bennett & Rolheiser, 2001). Figure 6.11 shows a filled-out placemat for a unit on endangered species.

Figure 6.11 Graffiti Placemat for Lesson on Endangered Species

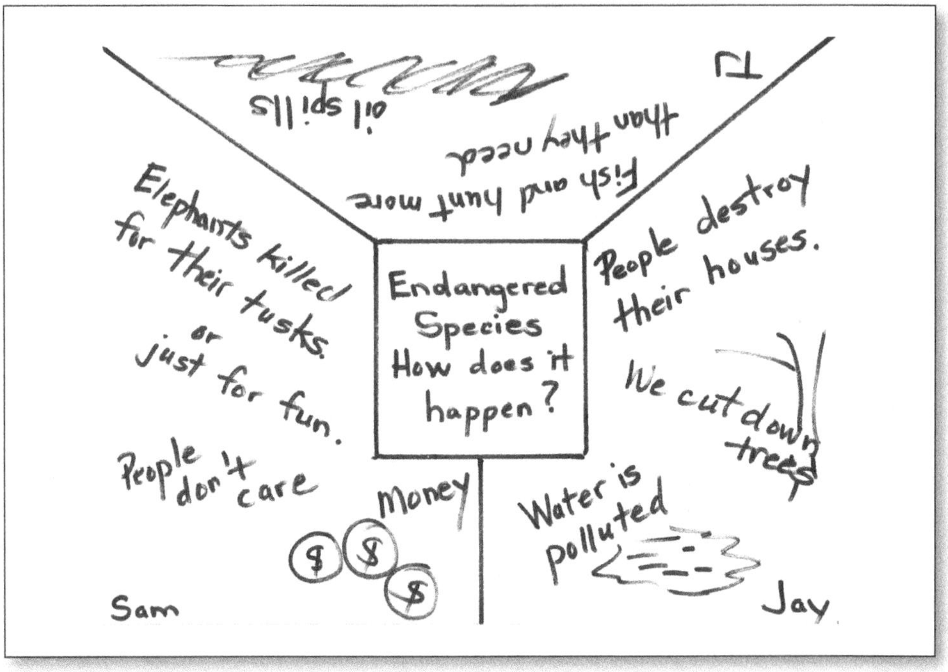

Four Squares

Create a card with four sections and four prompts or give each a piece of paper and have students fold it in four sections. Each student responds to the prompts, one in each corner of the card. When everyone is completed they can walk about and share their four corners with four other students. This also provides resources for instructional planning by responding to the needs and interests of students. Four Squares can also be used as a pre-assessment tool. The example in Figure 6.12 would be for a pre-assessment before a unit on Canada. The example in Figure 6.13 might be for a check for understanding (formative assessment) in math.

Quick Checks for Understanding

As mentioned earlier, formative assessment can be as simple as wandering around the room eavesdropping while students do pair or group

Figure 6.12   Four Squares on Canada

Why would you like to visit Canada?	What do you want to see there?
What question do you have about Canada?	What are three facts you know or think you know about Canada?

Figure 6.13   Four Squares on Math

Math problem	Was this difficult or easy for you? Why or why not?
What strategy did you use to solve the problem?	What question do you have about this type of problem? What suggestion could you make to someone who was struggling with this problem?

work or even simply noticing puzzled looks on students faces and asking a follow-up question. Here are some other quick, small checks for understanding that can be incorporated into day-to-day lessons:

- **Quick writes:** Give students a file card and ask them to jot down anything they know or are interested in related to the topic. This is a free-flow writing activity to open mental files and access prior knowledge. It can also be used to access a skill by giving students a problem to solve and asking them to try to solve it. It might be a formative check for understanding so teachers get information about "Where are we now?"
- **Student-made quiz:** Using Bloom's revised taxonomy of thinking chart from Chapter 3, students write higher-order questions about the text or task.
- **Defining key vocabulary:** Students select a number of domain-specific (key) vocabulary words from the text and provide definitions in their own words.
- **Compare and contrast:** Students identify the theme of a story and contrast it with the last one they read.
- **Examples and non-examples:** Students list three things that are examples of something and three things that are not.
- **Four corners:** The teachers designates each corner of the room as Good to go, Getting there, Trying hard, and Need some help. Students go to the corner that they think best represents their current expertise. This also will help students become good self-assessors.
- **Illustration:** Students create a diagram or graphic to represent an idea.
- **Study guide:** Students create a study guide to list and summarize the main points of a text and provide page numbers for references.
- **Mindmap key points:** Using a mindmap program like kidspiration, create a set of symbols to represent characteristics of a concept.
- **Talk a mile a minute:** Summarize what they know about . . . talking quickly with a partner.
- **Response cards (red, yellow, green):** Students display a colored card representing how competent they feel about their learning (red = I'm stuck, yellow = I'm moving along, and green = I'm good to go).
- **Fist of five:** Students use their fingers to show their level of confidence about a topic or skill (5 = I'm great, 4 = I know it well, 3 = I'm good, 2 = not there yet, 1 = I need help). Students respond on a piece of paper or index card: 3 things you found out, 2 interesting things, and 1 question you still have.
- **Thumbs up–thumbs down:** Students respond with thumbs up or thumbs down to questions or statements provided by the teacher,

depending on whether or not they agree or disagree with the statement. Variations include "response cards" that are green (for agree) and red (for disagree) or a "happy face" for understanding and "frowny face" if still a bit confused or unclear. This is a quick way that teachers can scan of the room to get a sense of progress. Thumbs can be displayed close to the chest, so students don't feel that their response is on public display.

- **Journaling:** Students complete a quick write in a journal or portfolio reflecting on their progress in relation to the rubric or success criteria. 3–2–1 can also be used: 3 things I can do or understand, 2 connections I've made, 1 question I still have.

- **Give one, get one:** Students have a numbered list or form with blanks. Students jot down two things they know about the topic under discussion, then meet with a partner to share one of their ideas and vice versa. Each partner adds the other's idea to their list, and the students continue meeting new partners until they have enough ideas to complete the form or the time allowed is finished.

- **Carousel brainstorming (Gibbs, 2006a):** Chart paper is posted around the room on the walls. Students work in small groups of three or four. A different topic or question related to the unit of study is posted on each piece of paper. Each groups starts at one of the charts and with a colored marker responds to the question or prompt in the amount of time given by the teacher. Then they rotate to the next chart and with the same colored marker they read what has been written and add to it. They rotate to each chart until they are back at the original one. The different colors of marker help the teacher identify which small group wrote the responses.

- **Be a detective:** Students circulate in the classroom with a bingo card or list of concepts or information. They try to find other students who can provide the pieces of information that they need. They also provide information to others. Afterward they report on what they learned and from whom they learned it. This fosters dialogue, rehearsal, and attentive listening.

Data from standardized testing does help teachers know which skills and knowledge have been attained in a summative sense. It is the day-to-day collection and recognition of how students are doing and where to next that is vital to teacher planning and student success. Remember, you don't fatten the pig by weighing it. Make the "diet" rich after you assess students' needs.

SUMMARY

Teachers need to know where students are in their learning, but students need to know too. Using formative assessment in the classroom allows both to adjust content and strategies to make sure that students don't get lost. Tools like fishbones and four squares can give insight into students' current levels of knowledge, and quick tools like thumbs up–thumbs down can provide checks for understanding.

DISCUSSION POINTS

- Discuss the DRIP syndrome and its implications for student learning.

- What is an assessment-capable learner? Does this describe your students? What would be the characteristics?

- Discuss of the idea of formative assessment and its role in teacher planning and student engagement and continued progress.

- Read the research on prior knowledge and its relationship to activating learning.

- Examine the strategies for pre-assessment and decide which you might use in the classroom.

- Create an anticipation guide to use with a new topic or reading.

- Discuss advance organizers and their uses. Develop a fishbone or other graphic organizer and have your classmates fill it out.

- Select several strategies for checking for understanding and use them with your students. Report back about how they worked and what you did as a result of the information.

7 Activating Feedback

Feedback and assessment go hand in hand. As seen in Chapter 6, assessments can serve to refine a teacher's lesson plans or instructional approach, and they can engage students in their own educational journey if self-assessment skills are taught. But assessment is also important to provide valuable quality feedback to students. As students are working on a task they need feedback from the teachers, peers, and themselves to continue to reach the success criteria and continue to be engaged and motivated. Assessment evolves from the Latin verb "assidere," to sit by—meaning to sit beside, as the Roman tax collector did to assess taxes owed. In classrooms, assessment should mirror this, as the student sits besides a teacher or peer who is providing feedback.

Feedback is powerful but has a huge variability when we examine the effects. Wiliam (2007) asserts that effective feedback can potentially double the growth of student learning. The key word here is "effective." First we must be sure there are clear expectations that students understand and that the learning tasks are focused on their achievement. Feedback must be ongoing, timely, and personalized for students. It should also activate students to be owners of their own learning paths and to become self-assessors as well as helping students foster collaboration as instructional resources for each other.

We need to examine those variables to make sure we are getting the greatest pay-off with feedback. Sadler (1989) coined the notion of gap feedback—feedback that addresses the gap between where a student is and where they should be. He suggested that feedback would be helpful if these conditions are met:

- Teachers are aware of where students are related to the goals.
- Students can be self-directed to plan next steps.

- Teachers provide clues that help students refocus.
- Teachers direct attention to the processes the student will need.
- Teachers provide information to clarify misconceptions.
- The feedback is motivational and helps students see which specific efforts will increase chances of being successful.

Although Hattie's meta-analysis unearthed the importance and power of feedback and student achievement with an effect size of 0.75, its impact was dependent on the effectiveness and type of feedback. Feedback that is given as reward and for motivational purposes is not helpful. But feedback that provides information to enable the student to adjust or change their efforts to get closer to the goal has a far greater impact. This is feedback that causes the student to feed-forward and self-regulate and fosters perseverance. Ongoing assessment is critical: It allows students to modify their approach and teachers to adjust the lessons and curriculum to respond to the learners' needs.

Students need feedback that paints a picture of what success looks like: from worked examples to samples of student work that meets the criteria for success. Like the video games they love, we need to get better at helping them see the level they are at presently and then the steps to attain the next level. Feedback's power is in three vital elements (Hattie & Timperley, 2007) for student success:

- Clear target: what success looks like
- Reducing the gap: where am I and where do I need to be?
- Providing information about "where to next?"

INEFFECTIVE FEEDBACK: WHAT TO AVOID

As important as feedback is, it is only useful if it helps accomplish the goals that Sadler (1989) discusses. There are lots of types of feedback that are not effective. These are common types that should be avoided.

Overly General Feedback

Feedback that is overly general, global, or delivered to the whole class isn't always helpful to the individual student and is often ignored (Carless, 2006).

Written Feedback

The same can be said for written feedback, for example on a paper; students often don't read the feedback and simply consider the task complete instead of considering revising the work, incorporating the feedback (Duncan, 2007). Some written feedback is inevitable. But care should be taken not to rely upon it entirely.

Summative Feedback

Summative feedback—like grades at the end of a semester or quarter or even grades on a specific project or paper—are a necessary part of schooling. But summative feedback has limitations. It can often be seen as final and does not mean much to the learning process from the student's perspective.

One idea is to give only feedback on student work instead of giving grades on individual projects. Teachers may struggle with this idea because they fear that students won't work as hard without the motivation of grades. But studies have shown that once the grade is placed on the paper, students often don't pay attention to the feedback as they are comparing their work with other students, celebrating their success, accepting mediocrity, or feeling shamed or discouraged (Taras, 2003; Black & Wiliam, 1998b; Butler, 1988). In these cases the feedback is ignored and wasted as a growth opportunity and loses its impact.

Praise

Conventional wisdom emphasizes the benefits of praise in the classroom. Many people assume that praise helps students learn more and is needed to foster feelings of self-worth. Surprisingly, it turns out that while praise might motivate you and make you feel happier at the moment, praise doesn't actually help you learn at all. Brophy (1981) distinguishes between praise as a management technique in terms of interpersonal relationships and praise as an *instructional* technique. Dweck found that some praise could actually be a detriment to learning because it provides immediate gratification instead of developmental persistence. Praise becomes meaningless over time as students hear a random "good job" with no direction for improvement or insight into what was good. And it conveys the message that the praise is the reward rather than the learning itself. In fact, praise may have a negative affect as it can actually lower engagement and effort (Kessels et al., 2008).

INSTRUCTIONAL FEEDBACK: FEEDBACK DONE RIGHT

If, from a learning standpoint, praise equals empty calories, it is quality instructional feedback that provides a nutritious meal. Praise, like sugar, is appealing but doesn't foster growth. Task, process, and self-regulation feedback provides what students need to grow and thrive.

Nicol and Macfarlane-Dick (2005) suggest that formative assessment—assessment that takes place throughout the learning process—is the most important type of feedback that students can receive. It answers the three questions that Hattie and Timperley consider key:

1. Where am I going? (What are the learning intentions? Success criteria?)

2. How am I going? (What progress have I made?)

3. Where to next? (What knowledge or skills need to be acquired?)

Instructional feedback is critical because we are not generally proficient after one practice. We may make errors. That isn't a deficiency; it's part of the process for every person learning something new. Errors move us forward and show us what we need to correct and not repeat. Understanding this allows teachers to embrace their role as feedback providers and convey to the students that this is a normal part of the educational process. Classroom skills can be coached just as a sport is. Coaches in basketball, tennis, or hockey don't give a grade; they give specific feedback related to the skill or task. Specific feedback helps the player or learner know what is correct and what needs to be improved.

Instructional feedback can address many different aspects of learning. Hattie (2012) divides these aspects into four categories: feedback related to task, process, self-regulation, and self (Figure 7.1). The first three have much more impact on feeding forward and improving performance.

- **Task:** Where am I going? This feedback is information about how the task is being performed, noting whether things are correct or incorrect and what other information or resources should be considered. Information is the foundation for the processing and self-regulation levels. All levels are important and all need to be addressed. At this level simplistic, clear, concise feedback should enable the learner to internalize and act on the feedback.

- **Process:** How am I doing? This deals with the process of learning, including the procedures and strategies the student is using and how the process may be better aligned with developing toward the goal. This also includes set-backs and error identification. This level fosters deeper understanding of material and improves student confidence in the task.

Figure 7.1 Feedback Areas: Task, Process, Self-Regulation, and Self

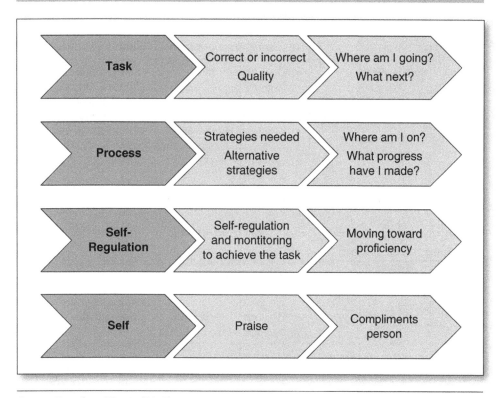

Source: Based on Hattie (2012).

- **Self-regulation:** This feedback fosters the student's ability to reflect and self-regulate toward the goal. At this level students develop autonomy, self-control, and direction. It is also key in developing a student's ability to create internal dialogue (self-talk) and respond with effort and action to feedback received and sought. Students should become more confident self-assessors and see themselves as learners and their own teachers. They appreciate feedback and seek it to improve their learning and success.

- **Self:** This feedback is general praise directed to the student and offers little to help the student improve. These general comments can enhance the student's sense of self or, if negative, deflate it. More focus on the first three levels will bring better results for students. As we discussed earlier, praise can even have negative effects on learning (Dweck, 2006).

Figure 7.2 lists the characteristics of each level and some considerations for teachers in providing feedback on the three critical categories and shows a sample feedback scenario.

Figure 7.2 Teacher Considerations for Feedback at Task, Process, and Self-Regulation Levels

Feedback Type	Teacher Considerations	Sample Feedback
Task-Level Feedback • Identify correct or incorrect answers • Get additional information • Re-teach; add more surface knowledge	• Does answer meet criteria? • Is the answer correct or incorrect? • What was done well? • What was missing? • Can the answer be improved?	I see you are checking with the rubric to make sure all the details are included. You might want to check another source for additional information.
Process-Level Feedback • Finding connections between ideas • Finding errors using a variety of strategies • Explicit learning • Learn from errors made • Cueing the student to other strategies	• What's wrong? • Why is it wrong? • What strategies were used? • How did they get the correct answer? • What other questions are there? • What connections can be made within the task?	Your project needs to incorporate multimedia. Perhaps creating a checklist of the types of multimedia you plan to include will help you with decisions and the flow of your presentation.
Self-Regulation Feedback • Being able to create internal self-feedback • Being able to identify what is correct or incorrect • Being willing to invest effort in seeking and using feedback • Additional help to seek other resources or confirm answers	• How can work be self-monitored by the student? • What self-checking will be done? • How can students evaluate the information? • How can they reflect on their task and process? • What did they do to . . . ?	Have you thought about how people will react to your presentation? What affect do you want it to have? Perhaps you would like to show it to someone and assess his or her interest and reaction.

Source: Adapted from Gregory and Kuzmich (2014).

Promoting a Growth Mindset

Having a growth mindset is extremely important to activating learning. Students have to know that intelligence is not fixed; there are not simply smart students, average students, and less capable students. Intellectual growth comes from practice and persistence, not necessarily any kind of innate intelligence. Challenges along the way are normal and should never be discouraging.

To continue to foster a growth mindset for students, feedback should include precise, accurate statements related to the effort the students expend. Comments about their abilities should be avoided; instead teachers should focus on the effort and progress made, which is more likely to activate next steps in the attention to task, as there is hope and direction to be successful. Here are some types of statements a teacher can make to a student, at various stages, regarding effort.

When a student is struggling even with a strong effort:

"When something is really new, it's not easy."

"I know you can do this! It's big, but you can eat an elephant one bite at a time."

"Wow, look how far you have come."

When students are struggling and need assistance:

"Let me help you. Tell me what you've been doing, please."

"Some parts of this are difficult. Show me what has you stumped."

"Here's another way that might work . . . maybe this will work for you."

When they are making progress:

"You chose a good strategy. Keep up the great effort."

"You really persevered and it made all the difference."

"I can see your hard work."

When they succeed with strong effort:

"Your hard work and effort was what made the difference."

"Which strategy made the difference for you?"

"You never gave up. I'm proud of you."

When they succeed easily without effort:

"What's next? You're ready!"

"You've got that down pat. You're ready for a challenge."

"You aced it. What's your next goal?"

These suggestions are developed from examples of Emily Diehl, a mindset works trainer. The website Mindset Works offers more sample statements to consider (http://www.mindsetworks.com/free-resources).

Dweck (2006) suggests that teachers use the phrase "not yet" when students struggle with new challenges. We may need more time, more resources, or more direction. We're just not there YET, but with tenacity and effort we can get there. Of course, students have an array of challenges with coursework sometimes. Figure 7.3 shows some useful phrases for students experiencing particular challenges.

The Power of the Particular

Feedback isn't helpful if it isn't specific. We've discussed how teacher clarity has a huge impact on whether or not students achieve well in class. Teachers must be clear about the learning intentions, the relevance and real-world impact of the lessons, the criteria for success, and the rubrics and exemplars that students can turn to. The same goes for feedback.

My family had an opportunity to experience this. My daughter, in one of her courses at university, was eager to maintain her A average because she wanted to go into a master's program. She was most upset one night as she shared with me that she got a B+ on a paper that had just been returned to her. I asked her what comments were written on the paper; perhaps she could write a do-over. She said make-ups were not possible. She replied that the teacher had written only "B+ Good job" on the paper. That was it. I told to her make an appointment with the professor to discuss the paper. She did. During our next telephone conversation I asked her about the meeting. She told me that he was rather defensive when she asked about the grade and what she might do to improve. He said, "I know a B+ when I see one." She replied that she didn't, and so she needed to know what was right and what she had failed to do as well. I was proud of her tenacity and perseverance to get the feedback she needed to improve, but sorry that an educator could return a paper without any corrective or constructive feedback. Even if the paper were A+ she had the right to know what was good about it so that she could note and maintain these features in all her writing.

When teachers think about feedback they should think about offering:

- Clarifying the learning intentions and goals
- Conveying the success criteria
- Comments on the progress
- Commitment to providing resources
- Corrections in a positive, constructive way
- Creating dialogue about the work

Figure 7.3 Feedback and Responses: Just in Time, Just for YOU

Behaviors and Needs	Considerations for Teacher Support
Students who seem unclear about the task	• Go over the expectations and review the intentions and success criteria. • Show worked examples to make the expectations tangible. • Ask questions to understand the issues and roadblocks the student is facing.
Students who seem anxious about specific learning tasks	• Review the rubric or model. • Chunk the tasks so they are seen as manageable.
Students who seem self-conscious	• Keep your discussions private. • Allow students to have some autonomy about the demonstration of competency.
Students who cannot seem to get started	• Structure and limit the choices and have students describe the one with the most advantages.
Students who have been used to frequent praise	• Help them to self-assess using a checklist and to share when they have completed one or two steps. • Use feedback for effort and completion. • Help them to use positive self-talk. • Provide specific praise that comments on moving forward with tenacity and effort and/or a completed goal set by the student.
Students who resist change in process or method	• Give them a connection to the previous process and a real-world rationale for the change. • Have students suggest a viable method or process that does not compromise the standard or assessment.
Students who display anger about a task or issue	• Have a quiet private discussion in a neutral zone about their feelings about the task. • Encourage the student share their frustration or ask you questions, as this lowers the threat level.
Students who seem bored	• Discuss the reasons for the lack of interest. The task may be modified to be more challenging or tailored to the student's interests. Help the student re-focus and begin again, or collaboratively reframe it so that it is more personal for them.

Source: Adapted from the work of Hattie and Timperley (2007).

- Confirm the quality of the work
- Comments with suggestions: feeding forward
- Constructive reflection: where to next?

Positive Language

When you ask students about what they want from feedback, they want to know how to get better. What they don't find helpful is critique. Sometimes the critique references past failures and is viewed as personal and damaging to their ego. Sometimes a critique is just as vague as the learning objectives were and students feel that they were in a "gotcha" situation. If the target was not visible, it becomes a guessing game of "What does the teacher like or want?" If their work then comes up wanting, they may blame the teacher, believing that they weren't taught well enough or that they were required somehow to go beyond expectations that were not given. They may make social comparisons and come up lacking.

Instead of negative feedback, students need feedback that tells them what to work on next time. An example of negative feedback for a writing assignment would be a comment such as "the language was not varied or descriptive." A better way to state it would be "Your writing could benefit from more descriptive adverbs and adjectives that would make the ideas more vivid to the reader." This constitutes a real roadmap for the students. The urge to point out the flaws in student work may seem constructive; but if the negatives outweigh the positives, it is demoralizing—and unfortunately one negative seems to have four times the impact of one positive.

Simply pointing out errors and omissions is not helpful. The teacher's role is not simply to correct mistakes but to get the students to engage with the material and figure out things themselves. This involves making suggestions for next steps or asking students to think of alternatives. Pointing students in the right direction activates their own innate SEEKING instincts and conveys confidence that they can work it out.

Giving feedback isn't one size fits all either. Depending on the student's knowledge or skill level the feedback should be sensitive to the level of expertise to encourage rather than discourage. Hattie suggests corrective feedback for beginners (novice), process feedback for intermediary proficient learners, and feedback on conceptual issues for more competent learners.

What Students Think About Feedback

Higgins et al. (2001) investigated students' responses when asked about when and how feedback is least helpful. Feedback was deemed negative and unhelpful under these conditions:

- If it is not informative enough
- When it is impersonal and too general
- If it does not feed forward
- If it is only a list of what is wrong

Hattie and Timperley (2007) conducted interviews with students as well, and their research revealed what students wanted from classroom feedback:

- Concise, explicit explanations in student language (clarity)
- Validation and reinforcement that they can learn
- Tasks that help them connect new learning to prior knowledge
- More independence and autonomy in learning
- Instructional feedback is effective when it focuses on task, process, and self-direction; when it is specific; and when it is positive, stressing what needs to be done next rather than what went wrong last time

PEER FEEDBACK

Chapter 3 discussed the importance of peer interaction in the classroom, and feedback is no exception to the rule. Students often prefer, accept, and engage with feedback from peers rather than teachers (Leahy et al. 2005). Discussing the quality of their work, comparing it with precise criteria, and getting feedback from colleagues can lead to greater self-esteem, more positive student relationships, and self-efficacy. As students develop more positive peer relationships, feedback is received and perceived as constructive, useful, and less hurtful. Then feedback can be considered and internalized in order to feed forward (Falchikow & Goldfinch, 2000; Harelli & Hess, 2008). Feedback can motivate and activate renewed energy toward the goal. Chan (2006) found that self-efficacy is enhanced when peer feedback is of a formative nature and not a summative or judgmental one. Peers influence colleagues' commitment to their goals through modeling, pressure, and a friendly competition (Carroll, Houghton et al., 2009). This interaction also broadens students' perspective and provides them with a chance to see other students' work and how they have approached the task.

It's important to remember, however, that peer feedback is not risk-free. From classroom observations, Nuthall (2007) noted that 80% of feedback to students is from peers and can be inaccurate. Precise criteria such as rubrics can increase the chances that learners and peers make accurate judgments. Using rubrics with specific criteria gives students clear indicators for assessing and goal setting. Peer discussions focused on rubric criteria are more beneficial than just opinion.

The specific criteria help students see where they are and what to do next; this conveys to the student that the task is doable, which activates students' motivation.

STUDENT FEEDBACK: GIVING STUDENTS A VOICE

> When one has no stake in the way things are, when one's needs or opinions are provided no forum, when one sees oneself as the object of unilateral actions it takes no particular wisdom to suggest one would rather be elsewhere.
>
> —Seymour Sarason, 1990

Listening is just as important as speaking if you are the teacher. True listening garners information about students' reactions to instruction, their strategies of learning, their successes, their interactions with peers, and their views about teaching. When I taught high school, we asked students to do a course evaluation at the end of semester and I always learned things that I didn't know about the students, such as how they enjoyed or didn't enjoy some aspects of the course. However, in retrospect, the questions were not specific enough to get good information about the teaching and learning that went on. And sadly it was too late to do anything about it for those students, as we did the assessment on the last day of class.

Feedback from students can be elicited in a way that makes it helpful for both them and the teachers. Hattie suggests that activating a student's voice allows teachers to better understand their impact on their students. Teachers need to get into students' thinking so that they can assess where they are, what they are thinking, what their preferences are, and what is helpful or not. We also want to know the merits of the instructional strategies we used, how to improve them, or even whether to delete them from our instructional menu if they're not working. Students are our customers, and most businesses have a customer service department that surveys customers for their opinions and responds to their needs. Why shouldn't students have the same opportunity?

We need to ask students many things so that we can create classrooms and learning opportunities that are safe, familiar, and interesting to help them connect to the curriculum. Incorporating personal information and the preferences of students into the learning tasks will engage students who might otherwise be disenfranchised and will activate a sense of involvement, ownership, and collaboration in the classroom. Giving students a voice in the classroom also creates an environment of respect and provides a reciprocal conversation that guides learning and the decisions teachers make.

Quaglia and Corso (2014), in their valuable publication *Student Voice: The Instrument of Change*, contend that student voice has a great impact on student achievement. Russell Quaglia has surveyed thousands of students about their aspirations. Extensive analysis of the data gathered revealed eight student aspirations, which Quaglia then gathered under three overarching principles: self-worth, engagement, and purpose (see Figure 7.4). (More resource materials related to his research are available at http://www.qisa.org/framework/students.jsp.)

Teachers are beginning to be more conscientious about asking for student input in many areas of teaching and learning. But asking is not enough unless true listening takes place—listening not just for information, not just for validation or condemnation, but to take action and make adjustments and accommodations for students to better meet their learning needs and preferences.

The school is their environment, and they spend a lot of their lives there. Having a student voice on a school committee isn't enough; it doesn't get down to the daily learning in the classroom, and that's where

Figure 7.4 Quaglia and Corso's Three Principles and Eight Aspirations

Principles	Aspirations
Self-Worth: When valued, students can flourish. Trust between and among all class members and a belief that they can be successful.	• **Belonging:** Unique but included • **Heroes:** People who are there for you and believe in you • **Sense of Accomplishment:** Acknowledgement for what you have done and respect for it
Engagement: Enthusiastic and willing to commit to the learning process and move forward.	• **Fun & Excitement:** Being joyful at any task • **Curiosity & Creativity:** Wonderment of new ideas • **Spirit of Adventure:** Venturing forth with excitement, risking and trying new things
Purpose: Responsible and confident in the present but looking forward to future careers.	• **Leadership & Responsibility:** Accountability for decisions • **Confidence to Take Action:** Setting goals and a plan to reach them

Source: Quaglia and Corso (2014).

change needs to take place. Students often have very constructive ideas that might enhance the whole learning experience and certainly have personal specifics that will help them learn better. It can be as simple as incorporating personal information or likes and dislikes in the curriculum; it's surprising to see how disengaged students become engaged when they have input. I remember teaching a grammar lesson on quotation marks in an eighth-grade class. I noted some of the common sayings of the students and created exclamatory statements with the students' names in them. They worked with a partner and added quotation marks and other punctuation. They enjoyed hearing the other students read their own statement and easily put in the quotation marks. Then they went back to their own narratives and infused quotes and exclamatory statements. The exercise was not boring grammar because it was tailor made for them.

But you have to listen. Just giving them a chance for input isn't enough. We have to truly listen, empathize, and respond. Don't ask if you're going to do nothing; that's hypocrisy. It's also a waste of everyone's time and will only succeed in demoralizing and further frustrating students.

Students have the greatest stake in teacher effectiveness, and they know better than anyone else how the teaching is going. Asking the right questions, in the right way, is an invaluable aid to teachers in assessing their own work. Here are some methods to activate students' voices and get the most impact from their feedback.

Surveys

Teachers often use survey assessments to get to know students to get to know students' preferences—how they like to learn and interests they might have related to a topic. The surveys may get at interests in a particular subject or preferences related to environment such as lighting, noise level, ability to work independently, or why or why not they feel comfortable or welcome at school.

In any written survey given to students, there are two questions in particular that are helpful with feedback issues:

- What kind of feedback is most valuable to help you improve?
- What is most helpful when you are working on something difficult?

Teachers can make use of online surveys like Survey Monkey or the survey tools on MetProject, posting questions that students can respond to with Strongly Agree, Agree, Disagree, and Strongly Disagree. They can also use the state of Kentucky's Student Voice Survey materials. Their website (State of Kentucky, 2014) provides a lot of information about survey procedures and provides samples for various grade levels as well.

Focus Groups

Some schools use focus groups to elicit student opinions. Focus groups bring together small groups of students to answer questions put forth by a moderator. Members of the focus group are allowed to talk freely and comment on each other's answers as well. Here are some questions a moderator might ask of a student focus group:

- What are your teachers doing that helps you learn?
- When are you finding learning difficult?
- How are you feeling about how you are doing?
- How do you set goals for the year?

Video Diaries

Having students record a video diary is another tool for eliciting student feedback. The video diaries don't have to be complicated. In one case, the teacher gave the students prompts to respond to:

- What are you grateful for . . . about school, this class. . . .
- What request might you have . . .
- What do you need from your teacher . . .
- One thing you'd like to add. . . .

Research on student voice from McIntyre, Peddler, and Rudduck (2005) showed that students appreciate a constructive focus on learning. They are not petty and complaining, but they want to talk about learning and how to get better at the tasks they are given.

Exit Cards

A quick way to get feedback is through exit cards or "tickets out." When the class ends, ask them what they liked about the day's class, what was frustrating, and something that they would like to see in the future (maybe even the next day). You can use a two-column T chart with one column titled *A Plus for Today* (what I enjoyed or appreciated) and another titled *A Wish for Tomorrow* (a request) (see Figure 7.5). It has quite an effect on a student when they realize that the teacher actually heard them and took their suggestion to heart and acted on it.

Figure 7.5 Feedback T Chart

A Plus for Today	A Wish for Tomorrow

Exit cards can ask students for details relating to a learning experience or content or skills and where they are feeling capable or need some help. These responses give the teacher a check for understanding but also help identify next steps, groupings, or instructional processes that are needed.

METACOGNITION: THE KEY TO SELF-FEEDBACK

> When we no longer know what to do we have come to our real work and when we no longer know which way to go we have begun our real journey. The mind that is not baffled is not employed. The impeded stream is the one that sings.
>
> —Wendell Berry

> When the mind is thinking it is talking to itself.
>
> —Plato

Piaget proposed that intelligent people know what to do when they don't know what to do. Art Costa thought that if students developed "habits of mind" that they would be able to handle the unexpected problems and situations that we face in life and that children could be taught these habits from an early age.

Metacognition is the ability to think about the way we think. It is the key to developing the kinds of habits of mind that Costa talks about. It allows students to figure out what to do when they don't know. Hattie assigns an effect size of 0.69 to metacognitive strategies.

Designed originally by Anderson, Costa, and Kallick (in Costa & Kallick, 2008), the 16 habits of mind are key skills to encourage in students of all ages. Developing these habits of mind allows students to tackle new and complex dilemmas. They foster self-monitoring skills and help students develop self-confidence as they begin to experience time and again the progress that the habits foster.

The 16 habits of mind identified by Costa and Kallick are as follows:

- **Persisting:** regardless of obstacles and setbacks
- **Thinking and communicating with clarity and precision:** specific, descriptive language for clear meaning
- **Managing impulsivity:** control physical and emotional responses so one can think
- **Gathering data through all senses:** exploring environment using all senses
- **Listening with understanding and empathy:** to feel for and with another person
- **Creating, imagining, innovating:** to use knowledge and skills to create
- **Thinking flexibly:** to adjust and see others' points of view
- **Responding with wonderment and awe:** being intrigued and wonderstruck
- **Thinking about thinking (metacognition):** awareness of one's own thinking
- **Taking responsible risks:** stretching competencies for growth
- **Striving for accuracy:** working toward clarity, quality, and correctness
- **Finding humor:** laughing and whimsy
- **Questioning and posing problems:** being inquisitive
- **Thinking interdependently:** using reciprocal learning to grow
- **Applying past knowledge to new situations:** being conscious of the past to help future situations
- **Remaining open to continuous learning:** humility, avoiding complacency

The self-reflection that these habits suggest is at the center of self-feedback. Effective teachers will activate this kind of metacognition in their classrooms, asking students to devise a strategy to attack a problem and then to assess its effectiveness and impact (Newell, 1990). The time spent reflecting on strategies used and possible transfer to other situations enables the learner to be more able to self-direct in the future.

Dignath and Buttner (2008) caution that metacognitive strategies are not a quick fix. They take months of practice and repetition to become second nature for students. In elementary schools metacognition as part of instruction is more challenging, as younger students don't seem to use these strategies as effectively. Given that adolescents are approaching the abstract thinking stage they tend to do better with them. All learners receive stronger effects when the metacognitive strategies are embedded in the instructional process. Here are some ways to employ them in the classroom.

Metacognitive Thinking Prompts

Metacognition has three elements: developing a plan, executing and monitoring the plan, and evaluating the plan. In other words: Before, During, and After.

Teachers can draw on this tripartite structure to get students to think about their process. Prompts that foster metacognitive thinking might be those shown in Figure 7.6.

Researchers and educators have suggested other prompts. These may be prompts for exit cards or in journal entries or self-assessments related to tasks and assignments. Some students have self-talk well instilled in their learning process, but many don't. Repeated reflections will help strengthen metacognitive processing.

Figure 7.6 Metacognitive Thinking Prompts

Before: Development	During: Implementing	After: Evaluating
What am I suppose to do?	Is this the right way to go about this?	Did I do what was asked?
What are the criteria for success?	How well am I doing?	How successful was I?
What kind of product will I create?	What don't I understand?	If I did this again, what would I change?
With whom will I work?	What help do I need?	What is a goal that will help me?
What resources do I need?	What additional resources would help me? Who? What?	Whom do I need to help me?

Beyer (1987) offers these possible prompts:

- What am I doing?
- Why am I doing it?
- What other way could I do it?
- Can I use this somewhere else?
- How would you help someone else do it?

Bellanca and Fogarty (1986) offer the following reflective strategies, derived from James Bellanca's fifth-grade teacher, Mrs. Potter:

- What were you asked to do?
- What did you do well?
- What would you do differently if you did it again?
- What help do you need?

De Bono (1991) suggests some prompts that can be used after a learning task or assignment (see Figure 7.7).

Figure 7.7 Plus, Minus, and Interesting Prompts

Plus

- The main ideas make sense because . . .
- This fits with what else I know about . . .
- I never knew that . . .
- This causes me to think about . . .

Minus

- I don't agree with . . .
- This doesn't fit with what I know about . . .
- My question is . . .
- My concern is . . .

Interesting

- I never thought about . . .
- Does that mean . . .
- This is a new idea for me and . . .

(Continued)

Figure 7.7 (Continued)

Here are some other possible prompts:

Thinking Prompts	Metacognitive Prompts
• I wonder . . .	• Why would you use . . . ?
• What puzzles me . . .	• Where would you use . . . ?
• What I am curious about . . .	• How would you use . . . ?
• This reminds me of . . .	• How would you adapt/modify . . . ?
• What interests me here . . .	
• I feel . . .	
• What would happen if . . .	

Think-Alouds

Self-verbalization is the self-talk that students engage in that will strengthen their ability to self-regulate. Thinking becomes more visible when we activate student self-talk. According to the meta-analysis from Hattie (2009), self-verbalization and self-questioning have an effect size of 0.64.

Teachers often model this in "think-alouds." It is like eavesdropping on what someone is thinking. Teachers verbalize out loud as they work through a process or demonstrate a skill. They describe clearly what they are doing and thinking so that students hear the details of the process that observation may not provide. This models for students what people do as they read or think about a process. Think-alouds modeled by the teacher afford students permission and strategies to engage in this process themselves. If you haven't tried think-alouds, check out some of the YouTube videos on the topic or websites like www.readingrockets.org for more details.

The Recovery Strategy

At the end of a lesson or activity, teachers often ask, "Tell me how you solved that" or "What went on in your head?" Some students can't answer those questions. They may be nervous when suddenly asked to express themselves. Some may let their minds wander while they read, merely moving through the print with no recognition or comprehension.

Sometimes a student may just need a minute to collect her thoughts before responding. But if a student has truly lost the thread of a topic, he can use what is known as the recovery strategy. The recovery strategy involves the student going back to the point where his mind wandered and matching that point to his last connected thought. From there he can read on and catch up.

The recovery strategy doesn't simply catch students up on the content under discussion. It instills in them a growth mindset, showing them that careful effort can catch them up and that losing the thread of a topic doesn't mean they have to be lost forever.

Right Angles

Right angle is a reflection tool for students and a great scaffolding method. It allows students to look at a concept or issue and respond to it on both a factual and evaluative level. It is a graphic organizer that works well with individual students and in small cooperative groups. It is also a great literacy tool, since a piece of text (fiction or nonfiction) or a nonprose source (charts, maps, websites, etc.) can be used for the facts. This tool helps students with inferential thinking as they pull the most important facts from a resource and then demonstrate their understanding of those facts as they offer or develop consensus around opinions, reactions, implications, and solutions.

Here are the steps to implementing a right angle:

1. Read or view a source of information about a topic in the class's current unit.

2. Have students highlight the most important information in the text or visual material.

3. Pass out the right angle graphic in Figure 7.8. Have one person in each group fill in the facts related to the topic or issue (e.g., a social studies topic or a character in a story) with the help of his group members.

4. Have the group brainstorm opinions, reactions, implications, or solutions depending on the prompt or question being address by the student or learning team.

5. At the bottom, have the group respond to the issue with opinions, reactions, or feelings.

Students can improve their cognitive skills by participating in other group reflections as well. They can discuss their thinking process with others, asking, for example, What are you doing? How is it helping you?

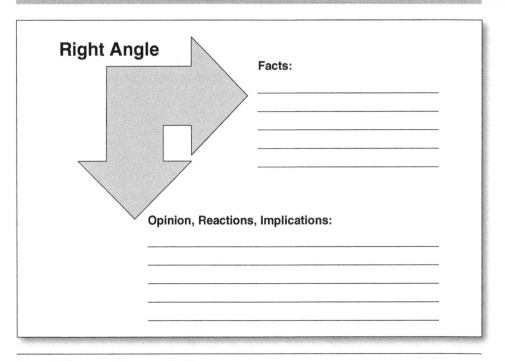

Figure 7.8 Right Angle

Source: Bellanca and Fogarty (2003).

Mindfulness

Mindfulness is a type of metacognition. According to Amy Saltzman, it consists of paying close attention to your own life, the here and now, with curiosity and kindness. In *Mindfulness: A Guide for Teachers,* she notes that teachers are constantly asking students for their attention, but we don't often overtly teach that skill. In elementary classes I remember that to show that we were ready to pay attention, we had to sit up straight, feet flat on the floor, hands folded on the desk, and look at the teacher. My body was ready and I looked compliant, but I'm not sure my brain was always engaged. Mindfulness is your ability to pay attention to both your external and internal environment. Mindful behavior is taking time to focus on your emotions and thoughts at the moment. Studies show that teaching mindfulness strategies to students K–12 is an essential element in helping children and adolescents to improve attention, social and learning behaviors, and executive function.

There is great value in thinking related to the affective domain, including to better understand one's feelings, physical well-being, and mental health, and to learn ways to settle the mind.

In Piagetian terms, many of us don't reach the stage of formal operations (Chiabetta, 1976) and not all adults metacogitate (Whimbey, 1976). The most likely reason is that many people have never been taught strategies to do so, and others are overscheduled with very little downtime (as in Elkind's [2006] *The Hurried Child*). The brain needs breaks from activity in order to reboot and consider ideas and processes as well as decisions made and reasons why.

In the daily rush students seldom question themselves or wonder about what they are doing and why. Some children have no clue about what to do when they encounter a problem, and they cannot articulate the strategies they use in problem solving or decision making (Sternberg and Wagner, 1982). Mindfulness and the other methods of self-feedback discussed here will help them connect with their own thinking and give them confidence.

SUMMARY

Feedback is one of the most important tools teachers have to activate learning. General feedback, grades, and praise are traditional forms of feedback, but recent research has shown that they are not the most effective types. Instead, instructional feedback provides students with timely, personalized information that helps them understand goals, explore next steps, and brainstorm their own solutions. Teachers should also foster peer feedback and self-feedback, turning their students in assessment-capable learners.

DISCUSSION POINTS

- Read and discuss the value of feedback in the learning process and why it is key to activating student engagement and feeding forward.

- Consider the use of praise as a positive or negative influence on developing assessment-capable learners.

- Related to feedback, Hattie suggests focusing on three categories: task, process, and self-regulation. Examine the feedback prompts related to these three important feedback lens.

- Read and discuss how we might greater ensure attention to developing a growth mindset.

- Have a discussion about the types of feedback needed for specific situations listed in Figure 7.3. Do you have students in some of these categories? What might be useful to try?

- Discuss the role of teacher clarity in effective feedback. Which might you focus on to improve the quality and clarity of your feedback?

- How could you use information about what students need, want, and don't like to adjust your teaching and hone your own feedback?

- Peer feedback is important. What are some cautions regarding maintaining quality and accuracy of peer feedback?

- Discuss the role of the students' voice in the classroom where they spend so much time.

- What are you already doing to get student feedback? What are some additional strategies you could use to elicit feedback?

- Discuss Quaglia's eight aspirations and their impact on teacher/student relationships.

- Metacognition is imperative as students reflect on their work, progress, and feedback. Which of Costa and Kallick's habits of mind do you think are most necessary for your students?

- Consider the prompts for metacognition before, during, and after learning.

- What do you think are the most useful strategies to prompt metacognition?

8 Final Thoughts

Every student deserves a passionate, inspired teacher who is firmly committed to helping students learn and consistently focused on doing a better job each and every day. Knowledge of subject matter has less to do with an expert teacher than does passion and enthusiasm, the ability to design appropriate learning tasks while activating and facilitating thinking and learning.

Accomplished teachers have a powerful and passionate focus in cognitive engagement with content for students. They develop thinking skills and problem solving related to the content. They monitor the development of the concepts and skills students are learning providing feedback to increase proficiency in a timely manner.

STUDENT CENTERED

Inspired teachers are student-centered activators. Contrary to some thought, student centered does not mean leaving the teacher out of the equation. The effect sizes for student-centered learning is $d = 0.64$ between cognitive student outcomes and person-centered variables, whereas $d = 0.70$ with behavioral and affective student outcomes (Cornelius-White, 2007). The term used is *facilitative relationship*. The student-centered teacher is passionately aware of each and every student's engagement and their progress toward the learning intentions.

A student-centered teacher exhibits warmth, trust, and empathy. Warmth means showing students affection, inclusion, acceptance, positive regard, and respect. Trust means showing them that you understand their point of view and will stand by them as they accept and manage the challenges of learning. Empathy means understanding and feeling with them despite their confusion and frustration at times. Together, these traits create a safe haven for students and activate brain-friendly learning.

As educators we can help student be hopeful by helping them set goals, breaking goals down into manageable chunks, helping them to manage setbacks, and strategizing alternate ways to get there, as well as sharing success stories and keeping things positive.

Goals that students set based on personal, internal standards are more motivating and energizing that those imposed by others, whether peers, teachers, or parents. Helping and coaching students to set goals that stretch them beyond just "doing your best" is more beneficial. It's also important to help students develop self-talk in positive voices. They may use audiotaping or journaling. Promote peer interaction and share stories about people overcoming adversity and challenge. Help students strategize to create pathways and realize that there are many routes to any goal, roadblocks occur, effort matters more than talent, and they can ask for help.

WHAT STUDENTS WANT FROM TEACHERS

DuFour and Eaker (1998) reported some of the statements that students made about teachers who meant the most to them:

- He had a contagious enthusiasm.
- She had a clear sense of what she wanted to accomplish.
- She knew how to communicate in our terms.
- He believed in me and gave me confidence in myself.
- He was passionate about it. You could not remain detached around him.
- She never gave up on me. She was tenacious.
- He was a tremendous motivator.
- She was challenging, but she made it fun to meet the challenge.
- He was energizing. It was just great to be around him.

Being a inspirational, passionate, and encouraging teacher has already been discussed. These attributes contribute much to the notion of teachers as change agents, as like begets like. This also relies on a growth mindset communicated by the teacher to the student, ensuring that they know they can become capable and that intelligence is not fixed. Teachers don't have to be over-the-top bubbly, but students should be able to sense how connected and engaged they are (Steele, 2009).

Wilson and Corbett (2007) investigated students who did not do well in school and how they felt about their teachers. They felt that some teachers gave up on them or didn't persevere in helping to engage them and encourage them. They had six criteria for the type of teachers whom they wanted to see in schools:

1. Someone who stayed with them through to completion of tasks

2. Someone who managed the classroom behavior without getting off task

3. Someone who continued to help and strategize for success

4. Someone who remained tenacious until the light went on (the a-ha moment)

5. Someone who had a plethora of multimodal instructional strategies

6. Someone who cared about them and understood their situation

Anyone who stops learning is old, whether at twenty or eighty. Anyone who keeps learning stays young.

—Henry Ford

PARENTS AND THE GROWTH MINDSET

It is important that parents know about the concept of a growth mindset. In particular, parents need to understand the role of praise. Praise for children being smart or clever is no better than random praise for breathing or showing up. In fact, such praise can be a detriment to their intellectual growth if it ignores the role of perseverance and pushing through obstacles in success.

When progress and not having reached the goal is an issue, Dweck (2006) suggests we reinforce the concept of "not yet." Teachers should communicate to students that time and persistence will be needed to achieve their goals. Teachers can also reinforce the idea that the brain changes with effort and practice, just as a batter who wants to get better would focus on batting practice. They will allow the student to experience that all-important dopamine release as they activate their SEEKING systems and continue to move closer to the goal.

The importance of effort and practice was confirmed by Dweck (2006) in an experiment she conducted in New York. She asked teachers to tell one group of students "Wow, you're really smart" and another group, "Your hard work paid off." They found that those students who were praised for being smart were less likely to choose challenging tasks or test items so they could be sure of keeping their status as "a smart kid." They gave up when things challenged them and believed that if one was smart, things should be easy for you. They were frustrated and defensive and laid blame on others when things got tough. They often gave up and lacked persistence.

> When the dialogue in education becomes limited to the narrow framework of grades, test scores, and scientifically based research, then a great deal of what education is about gets left behind. Moreover, the excessive concentration on developing uniform standards, implementing a rigorous curriculum, and raising test scores has several negative consequences that are creating more harm to students and teacher than benefits. (Armstrong, 2006, p. 23)

COLLABORATION

One of Professor Hattie's recommendations to increase student achievement is that teachers *must* work collaboratively instead of in isolation (Hattie, 2012).

What we need for student success is to have teachers as well as school leaders who are highly expert, passionate, and inspired, who are collaboratively increasing the effect of their teaching by becoming a professional community of scholars endeavoring to maximize each other's success.

Hattie (2015) suggests that we are not asking teachers to attain dream standards but that "all teachers can make the same impact as our best teachers" (p. 2). None of us would want to go to a doctor who still used a scalpel when a laser would have a safer, better result. Teachers should not be working in isolation but in collaboration so we can examine student data, discuss key issues in student learning, develop and share strategies, and plan for success.

One of the greatest influences on learning is having high expectations for the learner whatever age, student or teacher (Rubie-Davies, 2014). You get what you expect. Some teachers mentally categorize students into levels of low, medium, and high expectations. We have all heard the tale of the teacher who told students that blue-eyed students do very well in school and the brown-eyed students . . . not so much. This was a self-fulfilling prophecy even though there was no truth in the comparison. Mindsets matter (Dweck, 2006). Teachers with "possibility mindsets" should be emulated.

Here are some of the things that Hattie (2015) discovered accelerated students' growth by more than a year:

- Collaborating to evaluate teachers' impact: ES = 0.93
- Setting goals with success criteria: ES = 0.77
- Developing of trust and accepting errors: ES = 0.72
- Providing quality feedback: ES = 0.72
- Balancing surface to deep learning correctly: ES = 0.71
- Providing appropriate challenges and intentional practice to meet goals: ES = 0.60

The only way a school staff can achieve the mission of learning for all students is by working together (DuFour et al., 2010). The purpose of schools is not to teach but to have students learn. So it behooves teachers to discuss their practices and procedures and continue to increase their efficacy in collecting evidence of learning or lack thereof, increasing a repertoire of multi-modal instructional strategies and problem solving around students who need interventions. The synergy that collective focus produces is far greater than what one teacher can muster in isolation; it's *our* students instead of *my* students. Beyond looking at data, we need the collective discussion of analyzing the data and who and what needs attention. The evidence may lead teachers to enrich students who are exceeding expectations or share strategies that have been successful in helping students who are not yet competent. It comes down to these questions:

- What do we want students to know, be able to do?
- How will they demonstrate competency, success?
- What interventions will we make if they are not proficient?
- How will we use the evidence we collect to improve student learning and our collective professional practice?

Discussion is a powerful strategy for student learners and just as powerful for teacher learners to develop knowledge.

Teacher reflection is imperative. According to John Dewey, we learn from experience only if we reflect on experience. The following questions are more powerful in collaboration with others than reflection in isolation.

- How do we know this is working?
- How can we compare "this" with "'that"?
- What is the merit and worth of this influence on learning?
- What is the magnitude of the effect?
- What evidence would convince us that we are wrong?
- Where is the evidence that shows this is superior to other programs?
- Where has anyone seen this practice used so that it produces effective results?
- Do we share a common conception of progress?

MICROTEACHING

High impact in student learning occurs when teachers engage in microteaching (impact of $d = 0.88$).

Microteaching involves teachers videotaping their own classes and reflecting on their performance as teachers and the students' reactions to their lessons. This helps teachers to see learning through the eyes of the learner. It also helps teachers become aware of which strategies they underuse and overuse (e.g., noting the ratio of monologue and dialogue in their classroom as well as the levels and types of feedback used).

HOPE AND SELF-PERCEPTION

Inspired teachers exhibit hope. Snyder et al. (1991) define hope as entailing the motivation and energy to meet personal goals and the perceived capacity to create success capacity to meet them.

Hope has a significant impact on students if teachers make the effort to cultivate it. Studies show that students high in hope have many benefits:

- Greater student achievement
- Better relationships
- More creativity
- Better problem-solving ability

They also show fewer signs of depression and anxiety and stay in school longer. Having hope helps with feelings of self-worth and a positive attitude toward life. Hope helps students develop grit and drive.

Scientists tell us that hope is not wishful thinking. The following characteristics are embedded in a hopeful attitude: having clear and attainable aspirations, and multiple strategies to get there, maintaining a positive perspective, using self-talk, and staying motivated when things are tough.

Teachers are not broken but we could always get better. Why wouldn't we want to get better in a profession we chose and love, as most teachers' altruistic intention is students' success?

Hopefully some of the "do tomorrow" strategies, ideas for further discussion, and long-term implementation goals in this book will help teachers activate learning and make it more visible to everyone—students and teachers alike—for ultimately everyone's success.

References

Absolum, M., Flockton, L., Hattie, J. A. C., Hipkins, R., & Reid, I. (2009). *Directions for assessment in New Zealand*. Wellington, NZ: Ministry of Education.

Achor, S. (2010). *The happiness advantage: The seven principles of positive psychology that fuel success and performance at work*. New York: Crown.

Achor, S. (2013). *Before happiness: The 5 hidden keys to achieving success, spreading happiness, and sustaining positive change*. New York: Crown.

Adams, G., & Engelmann, S. (1996). *Research on direct instruction: 25 years beyond DISTAR*. Seattle, WA: Educational Achievement Systems.

Ainsworth, L. (2003a). *Power standards: Identifying the standards that matter most*. Englewood, CO: Lead + Learn Press.

Ainsworth, L. (2003b). *"Unwrapping" the standards: A simple process to make standards manageable*. Denver, CO: Advanced Learning Press.

Ainsworth, L. (2011). Keynote address, Rigorous Curriculum Design conference, April.

Ainsworth, L. (2015). *Common formative assessments 2.0*. Thousand Oaks, CA: Corwin.

Ainsworth, L., & Viegut, D. (2006). *Common formative assessments: How to connect standards-based instruction and assessment*. Thousand Oaks, CA: Corwin.

Alexander, R. J. (2008). *Essays on pedagogy*. New York: Routledge.

Alexander, R. J. (2008). *Towards dialogic teaching: Rethinking classroom talk* (4th ed.). York, UK: Dialogos.

Alfassi, M., Weissa, I., & Lifshitza, H. (2008). *The efficacy of reciprocal teaching in fostering the reading literacy of students with intellectual disabilities*. Oxford: Routledge.

Allaine, J. K., & Eberhardt, N. C. (2009). *Rti: The forgotten tier—a practical guide for building a data-driven tier 1 instructional process*. Stockton, KS: Rowe.

Amborse, S. A., Bridges, M. W., DiPietro, M., Lovett, M. C., & Norman, M. K. (2010). *How learning works: Seven research-based principles for smart teaching*. San Francisco: Jossey Bass.

AmeriCorps. (2001). Tutoring Outcomes Study, AbT Associates, Corporation for National and Community Service, February. http://www.abtassociates.com/reports/tutoring_0201.pdf

Amitay, S., Irwin, A., & Moore, D. (2006). Discrimination learning induced by training with identical stimuli. *Nature Neuroscience, 9*, 1446–1448.

Anderman, L. H., & Anderman, E. M. (1999). Social predictors of changes in students' achievement goal orientations. *Contemporary Educational Psychology, 25*, 21–37.

Anderson, L., Krathwohl, D., Airasian, P., . . . Wittrock, M. (2001). *A taxonomy for learning, teaching and assessment: A revision of Bloom's taxonomy of educational objectives.* New York: Longman.

Anderson, T. H., & Armbruster, B. B. (1984). Studying. In P. D. Pearson, R. Barr, M. L. Kamil, & P. Mosenthal (Eds.), *Handbook of reading research* (pp. 657–679). New York: Longman.

Antil, L. R., Jenkins, J. R., Wayne, S. K., & Vadasy, P. F. (1998). CL: Prevalence, conceptualizations, and the relation between research and practice. *American Educational Research Journal, 35,* 419–454.

Armstrong, J. S. (2012). Natural learning in higher education. In *Encyclopedia of the sciences of learning.* Heidelberg: Springer

Armstrong, T. (2006). *The best schools: How human development research should inform educational practice.* Arlington, VA: ASCD.

Aronson, E. (1978). *The jigsaw classroom.* Beverly Hills, CA: Sage.

Aronson, J., & Steele, C. M. (2005). Stereotypes and the fragility of human competence, motivation, and self-concept. In C. Dweck & E. Elliot (Eds.), *Handbook of competence and motivation.* New York: Guilford.

ASCD. (n.d.). Visuals. http://www.ascd.org/ASCD/pdf/journals/ed_lead/el200809_smith_pptpresentation.pdf.

Atkinson, R. K., & Renkl, A. (2007). Interactive example-based learning environments: Using interactive elements to encourage effective processing of worked examples. *Educational Psychology Review, 19,* 375–386.

Ausubel, D. P. (1968). *Educational psychology: A cognitive view.* New York: Holt, Rinehart, & Winston.

Bandura, A. (1986). *Social foundations of thought and action: A social cognitive theory.* Englewood Cliffs, NJ: Prentice-Hall.

Bandura, A. (1997). *Self-efficacy: The exercise of control.* New York: W. H. Freeman.

Barkley, F. E., Cross, K. P., & Major, C. H. (2005). *Collaborative learning techniques: A handbook for college faculty.* San Francisco: Jossey-Bass.

Barr, A. S. (1958). Characteristics of successful teachers. *Phi Delta Kappan, 39,* 282, 284.

Battistich, V., Schaps, E., & Wilson, N. (2004). Effects of an elementary school intervention on students' "connectedness" to school and social adjustment during middle school. *The Journal of Primary Prevention, 24*(3), 243–262.

Baumeister, R. F., & Leary, M. R. (1995). The need to belong: Desire for interpersonal attachments as a fundamental human motivation. *Psychological Bulletin, 117*(3), 497–529.

Bellanca, J., & Fogarty, R. (1986). *Catch them thinking: A handbook of classroom strategies.* Arlington Heights, IL: IRI Skylight Training and Publishing.

Bellanca, J., & Fogarty, R. (2003). *Blueprints for achievement in the cooperative classroom* (3rd ed.). Thousand Oaks, CA: Corwin.

Bennett, B., & Rolheiser, C. (2001). *Beyond Monet: The artful science of instructional integration.* Toronto: Author.

Bennett, B., Rolheiser, C., & Stevhan, L. (1991). *Cooperative learning: Where heart meets mind.* Toronto: Educational Connections.

Berndt, T. J. (2004). Children's friendships: Shifts over a half century in perspectives on their development and their effects. *Merrill Palmer Quarterly, 50,* 206–223.

Berry, D., & O'Connor, E. (2009). Behavioral risk, teacher–child relationships, and social skill development across middle childhood: A child-by-environment analysis of change. *Journal of Applied Developmental Psychology, 31*(1), 1–14.

Beyer, B. (1987). *Practical strategies for the teaching of thinking.* Boston: Allyn & Bacon.

Biggs, J., & Tang, C. (2007). *Teaching for quality learning at university.* Maidenhead: Open University Press/McGraw Hill.

Biggs, J. B., & Collis, K. F. (1982). *Evaluating the quality of learning—the SOLO taxonomy.* New York: Academic Press.

Birch, S. H., & Ladd, G. W. (1997). The teacher–child relationship and children's early school adjustment. *Journal of School Psychology, 35*(1), 61–79.

Black, P., & Wiliam, D. (1998a). Assessment and classroom learning. *Assessment in Education: Principles, Policy & Practice, 5*(1), 7–74.

Black, P., & Wiliam, D. (1998b). Inside the black box: Raising standards through classroom assessment. *Phi Delta Kappan,* October.

Black, P., & Wiliam, D. (2009). Developing the theory of formative assessment. *Educational Assessment, Evaluation and Accountability, 21*(1), 5–31.

Black, P., Harrison, C., Lee, C., Marshall, B., & Wiliam, D. (2004). Working inside the black box: Assessment for learning in the classroom. *Phi Delta Kappan, 86*(1), 9–21.

Bloom, B. S. (Ed.) (1956). *Taxonomy of educational objectives. Handbook 1: Cognitive domain.* New York: David McKay.

Blundell, N. (1980). *The world's greatest mistakes.* Portland, OR: Octopus Books.

Bradbury, T., and Greaves, J. (2009). *Emotional intelligence 2.0.* San Diego: Talent Smart.

Brady, M., & Tsay, M. (2010). A case study of cooperative learning and communication pedagogy: Does working in teams make a difference? *Journal of the Scholarship of Teaching and Learning, 10*(2), 78–89.

Bransford, J. D., Brown, A. L., & Cocking, R. R. (Eds.) (2000). *How people learn: Brain, mind, experience, and school.* Washington, DC: National Academy Press.

Brooks, R., & Goldstein, S. (2008). The mindset of teachers capable of fostering resilience in students. *Canadian Journal of School Psychology, 23,* 114–126.

Brophy, J. (1981). Teacher praise: A functional analysis. *Review of Educational Research, 51,* 5–32.

Brown, A. L. (1980). Metacognitive development and reading. In R. S. Spiro, B. B. Bruce, & W. L. Brewer (Eds.), *Theoretical issues in reading comprehension.* Hillsdale, NJ: Erlbaum.

Brown, B. (2005). Adolescent relationships with their peers. In R. M. Lerner and L. Steinberg (Eds.), *Handbook of adolescent psychology.* Hoboken, NJ: Wiley.

Brown, D. (2003). Urban teachers' use of culturally responsive management strategies. *Theory into Practice, 42*(4), 277–282.

Bryk, A. S., & Schneider, B. L. (2002). *Trust in schools: A core resource for improvement.* New York: Russell Sage Foundation.

Buhs, E. S. (2005). Peer rejection, negative peer treatment, and school adjustment: Self-concept and classroom engagement as mediating processes. *Journal of School Psychology, 43,* 407–424.

Buhs, E., Ladd, G., & Herald, S. (2006). Peer exclusion and victimization processes that mediate the relation between peer group rejection and children's classroom engagement and achievement. *Journal of Educational Psychology, 98,* 1–13.

Butler, R. (1988). Enhancing and undermining intrinsic motivation: The effects of task-involving and ego-involving evaluation on interest and performance. *British Journal of Educational Psychology, 58,* 1–14.

Butler, R., & Nisan, M. (1986). Effects of no feedback, task-related comments, and grades on intrinsic motivation and performance. *Journal of Educational Psychology, 78*, 210–216.

Caine, G., Caine, R. N., & Crowell, S. (1994). *Mindshifts: A brain-based process for restructuring schools and renewing education.* Tucson, AZ: Zephyr.

Caine, R. N., & Caine, G. (1994). *Making connections: Teaching and the human brain.* Reading, MA: Addison-Wesley.

Caine, R. N., & Caine, G. (1997). *Education on the edge of possibility.* Alexandria, VA: ASCD.

Carless, D. (2006). Differing perceptions in the feedback process. *Studies in Higher Education, 31*(2), 219–233.

Carroll, A., Houghton, S., Durkin, K., & Hattie, J. A. C. (2009). *Adolescent reputations and risk: Developmental trajectories to delinquency.* New York: Springer.

Carroll, C. W., Silva, M. C., Godek, K. M., Jansen, L. E., & Straight, A. F. (2009). Centromere assembly requires the direct recognition of CENP-A nucleosomes by CENP-N. *Nat. Cell Biol., 11*, 896–902. doi:10. 1038/ncb1899.

Carter, C. (1997). Why reciprocal teaching? *Educational Leadership, 54*, 64.

Casey, B. J. , Somerville, L. H., Gotlib, I. H., et al. (2011). From the cover: Behavioral and neural correlates of delay of gratification 40 years later. *Proceedings of the National Academy of Sciences, 108*(36), 14998–15003. doi:10.1073/pnas .1108561108.

Cawelti, G., Ed. (2004). *Handbook of research on improving student achievement* (3rd ed.). Arlington, VA: Educational Research Service.

Center on Education Policy. (2006). *A public education primer: Basic (and sometimes surprising) facts about the U.S. education system.* Washington, DC: Author.

Chan, C. Y. J. (2006). *The effects of different evaluative feedback on student's self-efficacy in learning.* Unpublished PhD, University of Hong Kong.

Charney, R. (2002). Teaching children to care: Classroom management for ethical and academic growth, K–8. Turner Falls, MA: Northeast Foundation for Children.

Chen, J. (2008). Flow in Games website. http://www.jenovachen.com/flowingames/.

Chiabetta, E. L. A. (1976). Review of Piagetian studies relevant to science instruction at the secondary and college levels. *Science Education, 60*, 253–261.

Chick, N., & Headrick Taylor, K. (2013). Making student thinking visible: Metacognitive practices in the classroom. Center for Teaching, Vanderbilt University, March 11, 2013, http://cft.vanderbilt.edu/2013/03/making-stu dent-thinking-visible-the-impact-of-metacognitive-practice-in-the-classroom.

Clarke, S., Timperley, H., & Hattie J. (2001). *Unlocking formative assessment: Practical strategies for enhancing students' learning in the primary and intermediate classroom.* London: Hodder and Stoughton.

Cloze statements. www. schoolhousetech.com/Vocabulary/?gclid=CK-3h5rR78g CFZKIaQodhggOvw.

Cohen, K. D'A., Neir, E., Luka, J., Lenartowicz, A., Nystrom, L. E., & Cohen, J. D. (2011). Role of prefrontal cortex and the midbrain dopamine system in working memory updating. Department of Chemistry, Princeton Neuroscience Institute; Department of Molecular Biology and Department of Psychology, Princeton University; and Virginia Tech Carilion Research Institute.

Cohn, S. J., George, W. C., & Stanley, J. C. (1979). *Educating the gifted: Acceleration and enrichment.* Baltimore: Johns Hopkins University Press.

Collins, A., Brown, J. S., & Newman, S. (1989). Cognitive apprenticeship: Teaching the craft of reading, writing, and mathematics. In L. Resnick (Ed.), *Knowing, learning and instruction: Essays in honor of Robert Glaserm* (453–494). Hillsdale, NJ: Erlbaum.

Combs, A. W. (1982). Affective education or none at all. *Educational Leadership, 39*(7), 494–497.

Cooper, B., & Cowrie, B. (2010). Collaborative Research of Assessment for Learning; *Teaching and Teacher Education, 26*(4), 979–986.

Cornelius-White, J. (2007). Learner-centered teacher-student relationships are effective: A meta-analysis. *Review of Educational Research, 77*(1), 113–143.

Costa, A., & Kallick, B. (2008). *Learning and leading with habits of mind.* Alexandria, VA: ASCD.

Covey, S. (1989). *The seven habits of highly effective people: Restoring the character ethic.* New York: Simon & Schuster.

Covili, J. (2012). *Going Google: Powerful tools for 21st century learning.* Thousand Oaks, CA: Corwin.

Cowan, G., & Cowan, E. (1980). *Writing.* New York: John Wiley.

Cowie, B., & Bell, B. (1999). A model of formative assessment in science education. *Assessment in Education, 6,* 101–116.

Crooks, T. J. (1988). The impact of classroom evaluation practices on students. *Review of Educational Research, 58*(4), 438–481.

Croninger, R. G., & Lee, V. E. (2001). Social capital and dropping out of high school: Benefits to at-risk students of teachers' support and guidance. *Teachers College Record, 103*(4), 548–581.

Csikszentmihalyi, M. (1990). *Flow: The psychology of optimal experience.* New York: HarperCollins.

Csikszentmihalyi, M. (1993). *The evolving self: A psychology for the third millennium.* New York: HarperCollins.

Damasio, A. R. (1994). *Descartes' error: Emotion, reason, and the human brain.* New York: Putnam.

Damasio, A. (2003). *Looking for Spinoza: Joy, sorrow, and the feeling brain.* Orlando, FL: Harcourt.

Daniels, D. H., & Perry, K. E. (2003). "Learner-centered" according to children. *Theory Into Practice, 42*(2), 102–108.

Darling-Hammond, L. (2006). *Powerful teacher education: Lessons from exemplary programs.* San Francisco: Jossey-Bass.

de Bono, E. (1991). The CoRT thinking program. In A. Costa (Ed.), *Developing minds: Programs for teaching thinking* (rev. ed., Vol. 2, 27–32). Alexandria, VA: ASCD.

de Bruin, A. B. H., Rikers, R. M. J. P., & Schmidt, H. G. (2007). The effect of self-explanation and prediction on the development of principled understanding of chess in novices. *Comtemporary Educational Psychology, 32*(2), 188–205.

Dean, C. B., Hubbell, E. R., Pitler, H., & Stone, B. (2012). *Classroom instruction that works: Research-based strategies for increasing student achievement* (2nd ed.). Alexandria, VA: ASCD.

Deci, E. L., & Ryan, R. M. (1985). *Intrinsic motivation and self-determinaton in human behaviour.* New York: Plenum.

Deci, E., & Ryan, R. (Eds.) (2002). *Handbook of self-determination research.* Rochester, NY: University of Rochester Press.

Dennison, P., & Dennison, G. (1986). *Brain gym: Simple activities for whole-brain learning*. Ventura, CA: Edu-Kinesthetics.

DePorter, B., Reardon, M., & Singer-Nourie, S. (1998). *Quantum teaching*. Boston: Allyn & Bacon.

DeVillar, R. A., & Faltis, C. (1991). Organizing the classroom for communication and learning. In *Computers and cultural diversity: Restructuring for school success* (9). Albany: State University of New York Press.

Dewey, J. (1915/1956). *The child and the curriculum*. Chicago: University of Chicago Press.

Dewey, J. (1938). *Experience and education*. Indianapolis: Kappa Delta Pi.

Diamond, M. C. (1967). Extensive cortical depth measurements and neuron size increases in the cortex of environmentally enriched rats. *Journal of Comparative Neurology, 131*, 357–364.

Diamond, M., & Hopson, J. (1998). *Magic trees of the mind: How to nurture your child's intelligence, creativity, and healthy emotions from birth through adolescence*. New York: Penguin.

Diamond, M. (2001). Response of the brain to enrichment. *Annals of the Brazilian Academy of Sciences, 73*, 61.

Dignath, C., & Buttner, G. (2008). Components of fostering self-regulated learning among students. A meta-analysis on intervention studies at primary and secondary level. *Metacognition and Learning, 3*, 231–264.

Donohue, K. M., Perry, K. E., & Weinstein, R. S. (2003). Teachers' classroom practices and children's rejection by their peers. *Applied Developmental Psychology, 24*, 91–118.

Doolittle, P. E., Hicks, D., Triplett, C. F., Nichols, W. D., & Young, C. A. (2006). Reciprocal teaching for reading comprehension in higher education: A strategy for fostering the deeper understanding of texts. *International Journal of Teaching and Learning in Higher Education, 17*(2), 106–118.

Doyle, M., & Strauss, D. (1976). *How to make meetings work*. New York: Playboy.

Drubach, D. (2000). The brain explained. Upper Saddle River, NJ: Prentice-Hall.

Duckworth, A. L., Peterson, C., Matthews, M. D., & Kelly, D. R. (2007). Grit: Perseverance and passion for long-term goals. *Personality Processes and Individual Differences, 92*(6), 1087–1101.

Duckworth, A. L., & Quinn, P. D. (2009). Development and validation of the Short Grit Scale (GRIT–S). *Journal of Personality Assessment, 91*(2), 166–174.

Duckworth, A. L., & Seligman, M. E. P. (2005). Self-discipline outdoes IQ in predicting academic performance of adolescents. *Psychological Science, 16*, 939–944.

DuFour, R., DuFour, R., Eaker, R., & Many, T. (2010). *Learning by doing: A handbook for professional communities at work*. Bloomington, IN: Solution Tree.

DuFour, R., & Eaker, R. (1998). *Professional learning communities at work: Best practices for enhancing student achievement*. Bloomington, IN: Solution Tree.

Duncan, N. (2007). "Feed-forward": Improving students' use of tutor comments. *Assessment & Evaluation in Higher Education, 32*(3), 271–283.

Dweck, C. S. (1999). *Self-theories: Their role in motivation, personality and development*. Philadelphia: Taylor and Francis/Psychology Press.

Dweck, C. S. (2006). *Mindset: The new psychology of success*. New York: Random House.

Dweck, C. S. (2015). Carol Dweck revists the growth mindset. *Education Week, 35*(5), 20–24.

Eber, P. A., & Parker, T. S. (2007). Assessing student learning: Applying Bloom's taxonomy. *Human Service Education, 27*(1), 45–53.

Elkind, D. (2006). *The hurried child* (25th anniversary ed.). Cambridge, MA: Da Capo Press.

Falchikow, N., & Goldfinch, J. (2000). Student peer assessment in higher education: A meta-analysis comparing peer and teacher marks. *Review of Educational Research, 70*(3), 287–322.

Fendick, F. (1990). *The correlation between teacher clarity of communication and student achievement gain: A meta-analysis.* Unpublished dissertation, University of Florida.

Ford, D. Y. (2005). Welcome all students to room 202: Creating culturally responsive classrooms. *Gifted Child Today, 28*(4), 28–30.

Freedman, J. (2007). *At the heart of leadership: How to get results with emotional intelligence.* San Francisco: Six Seconds.

Frey, N., Fisher, D., & Everlove, S. (2009). *Productive group work: How to engage students, build teamwork, and promote understanding.* Alexandria, VA: ASCD.

Fuchs, D., Fuchs, L. S., & Burish, P. (2005). Peer-assisted learning strategies: An evidence-based practice to promote reading achievement. *Learning Disabilities Research & Practice, 15*(2), 85–91.

Fullan, M. (2013a). *Stratosphere: Integrating technology, pedagogy, and change knowledge.* Toronto: Pearson.

Fullan, M. (2013b). Great to excellent: Launching the next stage of Ontario's education agenda. Retrieved from www.edu.gov.on.ca/eng/document/reports/fullan.html.

Fullan, M. (2013c). The new pedagogy: Students and teachers as learning partners. *Learning Landscapes, 6*(2), 27.

Gallagher, S. A. (1997). Problem-based learning: Where did it come from, what does it do, and where is it going? *Journal for the Education of the Gifted, 20*(4), 332–362.

Galton, M., Morrison, I., & Pell, T. (2000). Transfer and transition in English schools: Reviewing the evidence. *International Journal of Educational Research 33*(4), 341–363.

Gardner, H. (2004). *Frames of mind: The theory of multiple intelligences* (20th anniversay ed.). New York: Basic Books.

Gardner, H. (2006). *Multiple intelligences: New horizons in theory and practice.* New York: Basic Books.

Gay, G. (2002). Preparing for culturally responsive teaching. *Journal of Teacher Education, 53*(2), 106–116.

Geake, J. G. (2009). *The brain at school: Educational neuroscience in the classroom.* New York: McGraw-Hill.

Gee, J. P. (2005). Learning by design: Good video games as learning machines. *E-Learning and Digital Media, 2*(1), 5–16. http://www.wwwords.co.uk/elea/.

Gee, J. P. (2012). Foreword. In C. Steinkuehler, K. Squire, & S. Barab (Eds.), *Games, learning, and society: Learning and meaning in the digital age* (Learning in Doing: Social, Cognitive and Computational Perspectives). Cambridge: Cambridge University Press.

George, W. C., Cohn, S. J., & Stanley, J. C. (1979). *Educating the gifted: Acceleration and enrichment.* Revised and expanded proceedings of the Ninth Annual Hyman Blumberg Symposium on Research in Early Childhood Education, Baltimore.

Gibbs, J. (1998). *Tribus—Spanish edition: Una nueva forma de aprender y convivir juntos.* Cloverdale, CA: CenterSource Systems.

Gibbs, J. (2006a). *Reaching all by creating tribes learning communities.* Cloverdale, CA: CenterSource Systems.

Gibbs, J. (2006b). *Tribes: A new way of learning and being together.* Cloverdale, CA: CenterSource Systems.

Gibbs, J. (2007). *Discovering gifts in middle school learning in a caring culture called tribes.* Cloverdale, CA: CenterSource Systems.

Gibbs, J., & Ushijima, T. (2008). *Engaging all by creating high school learning communities.* Cloverdale, CA: CenterSource Systems.

Giedd, J., Blumenthal, J., Jeffries, N., . . . Rappaport, J. L. (1999). Brain development during childhood and adolescence: A longitudinal MRI study. *Nature Neuroscience, 2,* 861–863.

Glasser, W. (1984). *Control theory in the classroom.* New York: Harper and Row.

Glasser, W. (1990). *Quality school: Managing students without coercion.* New York: Harper and Row.

Glasser, W. (1999). *Choice theory: A new psychology of personal freedom.* New York: Harper Collins.

Glasser, W. (2013). *Take charge of your life: How to get what you need with choice-theory psychology.* iUniverse/Author.

Glossary of Educational Reform. (2014). http://edglossary.org/scaffolding.

Goldin-Meadow, S., & Wagner, S. M. (2005). How our hands help us learn. *Trends in Cognitive Science, 9*(5), 234–241.

Goldin-Meadow, S. (2009). How gesture promotes learning throughout childhood. *Child Development Perspectives, 3*(2), 106–111.

Goldstein, R. Z., Cottone, L. A., Jia, Z., . . . Squires, N. K. (2006). The effect of graded monetary reward on cognitive event-related potentials and behavior in young healthy adults. *International Journal of Psychophysiology, 62*(2), 272–279.

Goleman, D. (1995). *Emotional intelligence.* New York: Bantam Books.

Goleman, D. (2006a). Aiming for the brain's sweet spot. *New York Times* blog, May 12, 2006, http://opinionator.blogs.nytimes.com/2006/12/27/aiming-for-the-brains-sweet-spot/.

Goleman, D. (2006b). Teaching to student strengths: The socially intelligent leader. *Educational Leadership, 64*(1), 76–81.

Good, T. L., & Brophy, J. E. (1995). *Contemporary educational psychology* (5th ed.). White Plains, NY: Longman.

Gopnik, A., Meltzoff, A. N., & Kuhl, P. K. (1999). *The scientist in the crib: What early learning tells us about the mind.* New York: HarperCollins.

Gordon, W. J. J. (1961). *Synectics: The development of creative capacity.* New York: Harper & Row.

Graesser, A. C., Halpern, D. F., Hakel, M. (2008). *25 principles of learning.* Washington, DC: Taskforce on Lifelong Learning at Work and at Home. Retrieved from www.psyc.memphis.edu/learning/whatweknow/index.shtm.

Greenough, W. T., & Volkmar, F. R. (1973). Pattern of dendritic branching in occipital cortex of rats reared in complex environments. *Experimental Neurology, 40,* 491–504.

Gregorc, A. (1982). *Inside styles: Beyond the basics.* Columbia, CT: Gregorc Associates.

Gregory, G. H. (2005). *Differentiating instruction with style.* Thousand Oaks, CA: Corwin.

Gregory, G. H. (2013). *Differentiated instructional strategies for professional development.* Thousand Oaks, CA: Corwin.

Gregory, G. H., & Chapman, C. (2013). *Differentiated instructional strategies: One size doesn't fit all* (3rd ed.). Thousand Oaks, CA: Corwin.

Gregory, G. H., & Kaufeldt, M. (2012). *Think big, Start small: Daily differentiation in a brain-friendly classroom.* Bloomington, IN: Solution Tree.

Gregory, G. H., & Kaufeldt, M. (2015). *The motivated brain: Improving student attention, engagement and perseverance.* Alexandria, VA: ASCD.

Gregory, G. H., & Kuzmich, L. (2005). *Differentiated literacy strategies for student growth and achievement in grades 7–12.* Thousand Oaks, CA: Corwin.

Gregory, G. H., & Kuzmich, L. (2007). *Teacher teams that get results: 61 strategies for sustaining and renewing professional learning communities.* Thousand Oaks, CA: Corwin.

Gregory, G. H., & Kuzmich, L. (2010). *Student teams that get results: Teaching tools for the differentiated classroom.* Thousand Oaks, CA: Corwin.

Gregory, G. H., & Kuzmich, L. (2014). *Data driven differentiation in the standards based classroom* (2nd ed.). Thousand Oaks, CA: Corwin.

Gregory, G. H., & Parry, T. (2006). *Designing brain-compatible learning* (rev. ed.). Thousand Oaks, CA: Corwin.

Gurian, M. (2001). *Boys and girls learn differently: A guide for teachers and parents.* San Francisco: Jossey-Bass.

Hallowell, E. (2011). *SHINE: Using brain science to get the best from your people.* Boston: Harvard Business Review Press.

Hamre, B., & Pianta, R. (2001). Early teacher–child relationships and the trajectory of children's school outcomes through eighth grade. *Child Development, 72,* 625–638.

Harelli, S., & Hess, U. (2008). When does feedback about success in schools hurt? The role of causal attributions. *Social Psychology in Education 11,* 250–272.

Hart, L. (1983). *Human brain and human learning.* New York: Longman.

Haskins, W. (2000). Ethos and pedagogical communication: Suggestions for enhancing credibility in the classroom. *Current Issues in Education, 3*(4).

Hastie, S. (2011). *Teaching students to set goals: Strategies, commitment and monitoring.* Unpublished doctoral dissertation, University of Auckland, New Zealand.

Hattie, J. (2009). *Visible learning.* New York: Routledge.

Hattie, J. (2012). *Visible learning for teachers: Maximizing impact on learning.* New York: Routledge.

Hattie, J. (2015). *What works best in education: The politics of collaborative expertise.* London: Pearson.

Hattie, J., & Timperley, H. (2007). The power of feedback. *Review of Educational Research, 77*(1), 81–112.

Hattie, J., & Yates, G. (2014). *Visible learning and the science of how we learn.* New York: Routledge.

Haystead, M. W., & Marzano, R. J. (2009). *Meta-analytic synthesis of studies conducted at Marzano Research Laboratory on instructional strategies.* Englewood, CO: Marzano Research Laboratory.

Hebb, D. (1949/2002). *The organization of behaviour: The neuropsychological theory.* Mahwah, NJ: Erlbaum.

Heritage, H. M., Kim, J., & Vendlinski, R. (2008). *Measuring teachers' mathematical knowledge for teaching* (SCE Technical Report in Preparation). Los Angeles:

Center for the Study of Evaluation and National Center for Research on Evaluation, Standards, and Student testing.

Higgins, R., Hartley, P., & Skelton, A. (2001). Getting the message across: The problem of communicating assessment feedback. *Teaching in Higher Education, 6*(2), 269–274.

Hill, S., & Hancock, J. (1993). *Reading and writing communities*. Armadale, Australia: Eleanor Curtain Publishing.

Hirschy, A. S., & Braxton, J. M. (2004). Effects of student classroom incivilities on students. *New Directions for Teaching and Learning, 99*, 67–76.

Holroyd, C. B., Larsen, J. T., & Cohen, J. D. (2004). Context dependence of the event-related brain potential associated with reward and punishment. *Psychophysiology, 41*(2), 245–253.

Hord, S., Rutherford, W. I., Huling-Austin, I., & Hall, G. E. (1987). *Taking charge of change*. Alexandria. VA: ASCD.

Huang, Z. (1991). *A meta-analysis of student self-questioning strategies*. Unpublished PhD dissertation, Hofstra University, New York.

Hunter, M. (1967). *Teach more—faster!* El Segundo, CA: TIP Publications.

Hunter, M. (1982). *Mastery teaching: Increasing instructional effectiveness in elementary, secondary schools, colleges, and universities*. Thousand Oaks, CA: Corwin.

Hunter, R. (2004). *Madeline Hunter's mastery teaching: Increasing instructional effectiveness in elementary and secondary schools* (rev. ed.). Thousand Oaks, CA: Corwin.

Hythecker, V. I., Dansereau, D. F., & Rocklin, T. R. (1988). An analysis of the processes influencing the structured dyadic learning environment. *Educational Psychologist, 23*, 23–37.

Inoue, N. (2007). Why face a challenge? The reason behind intrinsically motivated students' spontaneous choice of challenging tasks. *Learning and Individual Differences, 17*(3), 251–259.

Jagust, W. J., & Budinger, T. F. (1992). New neuroimaging techniques for investigating of brain-behavior relationships. *Nida Res Monogr, 124*, 95–115.

Jensen, E. (1998). *Teaching with the brain in mind*. Alexandria, VA: ASCD.

Johnson, D., Johnson, R., & Holubec, E. (1998). *Cooperation in the classroom*. Edina, MN: Interaction.

Johnson, D. W. (1981). Student-student interaction: The neglected variable in education, *Educational Researcher, 10*, 5–10.

Johnson, D. W., & Johnson, R. (1981). Effects of cooperative and individualistic learning experiences on interethnic interaction. *Journal of Educational Psychology, 73*, 454–459.

Johnson, D. W., & Johnson, R. T. (1989). *Cooperation and competition: Theory and research*. Edina, MN: Interaction.

Johnson, D. W., & Johnson, R. T. (1994). An overview of cooperative learning. In J. Thousand, A. Villa and A. Nevin (Eds.), *Creativity and collaborative learning*. Baltimore: Brookes.

Johnson, D. W., & Johnson, R. (2009). An educational psychology success story: Social interdependence theory and cooperative learning. *Educational researcher, 38*(5), 365–379.

Johnson, D. W., Johnson, R. T., & Sharan, S. (1990). Cooperative learning and achievement. In S. Sharan (Ed.) *Cooperative learning: Theory and research* (23–37). New York: Praeger.

Johnson, D. W., Johnson, R., & Smith, K. (1996). *Academic controversy: Enriching college instruction through intellectual conflict.* ASHE-ERIC Higher Education Report, Vol. 25, No. 3. Washington, DC: The George Washington University, Graduate School of Education and Human Development.

Johnson, D. W., Johnson, R. T., & Smith, K. (1998). Cooperative learning returns to college: What evidence is there that it works? *Change*, July-August, 27–35.

Johnson, D. W., Johnson, R. T., & Smith, K. A. (1991). *Active learning: Cooperation in the college classroom.* Edina, MN: Interaction.

Jones, C. (1994). *Mistakes that worked: 40 inventions and how they came to be.* New York: Delacorte.

Joyce, B., & Showers, B. (2002). *Student achievement through staff development* (3rd ed.). Alexandria, VA: ASCD.

Kagan, S. (1991). *Cooperative learning: Resources for teachers.* Laguna Niguel, CA: Resources for Teachers.

Kagan, S. (1992). *Cooperative learning.* San Clemente, CA: Kagan Publishing.

Kagan, S. (1995). *We can talk: Cooperative learning in the elementary ESL classroom.* Eric Clearinghouse on Language and Linguistics, ED382035.

Kalkowski, P. (1995). *Peer and cross-age tutoring.* School Improvement Research Series. http://www.nwrel.org/scpd/sirs/9/c018.html.

Kaplan, F., & Oudeyer, P. Y. (2007). In search of the neural circuits of intrinsic motivation. *Frontiers in Neuroscience, 1*(1), 225–236. doi: 10.3389/neuro.01/1.1.017.2007.

Kaplan, S., Gould, B., & Siegel, V. (1995). *The flip book.* Educator to Educator.

Kessels, U., Warner, L. M., Holle, J., & Hannover, B. (2008). Threat to identity through positive feedback about academic performance. *Zeitschrift fur Entwicklungspsychologie und Padagogische Psychologie, 40*(1), 22–31.

Kirby, E. D., Muroy, S. E., Sun, W. G., . . . Kaufer, D. (2013). Acute stress enhances adult rat hippocampal neurogenesis and activation of newborn neurons via secreted astrocytic FGF2. doi: http://dx.doi.org/10.7554/eLife.00362.

Klem, A. M., & Connell, J. P. (2004). Relationships matter: Linking teacher support to student engagement and achievement. *Journal of School Health, 74*(7), 262–273.

Kohn, A. (1993/1999). *Alfie: Punished by rewards.* Boston: Houghton Mifflin.

Kohn, A. (2014). The myth of the spoiled child: Challenging the conventional wisdom about children and parenting. *EdWeek, 34*(3), 25.

Kohn, A. (2004). Challenging students . . . and how to have more of them. *Phi Delta Kappan*, November.

Koutselini, M. (2009). Teacher misconceptions and understanding of cooperative learning: An intervention study. *Journal of Classroom Interaction, 43*(2), 34–44.

Krashen, S. (1982). *Principles and practice in second language acquisition.* Oxford: Pergamon Press.

Kulik, C. L. C., & Kulik, J. A. (1984). *Effects of ability grouping on elementary school pupils: A meta-analysis.* Paper presented at the Annual Meeting of the American Psychological Association, Toronto.

Kunsch, C. A., Jitendra, A. K., & Sood, S. (2007). The effects of peer-mediated instruction in mathematics for students with learning problems: A research synthesis. *Learning Disabilities Research and Practice, 22*, 1–12.

LaFrance, M (2011). *Lip service: Smiles in life, death, trust, lies, work, memory, sex and politics.* New York: Norton.

Langer, F. J. (1989). *Mindfulness.* Reading, MA: Addison-Wesley.

Langer, R. (1989). Biomaterials in Controlled Drug Delivery: New perspectives from biotechnological advances. *Pharm. Techn., 13,* 22–30.

Leahy, S., Lyon, C., Thompson, M., & Wiliam, D. (2005). Classroom assessment: Minute-by-minute and day-by-day. *Educational Leadership, 63*(3), 18–24.

Levin, B. (2008). *How to change 5000 schools.* Cambridge, MA: Harvard Education Press.

Levine, M. (1990). *All kinds of minds.* Cambridge, MA: Educators Publishing Service.

Levy-Tossman, I., Kaplan, A., & Assor, A. (2007). Academic goal orientations, multiple goal profiles, and friendship intimacy among early adolescents. *Contemporary Educational Psychology, 32,* 231–252.

Lie, A. (2008). *Cooperative learning: Changing paradigms of college teaching.* http://faculty.petra.ac.id/anitalie/LTM/cooperative_learning.htm.

Locke, E. A., & Latham, G. P. (1990). Building a practically useful theory of goal setting and task motivation: A 35-year odyssey. *American Psychologist, 57*(9), 705–717.

Loh, K. K., & Kanai, R. (2014). High media multi-tasking is associated with smaller gray-matter density in the anterior cingulate cortex. *Plos One,* September 24.

Lou, Y., Abrami, P. C., & d'Apollonia, S. (2001). Small group and individual learning with technology: A meta-analysis. *Review of Educational Research, 71*(3), 449–521.

Lou, Y., Abrami, P. C., Spence, J. C., Poulsen, C., Chambers, B., & d'Appolonia, S. (1996). Within-class grouping: A meta-analysis. *Review of Educational Research, 66*(4), 423–458.

Lyman, F., & McTighe, J. (1988). Cueing thinking in the classroom: The promise of theory-embedded tools. *Educational Leadership,* April 7.

Marshmallow test points to biological basis for delayed gratification. (2011) *Science Daily,* September 1.

Martin, A. J. (2006). Personal bests (PBs): A proposed multidimensional model and empirical analysis. *British Journal of Educational Psychology, 76,* 803–825.

Marzano, R. J. (2003). *Classroom management that works: Research-based strategies for every teacher.* Alexandria, VA: ASCD.

Marzano, R. J. (2006). *Classroom assessments and grading that work.* Alexandria, VA: ASCD.

Marzano, R. J. (2009). *Designing and teaching learning goals and objectives.* Englewood, CO: Marzano Research Laboratory.

Marzano, R. J. (2010). Meeting students where they are. *Education Leadership, 67*(5), 71–72.

Marzano, R. J. (n.d.). Proficiency Scales for the Common Core. Solution Tree Webinar. http://pages.solution-tree.com/rs/solutiontree/images/LOWRES_35MEU_MRL_ProficiencyScalesForCC_webinar.pdf.

Marzano, R. J., & Brown, J. L. (2009). *A handbook for the art and science of teaching.* Alexandria, VA: ASCD.

Marzano, R. J., & Pickering, D. L. (2005). *Building academic vocabulary: Teacher's manual.* Alexandria, VA: ASCD.

Marzano, R. J., Pickering, D. J., & Pollock, J. E. (2001). *Classroom instruction that works: Research-based strategies for increasing student achievement.* Alexandria, VA: ASCD.

Marzano, R. J., Yanoski, D. C., Hoegh, J. K., & Simms, J. A. (2012). *Using Common Core Standards to enhance classroom instruction and assessment.* Bloomington, IN: Solution Tree.

Maslow, A. (1968). *Toward a psychology of being* (2nd ed.). New York: Van Nostrand.

Mayer, R. E. (1996). Learning strategies for making sense out of expository text: The SOI model for guiding three cognitive processes in knowledge construction. *Educational Psychology Review, 8*(4), 357–371.

Mayer, R. E. (2008). *Learning and instruction.* (2nd ed.). Upper Saddle River, NJ: Prentice Hall.

Mayer, R. E. (2010). Applying the science of learning to instruction in school subjects. In R. Marzano (Ed.), *On excellence in teaching* (93–112). Bloomington, IN: Solution Tree Press.

McCarthy, B. (2000). *About teaching: 4MAT in the classroom.* Wauconda, IL: About Learning.

McCombs, B. L., & Whisler, J. S. (1997). *The learner-centered classroom and school.* San Francisco: Jossey-Bass.

McIntyre, D., Peddler, D., & Rudduck, J. (2005). Pupil voice: Comfortable and uncomfortable learning for teachers. *Research Papers in Education, 20*(2), 149–168.

Mcleod, S. A. (2007). Vygotsky. http://www.simplypsychology.org/vygotsky.html.

McTaggart, L. (2008). *The intention experiment: Using your thoughts to change your life and the world.* New York: Atria Books.

McTighe, J., & Wiggins, G. (2013). *Essential questions. Opening doors to student understanding.* Alexandria, VA: ASCD.

Medina, J. (2008). *Brain rules: 12 principles for surviving and thriving at work, home, and school.* Seattle: Pear Press.

Meehan, H. (1979). What time is it, Denise? Asking known information questions in classroom practice. *Theory into Practice, 18,* 285–294.

Metlife Foundation. (2012). MetLife Survey of the American Teacher. https://www.metlife.com/metlife-foundation/about/survey-american-teacher.html?WT.mc_id=vu1101.

Miller, G. A. (1956). The magic number seven plus or minus two: some limits on our capacity to process information. *Psychological Review, 63*(2), 81–97.

Mischel, W., Ebbeson, E. B., & Raskoff Zeiss, A. (1972). Cognitive and attentional mechanisms in delay of gratification. *Journal of Personality and Social Psychology, 21*(2), 204–218.

Mischel, W., Shoda, Y., & Rodriguez, M. L. (1989). Delay of gratification in children. *Science, 244,* 933–938.

Montgomery, W. (2000). Literature discussion in the elementary school classroom: Developing cultural understanding. *Multicultural Education, 8*(1), 33–36.

Moss, C. M., & Brookhart, S. M. (2012). *Learning targets: Helping students aim for understanding in today's lesson.* Alexandria, VA: ASCD.

Multitasking May Not Mean Higher Productivity. (2009). *Talk of the Nation,* National Public Radio. http://www.npr.org/templates/story/story.php?storyId=112334449.

Murphy, C. (2011). *Why games work and the science of learning.* McLean, VA: Alion Science and Technology Corp.

Naested, I., Potvin, B., & Waldron, P. (2004). *Understanding the landscape of teaching.* Toronto: Pearson Education.

Naglieri, J. A., & Das, J. P. (1997a). *Cognitive assessment system. Administration and scoring manual—interpretive handbook.* Itasca, IL: Riverside.

Naglieri, J. A., & Das, J. P. (1997b). Intelligence revised: The planning, attention, simultaneous, successive (PASS) cognitive processing theory. In R. F. Dillon (Ed.), *Handbook on testing* (136–163). Westport, CT: Greenwood Press.

Nakamura, J., & Csikszentmihalyi, M. (2002). The concept of flow. In C. R. Snyder & S. J. Lopez (Eds.), *Handbook of positive psychology* (89–105). Oxford: Oxford University Press.

National Council of Teachers of Mathematics. (2007). *Common Core State Standards.* http://www.nctm.org/ccssm.

National Institute of Mental Health (NIMH). (2001). *Teenage brain: A work in progress—A brief overview of research into brain development during adolescence.* Rockville, MD: NIMH.

National Research Council. (2003). *Engaging schools: Fostering high school students' motivation to learn.* Atlanta: National Academies Press.

Neumann, A. (2006). Professing passion: Emotion in the scholarship of professors at research universities. *American Educational Research Journal, 43*(3), 381–424.

Newell, A. (1990). *Unified theories of cognition.* Cambridge, MA: Harvard University Press.

Nicol, D., & Draper, S. (2008). *Redesigning written feedback to students when class sizes are large.* Paper presented at the Improving University Teachers Conference, July 29–August 1, Glasgow.

Nicol, D., & Macfarlane-Dick, D. (2005). *Rethinking formative assessment in HE: A theoretical model and seven principles of good feedback practice.* Gloucester, UK: Quality Assurance Agency for Higher Education.

Nieto, S. (1996). *Affirming diversity: The sociopolitical context of education.* White Plains, NY: Longman.

Nolen-Hoeksema, S., & Hilt, L. M. (Eds.) (2012). *Handbook of depression in adolescents.* New York: Routledge.

Nottingham, J. (2012). *Labels limit learning.* Video presentation. tedxtalks.ted.com/video/James-Nottingham-on-Labels-Limi.

Nuthall, G. A. (2007). *The hidden lives of learners.* Wellington: New Zealand Council for Educational Research.

O'Keefe, J., & Nadel, L. (1978). *The hippocampus as a cognitive map.* Oxford: Clarendon Press.

Oczuks, L. (2003). *Reciprocal teaching at work: Strategies for improving reading comprehension.* Newark, DE: International Reading Association.

Ogle, D. M. (1986). K-W-L: A teaching model that develops active reading of expository text. *Reading Teacher, 39,* 564–570.

Ophir, E., Nass, C. I., & Wagner, A. D. (2009). Cognitive in media multitaskers. *Proceedings of the National Academy of Sciences USA, 106*(37), 15583–15587.

Ornstein, R., & Thompson, R. (1984). *The amazing brain.* Boston: Houghton Mifflin.

Paley, V. (1992). *You can't say you can't play.* Cambridge, MA: Harvard University Press.

Palincsar, A. S. (1986). *Reciprocal teaching: Teaching reading as thinking.* Oak Brook, IL: North Central Regional Educational Laboratory.

Palincsar, A. S., & Brown, A. (1984). Reciprocal teaching of comprehension fostering and comprehension monitoring activities. *Cognition and Instruction, 1*(2), 117–175.

Palincsar, A. S., Ransom, K., & Derber, S. (1989). Collaborative research and development of reciprocal teaching. *Educational Leadership, 46*(4), 37–40.

Panksepp, J. (1998). *Affective neuroscience: The foundations of human and animal emotions.* New York: Oxford University Press.

Panksepp, J., & Biven, L. (2012). *The archaeology of mind: Neuroevolutionary origins of human emotions.* New York: Norton.

Parker, J. (2006). Developing perceptions of competence during practice learning. *British Journal of Social Work, 36* (6), 1017–1036.

Partnership for 21st Century Schools. (n.d.). *Learning for the 21st century guide.* Washington, DC. http://www.p21.org/storage/documents/P21_Report.pdf.

Peake, P. K., & Rodriguez, M. L. (2000). Regulating the interpersonal self: Strategic self-regulation for coping with rejection sensitivity. *Journal of Personality and Social Psychology, 79*(5), 776–792.

Pecina, S., & Berridge, K. (2013). Dopamine or opioid stimulation of nucleus accumbens similarly amplify cue-triggered "wanting" for reward. *European Journal of Neuroscience, 37*, 1529–1540.

Peer Research Laboratory. (2002). *Peer tutoring works both ways.* National Self-Help Clearinghouse, http://www.selfhelpweb.org/peer.html.

Perkins, D. (1991). What creative thinking is. In A. Costa (Ed.), *Developing minds: A resource book for teaching thinking* (rev. ed., vol. 1, 85–88). Alexandria, VA: ASCD.

Perkins, D. (1995). *Smart schools.* New York: Free Press.

Perry, K. E., & Weinstein, R. S. (1998). The social context of early schooling and children's school adjustment. *Educational Psychologist, 33*(4), 177–194.

Peterson, R. (2005). Investing lessons from neuroscience: fMRI of the reward system. *Brain Research Bulletin, 67* (5), 391–397.

Peterson, R. (2007). *Inside the investor's brain: The power of mind over money.* New York: Wiley.

Petty, G. (2009). *Evidence-based teaching: A practical approach.* Cheltenham, UK: Nelson Thomes.

Piaget, J. (1965/1941). *The child's conception of number.* New York: Norton.

Piaget, J. (1970). *Genetic epistemology.* New York: Norton.

Piaget, J. (1971/1967). *Biology and knowledge: An essay on the relations between organic regulations and cognitive processes* (B. Walsh, Trans.). Chicago: University of Chicago Press.

Piaget, J. (1972). *The psychology of the child.* New York: Basic Books.

Piaget, J. (1978/1976). *Behavior and evolution* (D. Nicholson-Smith, Trans.). New York: Random House.

Piaget, J. (1990). *The child's conception of the world.* New York: Littlefield Adams.

Pianta, R. C. (1999). *Enhancing relationships between children and teachers.* Washington, DC: American Psychological Association.

Pianta, R. C., & Hamre, B. (2001). *Students, teachers, and relationship support [STARS]: User's guide.* Lutz, FL: Psychological Assessment Resources.

Pillay, S. (2011). *The science behind the law of attraction: A step-by-step guide to putting the brain science behind the law of attraction to work for you.* Cambridge, MA: NeuroBusiness Group.

Pilonieta, P., & Medina, A. L. (2009). Reciprocal teaching for the primary grades: "We can do it too!" *The Reading Teacher, 63* (2), 120–129.

Popham, J. (2013). *Classroom assessment: What teachers need to know* (7th ed.). Boston: Pearson.

Poskitt, J. (2004). Book review: Clarke, S., Timperley, H., & Hattie J. (2003). Unlocking formative assessment: Practical strategies for enhancing students' learning in the primary and intermediate classroom (NZ ed.). Auckland, Hodder Moa Beckett. *New Zealand Journal of Teachers' Work, 1*(2), 116–118.

Posner, M. I., & Rothbart, M. K. (2007). Research on attention networks as a model for the integration of psychological science. *Annual Review of Psychology, 58,* 1–23.

Pratt, S., & George, R. (2005). Transferring friendships: Girls' and boys' friendships in the transition from primary to secondary school. *Children & Society, 19*(1), 16–26.

Prensky, M. (2001). *Digital game-based learning.* New York: McGraw-Hill.

Qin, Z., Johnson, D. W., & Johnson, R. T. (1995). Cooperative versus competitive efforts and problem solving. *Review of Educational Research, 65*(2), 129–143.

Quaglia, R. J., & Corso, M. J. (2014). *Student voice: The instrument of change.* Thousand Oaks, CA: Corwin.

Ratey, J. J. (2008). *Spark: The revolutionary new science of exercise and the brain.* New York: Little, Brown.

Raz, A., & Buhle, J. (2006). Typologies of attentional networks. *Nature Reviews Neuroscience, 7,* 367–379.

Reeve, J. (1996). The interest-enjoyment distinction in intrinsic motivation. *Motivation and Emotion, 13,* 83–103.

Reeve, J. (2002). Self-determination theory applied to educational settings. In E. L. Deci & R. M. Ryan (Eds.), *Handbook of self-determination research* (183–203). Rochester, NY: University of Rochester Press.

Reeves, D. B. (2002). *Making standards work: How to implement standards-based assessments in the classroom, school, and district* (3rd ed.). Denver, CO: Advanced Learning Press.

Rimm-Kaufman, S. E., & Chiu, Y. I. (2007). Promoting social and academic competence in the classroom: An intervention study examining the contribution of the responsive classroom approach. *Psychology in the Schools, 44*(4), 397–413.

Rimm-Kaufman, S. E., Early, D. M., Cox, M. J., Saluja, G., Pianta, R. C., Bradley, R. H., & Payne, C. (2002). Early behavioral attributes and teachers' sensitivity as predictors of competent behavior in the kindergarten classroom. *Journal of Applied Developmental Psychology, 23*(4), 451–470.

Robbins, P. M., Gregory, G. H., & Herndon, L. E. (2000). *Thinking inside the block schedule: Strategies for teaching in extended periods of time.* Thousand Oaks, CA: Corwin.

Rosenshine, B., & Meister, C. (1994). Reciprocal teaching: A review of the research. *Review of Educational Research, 64*(4), 479–530.

Rowe, M. B. (1986). Wait time: Slowing down may be a way of speeding up! *Educator,* Spring, 43.

Rubie-Davies, C. M. (2014). *Becoming a high expectation teacher: Raising the bar.* London: Routledge.

Rubinstein, J. S., Meyer, D. E., & Evans, J. E. (2001). Executive control of cognitive processes in task switching. *Journal of Experimental Psychology: Human Perception and Performance, 27*(4), 763–797.

Rudasill, K. M., Rimm-Kaufman, S. E., Justice, L. M., & Pence, K. (2006). Temperament and language skills as predictors of teacher-child relationship quality in preschool. *Early Education and Development, 17*(2), 271–291.

Rutledge. P. (2012). The positive side of video games: Part III. The Media Psychology Blog. http://rutledge103.rssing.com/browser.php?indx=9357935&item=1.

Sadler, D. R. (1989). Formative assessment and the design of instructional systems. *Instructional Science, 18*(2), 119–144.

Salamone, J. D. (1994). The involvement of nucleus accumbens dopamine in appetitive and aversive motivation. *Behavioural Brain Research, 61*(2), 117–133.

Salamone, J. D., & Correa, M. (2002). Motivational views of reinforcement: Implications for understanding the behavioral functions of nucleus accumbens dopamine. *Behavioural Brain Research, 137*, 3–25.

Saltzman, A. (n.d.). *Mindfulness: A guide for teachers.* http://www.pbs.org/thebuddha/teachers-guide.

Sanderson, D. (2003). Engaging highly transient students. *Education, 123*(3), 600–605.

Sapolsky, R. M. (1998). *Why zebras don't get ulcers.* New York: Freeman.

Sarason, S. (1971). *The culture of the school and the problem of change.* Boston: Allyn & Bacon.

Sarason, S. (1990). *The predictable failure of school reform.* San Francisco: Jossey-Bass.

Schaffer, O. (2013). Crafting fun user experiences: A method to facilitate flow. *Human Factors International Whitepaper.* Retrieved from http://www.humanfactors.com/whitepapers/crafting_fun_ux.asp.

Schlam, N. L., Wilson, S., Yuichi, M., Mischel, W., & Ayduk, O. (2013). Preschoolers' delay of gratification predicts their body mass 30 years later. *The Journal of Pediatrics, 162*, 90–93.

Seitz, A. R., & Watanabe, T. (2003). Psychophysics: Is subliminal learning really passive? *Nature, 422*(36).

Senge, P. M., Roberts, C., Ross, R. B., Smith, B. J., & Kleiner, A. (1994). *The fifth discipline fieldbook: Strategies and tools for building a learning organization.* New York: Doubleday/Currency.

Shachar, H., & Sharon, S. (1994). Talking, relating, and achieving: Effects of cooperative learning circles. *Instructional Science, 19*, 445–466.

Shachtman, T. (1995). *The inarticulate society: Eloquence and culture in America.* New York: Simon & Schuster.

Sharan, D., & Hertz-Lazarowitz, R. (1980). A group investigation method of cooperative learning in the classroom. In S. Sharan, P. Hare, C. D. Webb, & R. Hertz-Lazarowitz (Eds.), *Cooperatioin in education* (14–46). Provo, UT: Brigham Young University Press.

Sharan, S. (1980). Cooperative learning in small groups: Recent methods and effects on achievement, attitudes and ethnic relations. *Review of Educational Research, 50*(2), 241–271.

Sharan, S., & Sharan, Y. (1992). *Expanding cooperative learning through group investigation.* Colchester, VT: Teachers College Press.

Sharan, Y., & Sharan, S. (1990). Group investigation expands cooperative learning. *Educational Leadership, 47*(4), 17–21.

Sharon, S. (1994). *Handbook of cooperative learning methods.* Westport, CT: Greenwood Press.

Sheets, R. H., & Gay, G. (1996). Student perceptions of disciplinary conflict in ethnically diverse classrooms. *NASSP Bulletin*, May, 84–93.

Shernoff, D. J., & Csikszentmihalyi, M. (2009). Flow in schools: Cultivating engaged learners and optimal learning environments. In R. C. Gilman, E. S. Heubner & M. J. Furlong (Eds.), *Handbook of positive psychology in schools* (131–145). New York: Routledge.

Shernoff, D., Csikszentmihalyi, M., Shneider, B., & Shernoff, E. S. (2003). Student engagement in high school classrooms from the perspective of flow theory. *School Psychology Quarterly, 18*, 158–176.

Shoda, Y., Mischel, W., & Peake, P. K. (1990). Predicting adolescent cognitive and self-regulatory competencies from preschool delay of gratification: Identifying diagnostic conditions. *Developmental Psychology, 26*(6), 978–986.

Shute, V. J. (2008). Focus on formative feedback. *Review of Educational Research, 78*(1), 153–189.

Skinner, B. F. (1968). *The technology of teaching.* New York: Appleton-Century-Crofts.

Slater, W. H., & Horstman, F. R. (2002). Teaching reading and writing to struggling middle school and high school students: The case for reciprocal teaching. *Preventing School Failure, 46*(4), 163.

Slavin, R. E. (1990). *Cooperative learning: Theory, research, and practice.* Englewood Cliffs, NJ: Prentice Hall.

Slavin, R. E. (1994). *Collaborative learning: Theory, research and practice* (2nd ed.). Boston: Allyn & Bacon.

Slavin, R. E. (1995). *Cooperative learning.* Boston: Allyn & Bacon.

Smith, R., & Lambert, M. (2008). Assuming the best. *The Positive Classroom, 66*(1), 16–21.

Smith S. L. (2009). *Academic target setting: Formative use of achievement data.* Unpublished doctoral thesis, University of Auckland.

Snyder, C. R., Harris, C., Anderson, J. R., (1991). The will and the ways: Development and validation of an individual-differences measure of hope. *Journal of Personality and Social Psychology, 60*, 570–585.

Solms, M., & Panksepp, J. (2012). The "id" know more than the "ego" admits: Neuropsychoanalytic and primal consciousness perspectives on the interface between affective and cognitive neuroscience. *Brain Sciences, 2*, 147–175.

Sousa, D. (2006). *How the brain learns: A classroom teacher's guide* (3rd ed.). Thousand Oaks, CA: Corwin.

Sowell, E. R., Thompson, P. M., Holmes, C. J., Jernigan, T. L., & Toga, A. W. (1999). In vivo evidence for post-adolescent brain maturation in frontal and striatal regions. *Nature Neuroscience, 2*(10), 859–861.

State of Kentucky. (2014). Student Voice Survey materials. http://education.ky.gov/teachers/PGES/TPGES/Documents/2014-15%20Student%20Voice%20Survey%20Guide.pdf.

Steele, C. F. (2009). *The inspired teacher: How to know one, grow one or be one.* Arlington, VA: ASCD.

Sternberg, R. J. (1984). *Beyond I.Q.: A triarchic theory of human intelligence.* New York: Cambridge University Press.

Sternberg, R. J. (2006). Creativity is a habit. *Education Week,* February 22, 47, 64.

Sternberg, R., & Wagner, R. (1982). *Understanding intelligence: What's in it for education?* Paper submitted to the National Commission on Excellence in Education.

Sternberg, Robert J. (1996). *Successful intelligence: How practical and creative intelligence determines success in life.* New York: Simon & Schuster.

Stiggins, R. (2014). *Revolutionize assessment, empower students, inspire learning.* Thousand Oaks, CA: Corwin.

Stiggins, R., Arter, J. A., & Chappuis, J. (2007). *Classroom assessment for student learning: Doing it right—using it well.* Washington, DC: Educational Testing Service.

Storm, E., & Tecott, L. H. (2005). Social circuits: peptidergic regulation of mammalian social behavior. *Neuron, 47*(4), 483–486.

Stricklin, K. (2011). Hands-on reciprocal teaching: A comprehension technique. *The Reading Teacher, 64* (8).

Sweller, J. (1988). Cognitive load during problem solving: Effects on learning. *Cognitive Science, 12*(2), 257–285.

Sweller, J. (2008). Cognitive load theory and the use of educational technology. *Educational Technology, 48*(I), 32–34.

Synder, C. R., Harris, C., Anderson, J. R., et al. (1991). The will and the ways: Development and validation of an individual-differences measure of hope. *Journal of Personality and Social Psychology, 60,* 570–585.

Taras, M. (2003). To feedback or not to feedback in student self-assessment. *Assessment and Evaluation in Higher Education, 28*(5), 549–565.

Thorndike, E. (1932). *The fundamentals of learning.* New York: Columbia University Press.

Thousand, J., Villa, A., & Nevin A. (Eds). (2002). *Creativity and collaborative learning.* Baltimore, MD: Brookes.

Toga, A., & Thompson, P. (2003). Temporal dynamics of brain anatomy. *Annual Review of Biomedical Engineering, 5,* 119–145.

Topping, K. (2008). *Peer-assisted learning: A practical guide for teachers.* Newton, MA: Brookline Books.

Tortora, G., & Grabowski, S. (1996). *Principles of anatomy and physiology* (8th ed.). New York: Harper Collins.

Tough, P. (2011). What if the secret to success is failure? *The New York Times,* September 14. www.nytimes.com/2011/09/18/magazine/what-if-the-secret-to-success-is-failure.html.

Tough, P. (2012). *How children succeed: Grit, curiosity and the hidden power of character.* New York: Houghton-Mifflin,

Trzcinksi, L. S. (2013). *Seeing is believing: The science behind visualization.* http://www.voler.com/connect/detail/li/SeeingIsBelievingTheScienceBehindVisu alization#sthash.otJa1p0I.dpuf.

University of California, Berkeley, Center for Teaching and Learning. (n.d.). *Learning goals/outcomes.* http://teaching.berkeley.edu/learning-goalsout comes#sthash.RdKreyaz.dpuf.

Vygotsky, L. S. (1978). *Mind in society: The development of higher psychological processes.* Cambridge, MA: Harvard University Press.

Vygotsky, L. S. (1987). Thinking and speech. In L. S. Vygotsky, *Collected works* (vol. 1, 39–285) (R. Rieber & A. Carton, Eds; N. Minick, Trans.). New York: Plenum. (Original works published in 1934, 1960.)

Waelti, P., Dickinson, A., & Schultz, W. (2001). Dopamine responses comply with basic assumptions of formal learning theory. *Nature, 412,* 43–48.

Wang, J., Rao, H., Wetmore, G. S., et al. (2005). Perfusion functional MRI reveals cerebral blood flow pattern under psychological stress. *Proceedings of the National Academy of Sciences USA, 102,* 17804–17809.

Wasserman, H., & Danforth, H. E. (1988). *The human bond: Support groups and mutual aid.* New York: Springer.

Watanabe, T., Nanez, J., & Sasaki, Y. (2001). Perceptual learning without perception. *Nature, 413,* 844–848.

Waterman, R. (1987). *The renewal factor: How the best get and keep the competitive edge.* New York: Bantam.

Whimbey, A. (1980). Students can learn to be better problem solvers. *Educational Leadership, 37*(7), 560–565.

Whimbey, A., Whimbey, L. S., & Shaw, L. (1975). *Intelligence can be taught*. New York: Erlbaum.

Wiggens, G., & McTighe, J. (1998). *Understanding by design*. Alexandria, VA: ASCD.

Wiliam, D. (2006). Assessment for learning: why, what and how. *Critical Quarterly, 42*(1), 105–127.

Wiliam, D. (2006). Formative assessment: Getting the focus right. *Educational Assessment, 11*(3–4), 283–289.

Wiliam, D. (2007). Content then process: Teacher learning communities in the service of formative assessment. In D. B. Reeves (Ed.), *Ahead of the curve: The power of assessment to transform teaching and learning* (183–204). Bloomington, IN: Solution Tree.

Wiliam, D. (2011). *Embedded formative assessment*. Bloomington, IN: Solution Tree Press.

Wilkinson, I. A. G., & Fung, I. Y. Y. (2002). Small-group composition and peer effects. *International Journal of Educational Research, 37*, 425–447.

Williams, J. (2010). Taking on the role of questioner: Revisiting reciprocal teaching. *The Reading Teacher, 64*(4), 278–281.

Willingham, D. (2009). *Why don't students like school? A cognitive scientist answers questions about how the mind works and what it means for the classroom*. San Francisco: Jossey-Bass.

Willis, J. (2007). *Research-based strategies to ignite student learning: Insights from a neurologist and classroom teacher*. Alexandria, VA: ASCD.

Wilson, B. L., & Corbett, H. D. (2007). Students' perspectives on good teaching: Implications for adult reform behavior. In D. Thiessen & A. Cook-Sather (Eds.), *International handbook of student experience in elementary and secondary school* (283–314). Dordrecht, Netherlands: Springer.

Wlodkowski, R. J. (1983). *Motivational opportunities for successful teaching* [Leader's Guide]. Phoenix, AZ: Universal Dimensions.

Wood, R., & Locke, E. (1990). Goal setting and strategy effects on complex tasks. In B. Staw & L. Cummings (Eds.), *Research in organizational behavior* (vol. 12, 73–109). Greenwich, CT: JAI Press.

Wood, R., Mento, A., & Locke, E. (1987). Task complexity as a moderator of goal effects. *Journal of Applied Psychology, 17*, 416–425.

Wood, R. E., & Lock, E. A. (1987). The relation of self efficacy and grade goals to academic performance. *Educational and Psychological Measurement, 47*(4), 1013–1024.

Wright, J. S., & Panksepp, J. (2012). An evolutionary framework to understand foraging, wanting, and desire: The neuropsychology of the SEEKING system. *Neuropsychoanalysis, 14*(1), 5–39.

Yeh, S. S. (2011). *The cost-effectiveness of 22 approaches for raising student achievement*. Charlotte, NC: Information Age.

Yu-Fen, Y. (2010). Developing a reciprocal teaching/learning system for college remedial reading instruction. *Computers and Education, 55*, 1193–1201.

Zakrzewski, V. (n.d.). Great Good blog. http://greatergood.berkeley.edu/author/vicki_zakrzewski.

Zull, J. (2002). *The art of changing the brain*. Sterling, VA: Stylus Publishing.

Index

Figures are indicated by f following the page number.

Ability grouping, 104–106
Academic controversy, 115–118, 117–118f
Academic support, 142–143
Acceleration, 130–131
Accountability, 108–109, 108f
Achor, Shawn, 59–60
Activation
  curricula change for, 7–8
  defined, 1
  facilitation compared, 4–5, 4f
  factors important for, 10–12
  instructional strategy change for, 6–7
  school change for, 5–6
  visible learning and, 8–10, 9f
Adaptive expertise, 62–63
Advance organizers. *See* Organizers
Agendas, 22, 23f
Alice's Adventures in Wonderland (Carroll), 122
Alphabet brainstorms, 155, 156f
Amygdalas, 18
Anoetic consciousness, 3, 3f
Anticipation guides, 159, 161–162f
Anticipatory anxiety, 21–26, 23f, 25f
Anxiety. *See* Stress
Appointment method, 86–88, 87–88f
Appreciation, 33–34, 33f
Armstrong, T., 196
Assessment
  basic elements for, 148–151
  clarity of, 62
  classroom climate and, 39–40, 41f
  data versus information, 147–148
  factors important for, 12
  formative assessment, 149–151, 158–167, 160–165f, 172
  goals and, 127, 130
  incorporation into classroom, 65, 151, 152f
  pre-assessment, 152–158, 156–158f

  self-assessment, 149
  summative assessment, 149–150
  See also Feedback
Attentive listening, 31–33, 33f

Barkley, F. E., 99
Before Happiness (Achor), 59
Belonging, need for, 73–74
Berry, Wendell, 184
Bloom's revised thinking taxonomy, 80, 81–83f
Blundell, Nigel, 56
Boredom, stress and, 20
Brainstorming, 155, 156f, 167
Brain structure and function
  classroom setting and, 17–18
  cooperative group learning and, 100–103, 102f
  dendrite connections, 3, 13–14, 24
  dopamine, 2, 58, 100, 154
  effort, praise for, 58
  extended practice, 66
  goals and, 123–124
  hippocampus, 45, 154
  importance of understanding, 6
  laughter and, 45
  movement and, 26
  multitasking and, 32
  neuroplasticity, 13–14, 55
  novelty and, 48
  processing of stimuli by, 43–44, 123
  repetition, 24
  reticular activating system, 2
  social interaction and, 74
  stress and, 18–19
  visualization and, 124
  visuals and, 22
  wait time, 34, 53, 76–77, 79–80

Bransford, J. D., 62, 65
Braxton, J. M., 20
Brown, A. L., 62, 65
Bryk, A. S., 48
Bulletin boards, 39

Caine, G., 21, 59
Caine, R. N., 21, 59
Caring, 50–54
Carousel brainstorming, 167
Carroll, Lewis, 122
Carter, Gene, 147
CCSS (Common Core State Standards), 126–127, 128–129f
CGL. See Cooperative group learning (CGL)
Chesterfield, G. K., 45
Choice, 22
Choice theory of Motivation, 28
Chunking content, 61, 63
Clarifiers, 95
Clarifying strategy, 94–95
Clarity, goals and, 132–133, 133–134f
Classroom climate
    overview, 14–15
    assessment of, 39–40, 41f
    brain research on, 17–18
    as environment for learning, 67
    factors important for, 11
    See also Social isolation; Stress
Classroom Instruction that Works (Dean et al.), 66–67
Cocking, R. R., 62, 65
Cognitive disequilibrium, 64
Cognitive load, 63
Collaboration, 11, 196–197
Common Core State Standards (CCSS), 126–127, 128–129f
Competence, 48, 49f
Concentric circles, 89–90, 90f
Conceptual understanding, 143–145, 144–145f
Concept webs, 158f
Concrete operational stage, 141
Concurrence, academic controversy compared, 115
Connectedness, 153
Constant assessment, 65
Controversy, academic, 115–118, 117–118f
Cooperative group learning (CGL)
    overview, 67, 99
    academic controversy to implement, 115–118, 117–118f
    beginning with, 103–104, 105f

brain structure and function and, 100–103, 102f
    elements for success of, 107–112, 108f, 110f
    group design for, 104–107
    group investigation to implement, 118–120, 119f
    importance of, 75
    jigsaw to implement, 112–115, 113–115f
    skepticism for, 100, 101f
    See also Peers
Corso, M. J., 181, 181f
Costa, Art, 184–185
Courtesy, 20
Covey, Stephen, 79, 91
Cowan, E., 81
Cowan, G., 81
Credibility of teachers, 46–48, 49–50f
Critiques, 178
Crooks, T. J., 148
Cross, K. P., 99
Csikszentmihalyi, Mihaly, 138
Cubing, 81, 84–85f
Cues, 68
Cultural responsiveness, 45, 53–54
Culture. See Classroom climate
Curricula, changing for activation, 7–8

Damasio, Antonio, 19
Data versus information, 147–148
Dean, C. B., 66–67
Debate, academic controversy compared, 115
Declarative objectives, 124
Deductive approach to hypotheses, 69–70
Deep learning, 7, 144–145, 144–145f
Demeanor, 12. See also Enthusiasm
Dendrite connections, 3, 13–14, 24
Detectives, 167
Dialogue, monologue compared, 75–78. See also Cooperative group learning (CGL)
Diamond, Marian, 6
Diehl, Emily, 176
Differences and similarities, identification of, 69
Differentiation, 130–131
Direct instruction, 65–70, 67–68f
Displays of student work, 39
Dopamine, 2, 58, 100, 154
DRIP syndrome, 147
Dropouts, 47
Dweck, Carol, 13–14, 55, 58, 195–196
Dynamism, 48, 49–50f

Eavesdropping, 91, 188
Educational neuroscience. *See* Brain structure and function
Effort
  growth mindset and, 56, 56f
  importance of, 195–196
  praise for, 57–58
Einstein, Albert, 56
Elbow partners, 86
Emotional processing. *See* SEEKING system; Stress
Empathy, 62, 194
Encouragement, 148
Endorphins, 45
Engagement, 75
Enrichment, 131
Enthusiasm
  of students, 5
  of teachers, 6, 44–46, 194–195
Errors, 56–57, 172
Essential Nine, 66–70, 67–68f
Ethnicity. *See* Cultural responsiveness
Ethos, 47
Evaluation, extending compared, 78–80
Examples, 61
Executive function, 3–4
Exercise, stress and, 26
Exit cards, 183–184, 184f
Expectations
  learning and, 196
  mindset and, 12–14, 14f
  stress and, 21–22, 23f
Expert jigsaw, 113–114, 114f
Explanations, clarity of, 61
Exploration, 2
Extending, evaluation compared, 78–80
Extraneous cognitive load, 63

Fab four (reciprocal teaching), 93–97, 96f
Face-to-face interaction, 108f, 112
Facilitators, activators compared, 4–5, 4f
FCQ (Flow Condition Questionnaire), 139, 139f
Feedback
  overview, 169–170
  benefits of, 169
  critiques and, 178
  factors important for, 12
  gap feedback, 169–170
  growth mindset and, 174–176, 177f
  importance of, 172
  ineffective types of, 170–171
  just in time and just for me, 64, 176–178, 177f

metacognition and, 184–191, 186–188f, 190f
  peer to peer, 179–180
  from students, 180–184, 181f, 184f
  student thoughts on, 178–179
  types of, 172–173, 173–174f
  See also Assessment
Feedback loops, 151
Feed-forward loops, 151
Fishbone, 157f
Fist of five, 166
Fixed mindset, 13–14, 14f, 55, 58–59
Flexibility, goals and, 135, 137
Flipped classrooms, 61–62, 158
Flow
  overview, 138–140
  conceptual understanding and, 143–145, 144–145f
  defined, 138
  Piaget and, 141–142
  support and, 142–143
  Zone of Proximal Development and, 140–141
Flow Condition Questionnaire (FCQ), 139, 139f
Flow: The Psychology of the Optimal Experience (Csikszentmihalyi), 138
Focal points, 127, 130
Focus groups, 183
Ford, Henry, 195
Formal operational stage, 141
Formative assessment, 149–151, 158–167, 160–165f, 172
Four corners, 166
Four squares, 164, 165f
Friendship, 72–73. *See also* Peers
Frustration, stress and, 20

Gap feedback, 169–170
Geake, John, 17–18
GEL charts, 159, 160f
Germane cognitive load, 63
Gestures, 45
Gibbs, Jeanne, 29–31
Give one, get one, 167
Glasser, William, 27–28, 27f
Glossary of Educational Reform, 142–143
Goals
  overview, 123–126, 194
  challenge level for, 140
  daily, setting of, 132–138, 133–134f, 136f
  growth mindset and, 57, 58f
  learning progressions and, 126–131, 128–129f, 131f
  need for, 122–123
  See also Flow

Goldilocks goals, 127
Grades, 148, 171
Graffiti placemats, 29, 30f, 162–164, 163–164f
Graphic organizers. *See* Organizers
Gregory, G. H., 74–75
Group investigation and processing, 108f, 111–112, 118–120, 119f. *See also* Cooperative group learning (CGL)
Growth mindset
 overview, 13–14, 14f
 feedback and, 174–176, 177f
 parents and, 195–196
 teachers and, 55–59, 56f, 58f

Habits of mind, 185–186
Happiness, 59–60
The Happiness Advantage (Achor), 59
Hart, Lesley, 6
Haskins, W., 47
Hattie, John, 4, 7, 8, 43, 46–47, 50–51, 54, 91, 141–142, 143, 172, 178, 196
Heterogeneous grouping, 106–107
Hiding avoidance, 51–52
Hierarchy of human needs, 27, 27f
Hippocampus, 45, 154
Hirschy, A. S., 20
Homework, 68–69
Hope, 198
How I got my Name activity, 35
How People Learn (Bransford, Brown, & Cocking), 65
Hubbell, E. R., 66–67
Humiliation, 46
Humor, 45–46
Hunter, Madeline, 7
Hunter's Seven, 65–66
Hypotheses, generating and testing of, 69–70

IEPs (individualized education programs), 143
Immediacy, 48, 50f
Inclusion, 73. *See also* Peers; Social isolation
Individual accountability, 108–109, 108f
Individualistic learning, academic controversy compared, 115–116
Individualized education programs (IEPs), 143
Information versus data, 147–148
Instructional feedback. *See* Feedback
Instructional intelligence, 7
Instructional standards, 7, 22, 126–127, 128–129f

Instructional strategies
 changing for activation, 6–7
 clarity, 60–62
 direct instruction, 65–70, 67–68f
 effect size of, 47
 growth mindset and, 57–59, 58f
 multimodal presentations, 62–65
 multisensory and pluralistic, 54
Interest surveys, 36, 37–38f, 182–183
Intrinsic cognitive load, 63
Intrinsic motivation, 138
IQ, 32, 59
Isolation. *See* Social isolation

Jensen, E., 19
Jigsaw, 112–115, 113–115f
Johnson method, 107–112, 108f, 110f
Jones, Charlotte, 57
Jordan, Michael, 56, 56f
Journaling, 167
Just in time feedback, 64, 176–178, 177f

Kaufeldt, M., 74–75
Kentucky Student Voice Survey, 182–183
Kindness, 20
Kirby, E. D., 19
KWL charts, 159, 160f

Labels, 54
Language learning, 78
Laughter, 45–46
Law of readiness, 149
Learning laws, 149
Levels of thinking, 80, 81–83f
Limbic systems, 18–19
Listening, 31–33, 33f, 181–182

Major, C. H., 99
Marzano, R. J., 62, 66
Maslow, Abraham, 27–28
Maximal cognitive efficiency, 19–21
McCroskey, James, 47–48
Memories
 chunking content, 61, 63
 cognitive load and, 63
 dendrite connections and, 3
 pre-assessment and, 153–158, 156–158f
Mentoring, 52–53
Metacognition, 184–191, 186–188f, 190f
Metacognition thinking prompts, 186–187, 186–188f
Microteaching, 198
Mindfulness, 190–191

Mindfulness: A Guide for Teachers (Saltzman), 190
Mindset, 12–14, 14f
Mindset: The New Psychology of Success (Dweck), 55
Mindset Works website, 55, 176
Minority groups. *See* Cultural responsiveness
Mirror neurons, 74, 124
Mistakes, 56–57, 172
Mistakes That Worked (Jones), 57
Monologue, dialogue compared, 75–78
Motivation, 2, 138, 149
Movement, 26
Multimodal presentations, 62–65
Multiple ways of interacting, 64
Multiple ways of knowing, 63
Multiple ways of practicing, 64
Multitasking, 31–32
Mutual respect, 34–36
Myelination, 24
My Favorite Shoe activity, 35

Names, using, 51
Names activity, 35
National Council of Teachers of Mathematics (NCTM), 127, 130
Neuroplasticity, 13–14, 55
Neuroscience. *See* Brain structure and function
Noetic consciousness, 3, 3f
Nonlinguistic representations. *See* Visuals
Norms, 26, 29–36, 30f, 32–33f
Note taking, 68, 117, 117f
Not yet concept, 176, 195
Novelty, 20–21, 48

Objectives, stress and, 22
Obstacles, growth mindset and, 56–57
Optimism, 59, 198
Organization, clarity of, 60–61
Organizers
    cooperative group learning and, 111
    as instructional strategy, 68, 70
    metacognition and, 189, 190f
    pre-assessment and, 155–157, 157–158f
Oxytocin, 100

Paley, Virginia, 73
Panksepp, Jaak, 2–5, 3–4f
Participation, 34
Partners, 81, 86, 87f, 103–104. *See also* Cooperative group learning (CGL)

Passing on participation, 34. *See also* Wait time
Passion, 12
Patterns of association (chunking), 61, 63
Peers
    appointment method, 86–88, 87–88f
    Bloom's revised thinking taxonomy and, 80, 81–83f
    cubing, 81, 84–85f
    evaluating versus extending, 78–80
    factors important for, 11
    feedback from, 179–180
    importance of, 72–75
    monologue, dialogue compared, 75–78
    partners, 81, 86, 87f, 103–104
    reciprocal teaching, 93–97, 96f
    tips for, 90–91
    turn and talk, 88–90, 90f
    tutoring by, 91–93
    See also Cooperative group learning (CGL)
Personal bests, 140–141
Personalization of goals, 137–138
PFC (prefrontal cortexes), 18
Piaget, Jean, 141–142, 152, 184
P.I.T. activity, 35
Pitler, H., 66–67
Placemats, 29, 30f, 162–164, 163–164f
Plato, 184
PNI (Princeton Neuroscience Institute), 124
Point-and-go, 86
Pop psychology, 54
Positive interdependence, 107–108, 108f
Power standards, 7
Power zones, 38
Practice
    extended practice, 66
    growth mindset and, 56, 56f
    homework and, 68–69
    importance of, 195–196
    instructional strategies and, 62
    multiple ways of practicing, 64
Praise, 78–79, 171, 195
Predictions, 93, 95
Predictors, 95
Prefrontal cortexes (PFC), 18
Preoperational stage, 141
Pre-tests, 155
Primary SEEKING process, 2–3, 3f
Princeton Neuroscience Institute (PNI), 124
Prior knowledge, 62, 65, 152–158, 156–158f
Procedural objectives, 124
Procedures, 22–26, 23f, 25f
Process feedback, 172, 173–174f

Professional learning communities, 123, 196–197
Prosumers, 92
Put-downs and put-ups, 33–34, 33f

Quaglia, Russell, 181, 181f
Questioners, 94
Questioning strategy, 94
Questions, 68, 132–133, 133–134f
Quick checks for understanding, 164–167
Quick writes, 166

Random grouping, 107
RAS (reticular activating system), 2
Readiness, law of, 149
Reciprocal teaching, 93–97, 96f
Recovery strategy, 188–189
Reeves, Doug, 12
Reflection, 54, 111–112, 197–198
Relational trust, 48
Relaxed alertness, 21
Repetition, 24
Respect, 34–36
Response cards, 166
Reticular activating system (RAS), 2
Right angles, 189, 190f
Routine expertise, 62–63
Routines, 21–26, 23f, 25f
Rubrics, 135, 136f, 159, 162, 179–180
Rules, norms compared, 26

Sadler, D. R., 169–170
Saltzman, Amy, 190
Sapolsky, Robert, 73
Sarason, S., 7, 180
Sarcasm, 46
Sarkazein, 46
Say and switch, 89
Say something, 89
Scaffolding, 142–143
Schaffer, O., 139
Schematas, 152
Schneider, B. L., 48
Schools, changing for activation, 5–6
Secondary SEEKING process, 3, 3f
SEEKING system
    overview, 2–5, 3–4f
    deep learning and, 145
    instructional strategies for, 68
    novelty and, 20–21
Self-assessment, 149
Self feedback, 173, 173f
Self-regulation feedback, 173, 173–174f

Self-talk, 188, 194
Sensorimotor stage, 141
Shepherding principle, 153
Shoes activity, 35
Shoulder partners, 86
Similarities and differences, identification of, 69
Simple jigsaw, 112–113, 113f
Smiling, 44–45
Social isolation
    catching students being good, 39
    identification of, 28
    importance of addressing, 28–29
    learning affected by, 26–28, 27f, 59
    norm creation, 29, 30f
    personal interest in students, 36–38, 37–38f
    teacher relationships with students and, 50–54
    tribes and, 29–36, 32–33f
Social skills, 73, 108f, 109–111, 110f
SOLO taxonomy, 144, 144–145f
Specificity of goals, 133–135
Standards, 7, 22, 126–127, 128–129f
Stone, B., 66–67
Stress
    friendship and, 73
    learning shut down by, 18–19
    management of, 20–26, 23f, 25f
    maximal cognitive efficiency and, 19–20, 21
    sarcasm and, 46
    social interaction and, 74–75
    success and, 60
Students
    assessment of, 62
    catching students being good, 39
    enthusiasm decreases in, 5
    feedback between, 179–180
    feedback from, 180–184, 181f, 184f
    growth factors for, 10
    input in procedures from, 24
    surveys of, 36, 37–38f, 182–183
    teachers, what is wanted from, 194–195
    visible learning and, 8
Student Voice: The Instrument of Change (Quaglia & Corso), 181, 181f
Subconscious mind, 123–124
Subject matter expertise, 47
Success, 59–60
Success criteria, 134–135
Summarization, 68, 95
Summarizers, 95

Summative assessment, 149–150
Summative feedback, 148, 171
Surface understanding, 144–145, 144–145f
Surveys, 36, 37–38f, 182–183
Sweller, J., 63

Table jigsaw, 115, 115f
Talk a mile a minute, 88
Task feedback, 172, 173–174f
T charts, 32–33, 32f
Teacher attitude
  overview, 43–44
  caring, 50–54, 137
  credibility, 46–48, 49–50f
  enthusiasm, 6, 44–46, 194–195
Teachers
  collaboration between, 196–197
  enthusiasm decreases in, 6
  factors important for, 11
  growth mindset and, 55–59, 56f, 58f
  happiness fostered by, 59–60
  student-centered learning and, 193–194
  supporting of, 7
  See also Instructional strategies;
    Teacher attitude
Team-building activities, 34–36
Tertiary SEEKING process, 3–4, 3f, 145
Think-alouds, 188
Think Pair Share, 76–77
Thorndike, E., 149
Thumbs up or down, 166–167
Tickets out, 183–184, 184f
Triangulation, 148
Tribes, 29–36, 32–33f
Trust, 47–48, 49f, 193–194

Turn and talk, 88–90, 90f
21st century skills, 101–102, 102f
Two by Ten strategy, 52

Uncertainty, stress and, 21–26, 23f, 25f

Video diaries, 183
Visible learning, 8–10, 9f
Visible Learning for Teachers (Hattie),
  46–47, 143
Visualization, 124
Visuals
  brain structure and function and, 22
  explanations and, 61
  as instructional strategy, 68
  routines, 24
  similarities and differences, identification
    of, 69
Vygotsky, Lev, 140, 143
Vygotsky's Zone of Proximal Development,
  96f, 140–141

W-5 charts, 159, 161f
Wait time, 34, 53, 76–77, 79–80
Why Don't Students Like School?
  (Willingham), 6
Why Zebras Don't Get Ulcers (Sapolsky), 73
Willingham, Daniel, 6
Wlodkowski, Ray, 52
The World's Greatest Mistakes (Blundell), 56

You Can't Say You Can't Play (Paley), 73

Zone of Proximal Development, 96f,
  140–141